PRACTICE for
AIR FORCE
PLACEMENT TESTS

★★★★★★★★★★★★★★★★★★★★★★★★★
ARCO Military Test Tutor
★★★★★★★★★★★★★★★★★★★★★★★★★

PRACTICE for AIR FORCE PLACEMENT TESTS

E.P. STEINBERG, M.A.

ARCO PUBLISHING, INC.
NEW YORK

Fifth Edition, Third Printing, 1983

Published by Arco Publishing, Inc.
215 Park Avenue South, New York, N.Y. 10003

Copyright © 1982 by Arco Publishing, Inc.

Library of Congress Cataloging in Publication Data

Steinberg, Eve P.
    Practice for the Air Force placement tests.

    Rev. ed. of: Practice for Air Force placement tests /
David R. Turner. 4th ed. c1977
        1. United States.   Air Force—Examinations.
2. Armed Services Vocational Aptitude Battery.
I. Turner, David Reuben, 1915–   .   Practice for Air
Force placement tests.   II. Title.
UG638.S73   1982   358.4′.0076   82-4068
ISBN 0-668-05355-0   AACR2

Printed in the United States of America

CONTENTS

WHAT THIS BOOK WILL DO FOR YOU

You want to join the Air Force. You want to travel and see the world. You want adventure and excitement. You want to serve your country. You want to prepare for a career, military or civilian. Congratulations! You have chosen the service that offers you all that you seek, and you have bought the book that will start you towards your goals.

The Air Force is a large, modern service. The types of jobs required to run, operate and maintain the sophisticated weapons system and technology of today's Air Force are varied and specialized, requiring skill, training and acceptance of responsibility. The Air Force trains its recruits to fill all of its jobs. The Air Force hopes, of course, that enlistees will recognize the challenge and advancement opportunities in the Air Force and that they will stay on for long military careers. With our all-volunteer military, this is the ideal. However, the enlistee is under no obligation to remain in the service once the original commitment has been fulfilled. The valuable training gained in the service is a bonus that you take with you if and when you go out into the modern industrialized civilian world.

Almost eighty percent of all military occupations have their counterparts in the civilian community. It is precisely these types of jobs that the Department of Labor projects will be in great demand between now and 1990. If you choose not to make the Air Force your permanent career, your Air Force training will equip you for a civilian career. For example, the combination of jobs required to run and operate a modern-day aircraft carrier is the same combination of jobs necessary to operate a medium sized U.S. city—electrician, plumber-steamfitter, chef, fire-fighter, forklift operator, electronic equipment repair technician, clerk, personnel specialist, accountant, computer operator, communications specialist—plus a variety of highly technical jobs that you will not find in your average American city but which you will find in highly specialized industries. As the nation's largest employer of young men and women, the military is also the nation's largest trainer of young men and women for the important and available careers of the future.

Enlistees in the Air Force may apply for a guaranteed training program in the field of their choice or may enlist without a training school preference and allow the Air Force to assign them to the school for which they are best suited. Either way, your ASVAB scores enter into your placement. If you apply for a guaranteed training program, you must achieve a minimum established score on the combination of test parts which the Air Force deems to be important to success in that area. Your high scores in those portions of the exam serve to convince the Air

Force that your goals are realistic. If you have not yet defined your goals, ASVAB helps you to explore your own interests and your own acquired skills in the mechanical, electronic, shop, automotive and other technical trade areas. ASVAB results can point out to you the best direction in which to head your talents, can identify the best training path and career for you. ASVAB results will help the Air Force in placing you where your training will yield the best results for both the Air Force and you.

This book will help you to pass the all-important qualifying test so that you will be accepted into the Air Force. Then, this book will help you to score high on the parts of the exam that are used in placing you in a training program. The higher you score in all the areas of the exam, the greater the number of choices open to you. The higher you score on the parts related to your area of interest, the more likely you are to be guaranteed training in that area.

Careful study of this book will give you instruction for answering the various questions you will meet and hints for dealing with the exam. The model exams in the book will give you practice and experience so that you can face the real exam calmly and with confidence. In short, this book will help you to earn a high score so that you can get from the Air Force all that you hope for while giving the Air Force the best that you can give.

HOW TO USE THIS BOOK

You will get the most benefit from this book if you use it with respect. By this we mean treat it seriously, follow instructions, observe time limits and do not cheat. We also mean that you should read every chapter and answer every question.

Find yourself a quiet spot with good light and a clear work space. Eliminate as many distractions as possible. Set aside specified periods of at least an hour at a time for your test preparation. If possible, try to set aside a couple of three-hour periods so that you can try working straight through one or two exams, just as you will on exam day.

Start at the beginning of the book. Read through each chapter carefully so that you can appreciate what you are studying, how to use the book and how to take the exam. Refer back to these chapters as needed. Be sure to reread the chapter on test-taking shortly before exam day.

Begin your active preparation by taking the first model exam. Sharpen two or three number 2 pencils with erasers and bring them to your work area along with a few pieces of scratch paper. If you have a portable kitchen timer, bring it to your work area, too. If you have no timer, put a clock or watch in an easily visible spot. Tear out the answer sheet. Then read the directions for part one and answer the practice questions. Carefully read the explained answers. Be sure that you understand the directions before you turn the page to the first question and set the timer. Use the full time allowed for each part. If you finish working before the time is up, check over your work. If time expires before you have finished, stop and mark the place where time ran out. Later on you will want to go back and answer the remaining questions just for the practice. When the time allowed for a part is up, turn the page to the directions, practice questions and explained answers for the next part. When you are sure that you understand what to do, turn the page, set the timer and answer the questions for the next part. Continue in this way through the model exam.

When you have completed all ten parts, check your answers against the correct answers which follow the exam. Look back at the questions to see where and why you went wrong. Fill out the score sheet so that you can compare your performance on the various parts of the exam.

Proceed through the entire book. Study the chapters which teach you how to answer the questions. Give extra time to those chapters dealing with the types of questions on which you showed weakness.

Work with a dictionary. Look up *every* unfamiliar word in this book. If you run across a word you do not know while doing the exams, circle the word and look it up later. Look up words you find in the reading passages, new words from among answer choices, words you find in the explanations, words you meet in the study chapters. You are far more likely to remember a word which you have looked up for yourself than a word you have attempted to memorize from a list. If you can understand every word used in this book, you have a broad-based vocabulary and are fully prepared for the verbal requirements of the exam.

Try another model exam. After checking your answers, return to the study chapters that deal with the areas in which you still need help.

Even if you feel that you have improved to the maximum of your ability, even if you are certain that you are ready, complete the book and read all the chapters. Any additional practice will add to your confidence and improve your scores.

ALL ABOUT THE EXAM

WHAT IS ASVAB?

ASVAB is the Armed Services Vocational Aptitude Battery. ASVAB is the exam given to all prospective members of the United States Air Force as well as to enlistees in the Marine Corps, Army, Navy, Reserves and National Guard.

The ASVAB is a series of ten parts or tests, each yielding a separate score. One combination of scores on the ASVAB serves as the AFQT, Armed Forces Qualifying Test. The AFQT is based upon scores on "Word Knowledge," "Arithmetic Reasoning," "Paragraph Comprehension" and "Numerical Operations" sections of ASVAB. Persons who score above a certain grade on the AFQT are accepted into the Air Force. Persons who score below a certain score are rejected from the Air Force, though they may still qualify for most of the other services. The Air Force and the Air National Guard have the highest standards of any of the services. The passing AFQT score varies from service to service and according to previous education. The holder of a high school diploma earned from a four-year high school does not need to earn as high an AFQT score as the holder of a GED diploma. The non-graduate is required to earn the highest score of all for acceptance into the Air Force. The Air Force applies its scoring standards equally to men and women.

Besides the AFQT, a number of other composite, or combined, scores are derived from the ASVAB. These composite scores serve to identify the areas in which you show the greatest aptitude. In other words, the composite scores are used to predict your success in various training programs and vocational areas. If you score above a certain grade on the appropriate combination of tests, you may be guaranteed admission to the training school for the specialty to which that combination applies.

For the **AIR FORCE** the crucial score combinations for the four major training and vocational areas are as follows:

Mechanical—General Science, Mechanical Comprehension and 2x Automotive/Shop (Automotive/Shop is so important that it counts twice in calculating your score.)

Administrative—Numerical Operations, Coding Speed and Verbal (Verbal is a combination of Word Knowledge and Paragraph Comprehension.)

General—Arithmetic Reasoning and Verbal

Electronics—General Science, Arithmetic Reasoning, Mathematics Knowledge and Electronics Information

Obviously, if you have your eye on a specific training school, you will want to prepare yourself very thoroughly so that you can earn a high composite score in the field of your choice.

WHO TAKES ASVAB?

Everyone who wishes to serve in the United States Air Force takes ASVAB. The AFQT serves as a screening test. It eliminates those who are not qualified to serve. The combined test scores help the Air Force to assign high school graduates and non-graduates to the training schools for which they are best suited. College graduates who wish to apply for officer's candidate training must then submit to further testing. There may be additional testing for various specialties, but ASVAB is the first step for everyone.

ASVAB 5 is unlike the regular ASVAB described up to now in that ASVAB 5 may be taken by persons who are unsure as to whether or not they wish to join the Air Force or even by persons who are sure that they do not want to enlist. ASVAB 5 is given only in high schools to high school students. It is a very worthwhile tool in the hands of the high school counselor. In the same way that ASVAB guides the Air Force in placement of recruits, ASVAB 5 guides the school counselor as he or she advises students towards their further training and career goals. If a high school student who has taken ASVAB 5 decides to join the Air Force, the student or graduate need not retake ASVAB. Where there are differences between the two exams, the forms are comparable and scores can be converted to yield all the same composites. On the other hand, the student who has taken ASVAB 5 is not stuck with the scores earned. Any recruit may take the ASVAB at the time of enlistment.

WHEN AND WHERE IT IS GIVEN

Shortly after you have indicated your sincere intent to join the Air Force, your recruiter will show you a few sample ASVAB questions. On the basis of how you handle these few questions, your recruiter will either discourage you from attempting to enlist in the Air Force or will tell you where and when to report for testing. If you have studied from this book before enlistment, you may be quite certain that the recruiter will not discourage you from joining the Air Force. You are the interested recruit that the Air Force is eager to have. The exam is not given by recruiters at recruiting offices. There are established examination centers at convenient locations throughout the country at which trained administrators administer the exam almost every day.

FORMAT OF THE EXAMINATION

The ASVAB is divided into ten parts or tests. Each part has its own instructions. Each part is timed and scored separately. Along with the instructions for each part, there are a few practice questions. At the examination, you will be given a chance to answer the practice questions before you take the timed test. The test administrator will go over the answers to the practice questions with you so that there should be no doubt in anyone's mind as to exactly what to do. You may ask questions during the instructional period.

The ASVAB is a multiple-choice type examination. For each question you are offered four answer choices. (Part 6, Coding Speed, has five answer choices.) Only one answer choice is absolutely correct. You must choose what you think is the *BEST* answer and mark the letter of that answer on your separate answer sheet.

Scoring of the ASVAB is based upon the number of questions you answer correctly. There is no penalty for wrong answers. A wrong answer simply is not a right answer, so you get no credit for it. Since wrong answers do not count against you, there is no harm in guessing. With the exception of the two highly speeded parts (Numerical Operations and Coding Speed) you should try to answer every question. The model exams in this book will give you experience so that you can learn to pace yourself to answer all questions.

The chart that follows describes the ASVAB. At this time there are three different forms of the ASVAB in use. Each form has the same ten parts in the same order. Each form has the same number of questions in each test and is timed the same. All the questions are of equal difficulty; only the actual questions are different. The use of different forms helps to discourage cheating. Your friend may have questions that are different from yours, but his exam is otherwise equal to yours in every way.

Part	Number of Questions	Working Time in Minutes
1. General Science	25	11
2. Arithmetic Reasoning	30	36
3. Word Knowledge	35	11
4. Paragraph Comprehension	15	13
5. Numerical Operations	50	3
6. Coding Speed	84	7
7. Auto & Shop Information	25	11
8. Mathematics Knowledge	25	24
9. Mechanical Comprehension	25	19
10. Electronics Information	20	9

NATURE OF THE QUESTIONS

The following questions are typical of those which you may expect on this exam. Each part begins with directions very much like those on the actual exam. The answer to each question is explained so that you may understand the kind of thinking that was involved in finding the answer.

PART 1

GENERAL SCIENCE

The general science part of your examination asks questions based upon the science you learned in high school. For each question there are four possible answers. Only one answer is correct. Choose the answer which you think is correct and mark the corresponding space on your answer sheet. Try these questions.

1. Of the following, the *most important* function performed for man by the bee is to

1-A produce beeswax
1-B pollinate plants
1-C produce honey
1-D destroy harmful insects

1. Ⓐ Ⓑ Ⓒ Ⓓ

1-B POLLINATE PLANTS is the correct answer. The words "most important" are key words in choosing the answer to this question. Bees do produce beeswax (A) and honey (C), both of which are useful to man, but their most important function is pollinating plants. Bees destroy other insects (D) only if those insects are threatening the nest.

2. At one time milk was called "the perfect food" because it contained so many nutrients vital to growth and health. Milk is no longer called "the perfect food" because

2-A the formula has changed
2-B pasteurization destroys its value
2-C calcium has been determined to be harmful
2-D it lacks iron

2. Ⓐ Ⓑ Ⓒ Ⓓ

2-D IT LACKS IRON is the correct answer. Infants do not require iron, so milk is still a "perfect food" for them. Children and adults must have iron in their diets to insure against anemia and to maintain their strength and health. Cows have not changed the formula by which they make milk (A); pasteurization (B) destroys bacteria, not food value; calcium (C) is vital to the formation and strength of bones and teeth.

3. Of the following, the one that expands when it freezes is:

3-A carbon dioxide
3-B iron
3-C glass
3-D water

3. Ⓐ Ⓑ Ⓒ Ⓓ

3-D WATER is the correct answer. Water expands its volume when it freezes. If a glass jar is filled with water, tightly capped and frozen, it will crack and burst. The glass (C) does not expand along with the water. Carbon dioxide (A) and iron (B) do not expand when frozen.

4. Proteins are used by the body *chiefly* to:

4-A build cells
4-B develop antibodies
4-C maintain body heat
4-D produce nutrients

4. Ⓐ Ⓑ Ⓒ Ⓓ

4-A BUILD CELLS is the correct answer. Proteins are called the building blocks of the body. They are essential parts of all living cells. Proteins do play a role in the development of antibodies (B), the body's defenses against specific diseases, and they may be burned to maintain body heat (C) when other sources of calories are not available, but these are not their *chief* uses. Proteins are nutrients (D), they do not produce nutrients.

PART 2

ARITHMETIC REASONING

The arithmetic reasoning questions require careful thinking as well as arithmetic calculation. Some problems require more than one step for their solutions. You must decide exactly what the question asks; then you must determine the best method for finding the answer; finally, you must work out the problem on your scratch paper. Be sure to mark the letter of the correct answer on your answer sheet. Try these questions.

1. Two cars start from the same point at the same time. One drives north at 20 miles an hour and the other drives south on the same straight road at 36 miles an hour. How many miles apart are they after 30 minutes?

   1-A less than 10
   1-B between 10 and 20
   1-C between 20 and 30
   1-D between 30 and 40

   1. Ⓐ Ⓑ Ⓒ Ⓓ

   1-C One car went 20 mph for $\frac{1}{2}$ hour = 10 miles. The other car went 36 mph for $\frac{1}{2}$ hour = 18 miles. Since they went in opposite directions, add the two distances to find the total number of miles apart. 10 + 18 = 28

2. A sportswriter claims that his football predictions are accurate 60% of the time. During football season, a fan kept records and found that the writer was inaccurate for a total of 16 games, although he did maintain his 60% accuracy. For how many games was the sportswriter accurate?

   2-A 15
   2-B 24
   2-C 40
   2-D 5

   2. Ⓐ Ⓑ Ⓒ Ⓓ

   2-B If 60% of the games were predicted accurately, then 40% of the games were predicted inaccurately.

   Let x = games played

$$.40x = 16$$
$$x = 40 \text{ games played}$$
$$40 - 16 = 24 \text{ games won}$$

Therefore, the sportswriter was accurate for 24 games.

3. A clerk can add 40 columns of figures an hour by using an adding machine and 20 columns of figures an hour without using an adding machine. What is the total number of hours it will take the clerk to add 200 columns of figures if $\frac{3}{5}$ of the work is done by machine and the rest without the machine?

   3-A 6 hours
   3-B 7 hours
   3-C 8 hours
   3-D 9 hours

   3. Ⓐ Ⓑ Ⓒ Ⓓ

   3-B $\frac{3}{5}$ of 200 = 120 columns by machine @ 40 columns per hour = 3 hours
   200 − 120 = 80 columns without machine @ 20 columns per hour = 4 hours
   3 hours + 4 hours = 7 hours to complete the job.

4. At the rate of 28.5 feet per second, how many seconds will it take a boy to run 100 yards?

   4-A 11.2
   4-B 10.5
   4-C 10.1
   4-D 9.5

   4. Ⓐ Ⓑ Ⓒ Ⓓ

4-B 28.5 feet per second ÷ 3 = 9.5 yards per second

Distance = Rate × Time

$$Time = \frac{Distance}{Rate}$$

$$Time = \frac{100}{9.5} = 10.5 \text{ seconds}$$

5. How many square yards of linoleum are needed to cover a floor having an area of 270 square feet?

5-A 24
5-B 28
5-C 30
5-D 33

5. Ⓐ Ⓑ Ⓒ Ⓓ

5-C 9 square feet = 1 square yard
270 sq. ft. ÷ 9 = 30 sq. yds.

6. A Major, U.S. Army, Ret., and his wife took a pre-paid bus trip from their home near Ft. Lauderdale to Disney World. The cost of the trip was $143 each. On the first evening, they ordered cocktails and a special dessert at a cost of $7.00. With their second dinner out they ordered cocktails costing $4.50. At the end of the trip, they tipped the bus driver $3.00. What was the total cost of their vacation?

6-A $ 14.50
6-B $157.50
6-C $300.50
6-D $315.00

6. Ⓐ Ⓑ Ⓒ Ⓓ

6-C The prepaid portion of the trip was $143 × 2 = $286. Out-of-pocket expenses were $7 + $4.50 + $3 = $14.50. Altogether the cost was $300.50.

PART 3

WORD KNOWLEDGE

The questions in this part test how well you understand the meanings of words. Each question has an underlined word. Read all four possible answers and decide which one has a meaning closest to the meaning of the underlined word. On your answer sheet mark the letter of the answer you choose. Try these questions.

1. Explode most nearly means

   1-A crash
   1-B cave in
   1-C crumble
   1-D burst

   1. Ⓐ Ⓑ Ⓒ Ⓓ

1-D BURST is the correct answer. *Crash* (A), *cave in* (B), and *crumble* (C) are common results of an *explosion.* When an object *explodes,* it *bursts.*

2. Because of a death in the family, the private's leave was extended.

   2-A denied
   2-B lengthened
   2-C dreary
   2-D publicized

   2. Ⓐ Ⓑ Ⓒ Ⓓ

2-B LENGTHENED is the correct answer. *To extend* means *to stretch out* or *to lengthen.* Under the circumstances the private's leave may well have been *dreary,* but that is not the meaning of *extended.* (A) and (D) are wrong.

3. The pitcher missed nearly the whole season because of chronic arm trouble.

   3-A painful
   3-B frequent
   3-C imaginary
   3-D dangerous

   3. Ⓐ Ⓑ Ⓒ Ⓓ

3-B FREQUENT is the correct answer. The condition of the pitcher's arm may or may not have been *dangerous* (D) and it most certainly was *painful* (A), but it was its *frequency,* its *chronic nature,* that made him miss so much of the season. *Imaginary* (C) is not the meaning of *chronic.*

4. Lyrics most nearly means

   4-A music
   4-B words
   4-C rhyme
   4-D song

   4. Ⓐ Ⓑ Ⓒ Ⓓ

4-B WORDS is the correct answer. The *lyrics* are the *words* of a *song* (D), not the song itself nor the *music* (A). The *lyrics* may *rhyme* (C).

5. The retiring teacher had taught for thirty-two years.

   5-A starting over
   5-B leaving
   5-C shy
   5-D promoted

   5. Ⓐ Ⓑ Ⓒ Ⓓ

5-B LEAVING is the best answer. *Retiring* can also mean *shy* (C), but in this sentence it makes more sense to conclude that after thirty-two years of teaching the teacher is ready to *leave.* (A) *starting over* and (D) *promoted* are not meanings of *retiring.*

6. The President has appointed his cabinet.

   6-A cupboard
   6-B shelves

6-C advisors
6-D conference room

6. Ⓐ Ⓑ Ⓒ Ⓓ

6-C ADVISORS is the correct meaning of *cabi-*

net as used in this sentence. *Cupboard* (A) and *shelves* (B) are meanings of *cabinet* in an entirely different sense. *Conference room* (D) might be a definition of *cabinet,* but in that case the President would simply choose the room, not appoint it.

PART 4

PARAGRAPH COMPREHENSION

The paragraph comprehension part of your test battery requires concentration and attention to detail. First you must read and understand the paragraph. Then you must read and understand each of the answer choices, noticing the differences of meaning or emphasis that are imparted by little words. There is one question based upon each paragraph. You must answer that question on the basis of what is stated or implied in the passage, even if you know a better answer and even if you know the information in the paragraph to be false. In some cases more than one answer might be correct, but you must choose the BEST answer and mark its letter on your answer sheet. Try these questions.

1. Since duplicating machines are being changed constantly, the person who is in the market for such a machine should not purchase offhand the kind with which he is most familiar or the one recommended by the first salesman who calls on him. Instead he should analyze his particular equipment situation and then investigate all the possibilities.

When duplicating equipment is being purchased,

1-A the purchaser should choose equipment that he can use with the least extra training

1-B the needs of the purchaser's office should determine the selection

1-C the buyer should have his needs analyzed by an office-equipment salesman

1-D the recommendations of salesmen should usually be ignored

1. Ⓐ Ⓑ Ⓒ Ⓓ

1-B The last sentence answers the question. It recommends that specific office needs be analyzed and that all types of equipment be investigated. Since the office-equipment salesman is necessarily biased toward whatever he sells, he is not the one to do the analysis.

2. In a lightning-like military advance, similar to that used by the Germans, the use of persistent chemicals is unnecessary. It might even be a considerable detriment to a force advancing over a broad front.

The paragraph best supports the statement that

2-A chemicals should not be used by a defending army

2-B the Germans advanced in a narrow area

2-C an advancing army may harm itself through the use of chemicals

2-D chemical warfare is only effective if used by an advancing army

2. Ⓐ Ⓑ Ⓒ Ⓓ

2-C In stating that the use of chemicals might be a detriment to an advancing force, the paragraph means that an advancing army might cause harm to itself with its own chemicals.

3. It is probably safe to assume that for most people mental growth ceases somewhere between fourteen and a half and sixteen. After that, any increase in ability to meet novel situations is gained from experience. Intellectual growth is likewise ascribed to wider experience and more information, rather than to an increase in mental capacity.

Most individuals somewhere between fourteen and a half and sixteen

3-A make demands on mere experience rather than on native ability

15

3-B show an increase rather than a decrease in general mental capacity

3-C have achieved their total mental growth

3-D cease to show increased capacity to meet novel situations

3. Ⓐ Ⓑ Ⓒ Ⓓ

3-C The first sentence states that for most people mental growth ceases between the ages of fourteen and a half and sixteen. The remainder of the paragraph explains that what may later appear to be increased capacity must be ascribed to greater experience and information.

4. Metered mail must bear the correct date of mailing in the meter impression. When metered mail bearing the wrong date or time is presented for mailing, it shall be run through the canceling machine or otherwise postmarked to show the proper date and time, and then dispatched. The irregularity shall be called to the attention of the mailer. If the irregularity is repeated, the mail may be refused.

The paragraph best supports the statement that if a first mailing of metered mail bears a wrong date or time,

4-A no action shall be taken by the postal service

4-B the mailing privileges of the sender may be canceled

4-C the mailer will be notified of the error before the mail is dispatched

4-D the postal service accepts the responsibility for correction

4. Ⓐ Ⓑ Ⓒ Ⓓ

4-D According to the paragraph, the post office must cancel mail with the proper date and time if it has been metered improperly. It then becomes the responsibility of the post office to notify the mailer of his error and to refuse any additional mail which is improperly metered. However, once the post office accepts the mail, it must make the correction.

PART 5

NUMERICAL OPERATIONS

The numerical operations part of your test battery consists of fifty very simple arithmetic questions which must be answered in only three minutes. Obviously, speed is a very important factor. You should not attempt to compute these answers using pencil and scratch paper. Instead, solve each problem in your head, then choose the correct answer from among the four choices and mark the letter of the correct answer on your answer sheet. If you are not sure of an answer, guess and go on to the next question. Do not skip any questions. You will most certainly not have time to go back to fill in. Since a wrong answer will not count against you, it cannot hurt to guess. Many people cannot complete all fifty questions in the three minutes allowed. Do not be upset if you cannot finish. Just answer as many questions as you can. Try these questions.

1. $7 + 6 =$

  1-A 11
  1-B 13
  1-C 15
  1-D 19

  1. Ⓐ Ⓑ Ⓒ Ⓓ

1-B $7 + 6 = 13$

2. $8 - 3 =$

  2-A 6
  2-B 11
  2-C 4
  2-D 5

  2. Ⓐ Ⓑ Ⓒ Ⓓ

2-D $8 - 3 = 5$

3. $4 + 1 =$

  3-A 2
  3-B 3
  3-C 4
  3-D 5

  3. Ⓐ Ⓑ Ⓒ Ⓓ

3-D $4 + 1 = 5$

4. $7 \times 6 =$

  4-A 11
  4-B 13

  4-C 24
  4-D 42

  4. Ⓐ Ⓑ Ⓒ Ⓓ

4-D $7 \times 6 = 42$

5. $10 - 3 =$

  5-A 7
  5-B 13
  5-C 8
  5-D 6

  5. Ⓐ Ⓑ Ⓒ Ⓓ

5-A $10 - 3 = 7$

6. $1 + 7 =$

  6-A 6
  6-B 7
  6-C 8
  6-D 9

  6. Ⓐ Ⓑ Ⓒ Ⓓ

6-C $1 + 7 = 8$

7. $4 + 5 =$

  7-A 1
  7-B 7
  7-C 9
  7-D 15

  7. Ⓐ Ⓑ Ⓒ Ⓓ

7-C 4 + 5 = 9

8. 6 − 3 =

8-A 3
8-B 9
8-C 18
8-D 24

8. Ⓐ Ⓑ Ⓒ Ⓓ

8-A 6 − 3 = 3

9. 7 × 2 =

9-A 5
9-B 9

9-C 12
9-D 14

9. Ⓐ Ⓑ Ⓒ Ⓓ

9-D 7 × 2 = 14

10. 8 + 8 =

10-A 0
10-B 16
10-C 18
10-D 26

10. Ⓐ Ⓑ Ⓒ Ⓓ

10-B 8 + 8 = 16

PART 6

CODING SPEED

The coding part of your exam is different from all other parts of the exam. Nothing that you have learned enters into your answering of these questions. Coding is a test of your memory, your eye-hand coordination and your working speed.

Before each set of questions you will find a "key." The key consists of ten words listed in alphabetical order. Each word has a four-digit code number assigned to it.

In the set of questions you will find the same ten words, scrambled and sometimes repeated. Following each word in the test are *five* answer choices in columns labelled "A" to "E." Each answer choice is a four-digit number. The answer choices are in ascending order; that is, the lowest number is always in column A, the next higher number is in column B, and so on to the highest number in column E. You must look at the word, find the correct code number among the choices and mark on your answer sheet the letter of the column in which you found the correct code number.

On the actual examination you must work very quickly. You have only seven minutes in which to try to answer eighty-four questions. Use the sample questions that follow to develop a system that works for you—memorization, some sort of word-number association, a mathematical formula or any private method that helps you work up speed and accuracy. Many people cannot finish this part in the time allowed. Do not be upset if you cannot finish. Just do your best. Try these questions.

Key

bay 7100	dark 1872	mole 4386
brain 3600	half 1492	nest 6663
calf 9012	igloo 1776	shoe 8080
	lemon 5486	

Answers

	A	B	C	D	E	
1. brain	1776	3600	4386	6663	8080	1. Ⓐ Ⓑ Ⓒ Ⓓ Ⓔ
2. igloo	1492	1776	1872	7100	9012	2. Ⓐ Ⓑ Ⓒ Ⓓ Ⓔ
3. shoe	3600	4386	5486	6663	8080	3. Ⓐ Ⓑ Ⓒ Ⓓ Ⓔ
4. mole	1872	3600	4386	5486	7100	4. Ⓐ Ⓑ Ⓒ Ⓓ Ⓔ
5. calf	1776	4386	6663	8080	9012	5. Ⓐ Ⓑ Ⓒ Ⓓ Ⓔ
6. lemon	3600	5486	7100	8080	9012	6. Ⓐ Ⓑ Ⓒ Ⓓ Ⓔ
7. nest	1776	3600	6663	7100	8080	7. Ⓐ Ⓑ Ⓒ Ⓓ Ⓔ
8. dark	1872	3600	5486	6663	7100	8. Ⓐ Ⓑ Ⓒ Ⓓ Ⓔ
9. bay	1776	1872	4386	5486	7100	9. Ⓐ Ⓑ Ⓒ Ⓓ Ⓔ
10. half	1492	1872	3600	4386	6663	10. Ⓐ Ⓑ Ⓒ Ⓓ Ⓔ
11. lemon	3600	4386	5486	6663	9012	11. Ⓐ Ⓑ Ⓒ Ⓓ Ⓔ
12. mole	1872	4386	5486	8080	9012	12. Ⓐ Ⓑ Ⓒ Ⓓ Ⓔ

The correct answers are:

1-B	4-C	7-C	10-A
2-B	5-E	8-A	11-C
3-E	6-B	9-E	12-B

Key

bubble 3393	eat 6912	oval 8003
crown 1465	hose 7577	steer 5665
dentist 3290	juice 2012	yellow 6872
	lap 4755	

Answers

		A	B	C	D	E	
13.	dentist	2012	3290	3393	6872	8003	13. Ⓐ Ⓑ Ⓒ Ⓓ Ⓔ
14.	yellow	3393	4755	5665	6872	7577	14. Ⓐ Ⓑ Ⓒ Ⓓ Ⓔ
15.	oval	3290	5665	6912	7577	8003	15. Ⓐ Ⓑ Ⓒ Ⓓ Ⓔ
16.	crown	1465	2012	3290	5665	6872	16. Ⓐ Ⓑ Ⓒ Ⓓ Ⓔ
17.	hose	3290	3393	4755	6912	7577	17. Ⓐ Ⓑ Ⓒ Ⓓ Ⓔ
18.	lap	1465	2012	3290	3393	4755	18. Ⓐ Ⓑ Ⓒ Ⓓ Ⓔ
19.	steer	1465	4755	5665	6872	6912	19. Ⓐ Ⓑ Ⓒ Ⓓ Ⓔ
20.	juice	2012	3290	4755	6872	6912	20. Ⓐ Ⓑ Ⓒ Ⓓ Ⓔ
21.	eat	4755	5665	6872	6912	7577	21. Ⓐ Ⓑ Ⓒ Ⓓ Ⓔ
22.	bubble	3290	3393	4755	5665	6912	22. Ⓐ Ⓑ Ⓒ Ⓓ Ⓔ
23.	dentist	1465	2012	3290	3393	6912	23. Ⓐ Ⓑ Ⓒ Ⓓ Ⓔ
24.	hose	2012	4755	5665	7577	8003	24. Ⓐ Ⓑ Ⓒ Ⓓ Ⓔ

The correct answers are:

13-B	16-A	19-C	22-B
14-D	17-E	20-A	23-C
15-E	18-E	21-D	24-D

PART 7

AUTO & SHOP INFORMATION

The auto and shop information questions test your knowledge and understanding of automobiles and of tools and shop practices. The answers to many questions come straight from your life experience. However, if this is not your area of interest, there will be questions to which you do not know the answer. Make the most sensible guess. Answer all questions. Mark the letter of your choice on your answer sheet. Try these questions.

1. Wheels should be balanced

   1-A only when they are new
   1-B whenever air pressure is low
   1-C every 10,000 miles
   1-D whenever tires are put onto rims

1. Ⓐ Ⓑ Ⓒ Ⓓ

1-D EACH TIME A TIRE IS PUT ONTO A RIM the wheel must be balanced. If you take your regular tires off the rims and mount snow tires on those same rims, the wheels must be balanced, even though the tires may not be new (A). If you answered (C), you were probably thinking of tire rotation, which is done according to schedule.

2. Black smoke coming from the muffler means that

   2-A there is too much lubricating oil
   2-B the car needs an oil change
   2-C the carburetor is delivering too rich a mixture
   2-D the carburetor is delivering too weak a mixture

2. Ⓐ Ⓑ Ⓒ Ⓓ

2-C If the carburetor is sending to the engine a mixture that contains TOO MUCH GASOLINE with TOO LITTLE AIR, the mixture is said to be *too rich* and black smoke will come from the muffler. If there is too much lubricating oil (A), bluish-gray smoke will come from the tailpipe.

3.

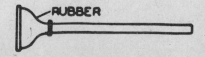

The tool below is most likely to be used by a

   3-A stonemason
   3-B plumber
   3-C carpenter
   3-D machinist

3. Ⓐ Ⓑ Ⓒ Ⓓ

3-B The tool is a plunger. It is used by a PLUMBER to dislodge material that is clogging drains.

4. The proper place for rope storage is

   4-A a dry, cool closet
   4-B a hot, dry attic
   4-C in the open air
   4-D a covered container of water

4. Ⓐ Ⓑ Ⓒ Ⓓ

4-A A DRY, COOL CLOSET is the best place to store rope. There it should not dry out and become brittle, as it might in a hot attic, yet it would be protected from weather and weakening moisture.

5. An engine is found to be missing on one cylinder. Of the following, what is the most likely cause?

   5-A vapor lock
   5-B a clogged exhaust
   5-C an overheated engine
   5-D a defective sparkplug

5. Ⓐ Ⓑ Ⓒ Ⓓ

5-D All of the choices might cause an engine to miss, but if it misses only on one cylinder a defective sparkplug is a likely cause.

6. The material used with solder to make it stick better is

6-A oakum
6-B lye
6-C oil
6-D flux

6. Ⓐ Ⓑ Ⓒ Ⓓ

6-D FLUX is used during soldering. It removes oxide as the solder contacts metal, making the solder stick better. Oakum (A) is a tar-treated rope used for sealing joints. Lye (B) is a caustic agent used for heavy cleaning. Oil (C) would be the wrong substance to make solder stick.

PART 8

MATHEMATICS KNOWLEDGE

To solve the problems in this part, you must draw upon your knowledge of high school mathematics. The problems require you to use simple algebra and geometry along with arithmetic skills and reasoning power. Some questions can be answered in your head. Others will require the use of scratch paper. If you use scratch paper for your calculations, be sure to mark the letter of the correct answer on your answer sheet. Try these questions.

1. What is the value of x when $5x = 5 \times 4 \times 2 \times 0$?

1-A 6
1-B 8
1-C 0
1-D 1

1. Ⓐ Ⓑ Ⓒ Ⓓ

1-C Any number multiplied by 0 equals 0. Since one multiplier on one side of the = sign is 0, the product on that side of the sign must be 0. The value on the other side of the = sign must also be 0.

$5x = 5 \times 4 \times 2 \times 0$
$5x = 40 \times 0$
$5x = 0$
$x = 0$

2. $r = 35 - (3 + 6)(-n)$
$n = 2$
$r =$

2-A 53
2-B 17
2-C −53
2-D −17

2. Ⓐ Ⓑ Ⓒ Ⓓ

2-A $r = 35 - (9)(-n)$
$r = 35 - (9)(-2)$
$r = 35 - (-18)$
$r = 35 + 18 = 53$

To subtract signed numbers, change the sign of the subtrahend and proceed as in algebraic addition.

3. When 81.3 is divided by 10 the quotient is

3-A 0.0813
3-B 0.813
3-C 8.13
3-D 813

3. Ⓐ Ⓑ Ⓒ Ⓓ

3-C

$$\begin{array}{r} 8.13 \\ 10\overline{)81.30} \\ 80 \\ \hline 13 \\ 10 \\ \hline 30 \\ 30 \\ \hline \end{array}$$

4. Change $\frac{5}{8}$ to a percent

4-A 60%
4-B $62\frac{1}{2}$%
4-C 75%
4-D 65%

4. Ⓐ Ⓑ Ⓒ Ⓓ

4-B To change a fraction to a percent, multiply the fraction by 100; reduce, if possible; then add a percent sign. Thus,

$\frac{5}{8} \times 100 = 500/8 = 62\frac{1}{2}$%

5. The area of a square has been increased from 36 square inches to 81 square inches. How many inches has the perimeter been increased?

5-A 6
5-B 8

23

5-C 10
5-D 12

5. Ⓐ Ⓑ Ⓒ Ⓓ

5-D Area of a square $= s^2$

Square 1: $s^2 = 36$
$s = 6$ inches

Square 2: $s^2 = 81$
$s = 9$

Perimeter of a square $= 4s$
$4 \times 6 = 24$ inches
$4 \times 9 = 36$ inches

Increase $= 36 - 24 = 12$ inches

6. A jet pilot wishes to cover a certain distance in 25% less time than he had previously taken to cover that distance. What percent must he increase his speed in order to accomplish this?

6-A 25%
6-B $33\frac{1}{3}$%
6-C 40%
6-D $66\frac{2}{3}$%

6. Ⓐ Ⓑ Ⓒ Ⓓ

6-B

$$Rate = \frac{Distance}{Time}$$

Let $D = 100$ and $T = 1$

$$R = \frac{100}{1 - \frac{1}{4}}$$

$$R = \frac{100}{\frac{3}{4}}$$

$$R = 100 \times \frac{4}{3} = \frac{400}{3} = 133\frac{1}{3}$$

$133\frac{1}{3} - 100 = 33\frac{1}{3}$% increase

PART 9

MECHANICAL COMPREHENSION

Part 9 consists of questions about your understanding of general mechanical and physical principles. Your understanding of these principles will come from your own observations, from experience in working with mechanical devices and from your reading and school courses. Answer all the questions as best you can, marking the letter of your choice on your answer sheet. Try these questions.

1.

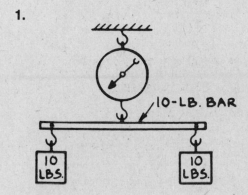

10-LB. BAR

10 LBS.

10 LBS.

The reading on the weighing scale will be approximately

1-A zero
1-B 20 lbs.
1-C 10 lbs.
1-D 30 lbs.

1. Ⓐ Ⓑ Ⓒ Ⓓ

1-D The scale is supporting the weight of two 10-pound weights and a 10-pound bar. Since 30 pounds is suspended from the scale, it should read 30 pounds. In actuality, the scale should read just slightly more than 30 pounds, because it will also register the weight of the hardware used for suspension.

2.

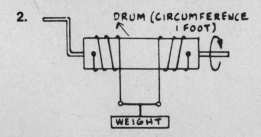

DRUM (CIRCUMFERENCE 1 FOOT)

WEIGHT

One complete revolution of the windlass drum shown at 2 will move the weight up

2-A ½ foot
2-B 1½ feet
2-C 1 foot
2-D 2 feet

2. Ⓐ Ⓑ Ⓒ Ⓓ

2-C Since the circumference of the drum is one foot, one complete revolution of the drum will take up one foot of each rope. As each of the separate ropes supporting the weight is shortened by one foot, the weight will move up one foot.

3.

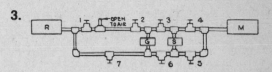

In the figure above, assume that all valves are closed. For air to flow from R, through G, then through S to M open

3-A valves 1, 2, 6 and 4
3-B valves 7, 3 and 4
3-C valves 7, 6 and 4
3-D valves 7, 3 and 5

3. Ⓐ Ⓑ Ⓒ Ⓓ

3-D The air from R must follow a route down through valve 7, up through G, then through valve 3, down through S, to the right through 5, then up and over to M. The air could not pass through valves 1 and 2 to G because it would escape through the opening between valves 1 and 2. If either valve 4 or valve 6 were to be opened, the air would be diverted from the appointed route.

4.

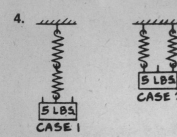

In the figure above, all 4 springs are identical. In Case 1 with the springs end to end, the stretch of each spring caused by the five lb. weight is

4-A $\frac{1}{2}$ as much as in Case 2
4-B the same as in Case 2
4-C twice as much as in Case 2
4-D four times as much as in Case 2

4. Ⓐ Ⓑ Ⓒ Ⓓ

4-C In Case 2, each spring bears one-half of the weight of the five pound weight. Each spring in Case 2 is therefore stretched by two and one half pounds. In Case 1, each spring bears a full five pound load. Each spring in Case 1 must be stretched twice as much as each spring in Case 2.

PART 10

ELECTRONICS INFORMATION

The questions in this part test your knowledge and understanding of electricity, radio and electronics. To answer some of the questions all you need is common sense. Other questions can be answered on the basis of experience, courses and reading. Answer all the questions. Mark the letter of your answer on the answer sheet. Try these questions.

1. An electric light bulb operated at *more* than its rated voltage will result in a

1-A longer life and dimmer light
1-B longer life and brighter light
1-C shorter life and brighter light
1-D shorter life and dimmer light

1. Ⓐ Ⓑ Ⓒ Ⓓ

1-C If an electric lightbulb is operated at more than its rated voltage, the extra surge of electricity will cause the bulb to burn more brightly. However, the same excess electrical force will weaken the filament and cause the bulb to burn out more quickly.

2. A battery consisting of four two-volt cells in series will have a voltage of

2-A ½ volt
2-B 4 volts
2-C 2 volts
2-D 8 volts

2. Ⓐ Ⓑ Ⓒ Ⓓ

2-D In a series connection, each member draws from or contributes equally to the voltage. Thus five light bulbs connected in series to a 300 volt source would each draw 60 volts. In this case, the four two-volt cells connected in series will produce 8 volts.

3. Asbestos is commonly used as the covering of electric wires in locations where there is likely to be high

3-A voltage
3-B humidity
3-C temperature
3-D current

3. Ⓐ Ⓑ Ⓒ Ⓓ

3-C Asbestos is an excellent insulator against heat. If electric wires are to be used under conditions where they are exposed to very high, possibly damaging, heat, the wires are covered with asbestos for their own protection.

4. A thermostat is caused to operate by changes in

4-A air pressure
4-B moisture
4-C temperature
4-D speed of rotation

4. Ⓐ Ⓑ Ⓒ Ⓓ

4-C The action of a thermostat in opening and closing a circuit is directed by changes in temperature. *Thermo* comes from a Greek word meaning *heat*. It is the same root found in *thermometer.*

5. Transistors are mainly employed in electrical circuits to take the place of

5-A resistors
5-B vacuum tubes
5-C condensers
5-D inductances

5. Ⓐ Ⓑ Ⓒ Ⓓ

5-B Modern technology has developed the transistor, which has just about completely taken over from the vacuum tube. Transistors are far less troublesome and do not burn out like vacuum tubes. Transistors have made possible miniaturization. Pocket size portable radios were among the first popular benefits of the transistor.

6. The principal objection to using water from a hose to put out a fire involving electrical equipment is that

6-A   serious shock may result
6-B   it may spread the fire
6-C   metal parts may rust
6-D   fuses may blow out

6. Ⓐ Ⓑ Ⓒ Ⓓ

6-A Water is not likely to spread an electrical fire (B), though it may be ineffective at putting it out. It is true that metal parts may rust if soaked with water (C) and fuses may blow (D), but there are not serious considerations. There is a real danger from fatal shock if water is used on an electrical fire. The danger is much greater still if that water comes from a hose, because there would then be a great deal of water on the floor and the firefighters would be standing in it. Electricity travels rapidly through water, and the people standing in the water would be its targets.

TEST-TAKING TECHNIQUES

Your last minute preparations for any exam are based strictly on common sense. They include getting a good night's sleep and leaving home early enough so that you do not need to rush or worry. It is a good idea to wear a watch to your exam so that you can keep track of your own time and pace yourself. There are no other materials you need bring to the exam. Pencils and scratch paper will be issued to you.

Once all examinees are seated in the examination room, the test administrator will hand out forms and will give instructions as to how to fill them out. Listen carefully and follow all instructions. Ask questions if necessary. The administrator will tell you of the procedure that will be followed when the exam begins. He or she will tell you how to recognize the *start* and *stop* signals, what to do if all your pencils break or if a page seems to be missing from your test booklet. The instructions will be step-by-step and should be very clear, but if you are uncertain about anything, do not hesitate to ask. No one keeps a record of who asks questions, even questions that seem to be foolish.

Before each part of the exam, there is a page of directions and practice questions. You will get a chance to read the page and answer the questions before timing begins on that part. The test administrator will go over the practice questions with the group and will explain the correct answers. This is your chance to ask questions. You must understand what you are to do before timing begins on a part. You cannot ask questions once testing is underway. Each part of your exam will be timed separately. You will have a chance to read instructions, answer practice questions and discuss both instructions and answers to the practice questions before actually taking each part.

When you do begin each part of the exam, we urge you to READ every word of every question. Be alert for exclusionary words which might affect your answer—words like "not," "most," "all," "every," "except."

READ all four choices before you mark your answer. It is statistically true that most errors are made when the correct answer is (D). Too many people mark the first answer that seems correct, without reading through all the choices to find out which answer is *best.*

The following list consists of important suggestions for taking this exam. Read the suggestions now before you attempt the model exams in this book. Read them again right before you take the exam. You will find them all useful.

1. Mark your answers by completely blackening the answer space of your choice.
2. Mark only ONE answer for each question, even if you think that more than

one answer is correct. You must choose only one. If you mark more than one answer, the scoring machine will consider you wrong.

3. If you change your mind, erase completely. Leave no doubt as to which answer you mean.

4. If you use scratch paper, be certain to mark the answer on the answer sheet.

5. Check often to be sure that the question number matches the answer space, that you have not skipped a space by mistake.

6. Try to answer every question. If you are unsure of an answer you mark, put a check next to the question in the question booklet. Then, if you have time, you can quickly spot those questions to which you would like to give some extra thought.

7. Guess if you must. If you do not know the answer to a question, eliminate the answers that you know are wrong and guess from among those remaining. If you have no idea whatsoever of the answer to a question, guess anyway. There is no penalty for a wrong answer, so even a wild guess gives you a 25% chance to be right. If you leave the space blank, you have no chance at all to be correct.

8. If you notice that time is about to run out and you have not completed all the questions, mark all the remaining questions with the same answer. Some will probably be correct. In doing this, choose an answer other than (A). (A) is generally the correct answer less often than the other choices.*

9. Stay alert. Be careful not to mark a wrong answer because you were not concentrating. An example of this type of error might be: The correct answer to a Mathematics question is (B) d, and you mark (D) instead of (B).

10. Do not panic. If you do not finish any part before time is up, do not worry. If you are accurate, you can do well without finishing. At any rate, do not let your performance on any one part affect your performance on any other part.

11. Check and recheck. If you finish any part before time is up, do not daydream. Check to be sure that each question is answered in the right space and that there is only one answer for each question. Return to the difficult questions and rethink them.

Good luck!

*Do not rush to complete Part 5, Numerical Operations, or Part 6, Coding Speed, in the manner described above. Use every second of those two parts to answer the questions according to the directions. You are not expected to finish those two tests, and accuracy is important.

FIRST MODEL EXAM

ANSWER SHEET—FIRST MODEL EXAM

PART 1—GENERAL SCIENCE

1 Ⓐ Ⓑ Ⓒ Ⓓ   6 Ⓐ Ⓑ Ⓒ Ⓓ   11 Ⓐ Ⓑ Ⓒ Ⓓ   16 Ⓐ Ⓑ Ⓒ Ⓓ   21 Ⓐ Ⓑ Ⓒ Ⓓ

2 Ⓐ Ⓑ Ⓒ Ⓓ   7 Ⓐ Ⓑ Ⓒ Ⓓ   12 Ⓐ Ⓑ Ⓒ Ⓓ   17 Ⓐ Ⓑ Ⓒ Ⓓ   22 Ⓐ Ⓑ Ⓒ Ⓓ

3 Ⓐ Ⓑ Ⓒ Ⓓ   8 Ⓐ Ⓑ Ⓒ Ⓓ   13 Ⓐ Ⓑ Ⓒ Ⓓ   18 Ⓐ Ⓑ Ⓒ Ⓓ   23 Ⓐ Ⓑ Ⓒ Ⓓ

4 Ⓐ Ⓑ Ⓒ Ⓓ   9 Ⓐ Ⓑ Ⓒ Ⓓ   14 Ⓐ Ⓑ Ⓒ Ⓓ   19 Ⓐ Ⓑ Ⓒ Ⓓ   24 Ⓐ Ⓑ Ⓒ Ⓓ

5 Ⓐ Ⓑ Ⓒ Ⓓ   10 Ⓐ Ⓑ Ⓒ Ⓓ   15 Ⓐ Ⓑ Ⓒ Ⓓ   20 Ⓐ Ⓑ Ⓒ Ⓓ   25 Ⓐ Ⓑ Ⓒ Ⓓ

PART 2—ARITHMETIC REASONING

1 Ⓐ Ⓑ Ⓒ Ⓓ   7 Ⓐ Ⓑ Ⓒ Ⓓ   13 Ⓐ Ⓑ Ⓒ Ⓓ   19 Ⓐ Ⓑ Ⓒ Ⓓ   25 Ⓐ Ⓑ Ⓒ Ⓓ

2 Ⓐ Ⓑ Ⓒ Ⓓ   8 Ⓐ Ⓑ Ⓒ Ⓓ   14 Ⓐ Ⓑ Ⓒ Ⓓ   20 Ⓐ Ⓑ Ⓒ Ⓓ   26 Ⓐ Ⓑ Ⓒ Ⓓ

3 Ⓐ Ⓑ Ⓒ Ⓓ   9 Ⓐ Ⓑ Ⓒ Ⓓ   15 Ⓐ Ⓑ Ⓒ Ⓓ   21 Ⓐ Ⓑ Ⓒ Ⓓ   27 Ⓐ Ⓑ Ⓒ Ⓓ

4 Ⓐ Ⓑ Ⓒ Ⓓ   10 Ⓐ Ⓑ Ⓒ Ⓓ   16 Ⓐ Ⓑ Ⓒ Ⓓ   22 Ⓐ Ⓑ Ⓒ Ⓓ   28 Ⓐ Ⓑ Ⓒ Ⓓ

5 Ⓐ Ⓑ Ⓒ Ⓓ   11 Ⓐ Ⓑ Ⓒ Ⓓ   17 Ⓐ Ⓑ Ⓒ Ⓓ   23 Ⓐ Ⓑ Ⓒ Ⓓ   29 Ⓐ Ⓑ Ⓒ Ⓓ

6 Ⓐ Ⓑ Ⓒ Ⓓ   12 Ⓐ Ⓑ Ⓒ Ⓓ   18 Ⓐ Ⓑ Ⓒ Ⓓ   24 Ⓐ Ⓑ Ⓒ Ⓓ   30 Ⓐ Ⓑ Ⓒ Ⓓ

PART 3—WORD KNOWLEDGE

1 Ⓐ Ⓑ Ⓒ Ⓓ   8 Ⓐ Ⓑ Ⓒ Ⓓ   15 Ⓐ Ⓑ Ⓒ Ⓓ   22 Ⓐ Ⓑ Ⓒ Ⓓ   29 Ⓐ Ⓑ Ⓒ Ⓓ

2 Ⓐ Ⓑ Ⓒ Ⓓ   9 Ⓐ Ⓑ Ⓒ Ⓓ   16 Ⓐ Ⓑ Ⓒ Ⓓ   23 Ⓐ Ⓑ Ⓒ Ⓓ   30 Ⓐ Ⓑ Ⓒ Ⓓ

3 Ⓐ Ⓑ Ⓒ Ⓓ   10 Ⓐ Ⓑ Ⓒ Ⓓ   17 Ⓐ Ⓑ Ⓒ Ⓓ   24 Ⓐ Ⓑ Ⓒ Ⓓ   31 Ⓐ Ⓑ Ⓒ Ⓓ

4 Ⓐ Ⓑ Ⓒ Ⓓ   11 Ⓐ Ⓑ Ⓒ Ⓓ   18 Ⓐ Ⓑ Ⓒ Ⓓ   25 Ⓐ Ⓑ Ⓒ Ⓓ   32 Ⓐ Ⓑ Ⓒ Ⓓ

5 Ⓐ Ⓑ Ⓒ Ⓓ   12 Ⓐ Ⓑ Ⓒ Ⓓ   19 Ⓐ Ⓑ Ⓒ Ⓓ   26 Ⓐ Ⓑ Ⓒ Ⓓ   33 Ⓐ Ⓑ Ⓒ Ⓓ

6 Ⓐ Ⓑ Ⓒ Ⓓ   13 Ⓐ Ⓑ Ⓒ Ⓓ   20 Ⓐ Ⓑ Ⓒ Ⓓ   27 Ⓐ Ⓑ Ⓒ Ⓓ   34 Ⓐ Ⓑ Ⓒ Ⓓ

7 Ⓐ Ⓑ Ⓒ Ⓓ   14 Ⓐ Ⓑ Ⓒ Ⓓ   21 Ⓐ Ⓑ Ⓒ Ⓓ   28 Ⓐ Ⓑ Ⓒ Ⓓ   35 Ⓐ Ⓑ Ⓒ Ⓓ

PART 4—PARAGRAPH COMPREHENSION

1 Ⓐ Ⓑ Ⓒ Ⓓ   5 Ⓐ Ⓑ Ⓒ Ⓓ   9 Ⓐ Ⓑ Ⓒ Ⓓ   13 Ⓐ Ⓑ Ⓒ Ⓓ

2 Ⓐ Ⓑ Ⓒ Ⓓ   6 Ⓐ Ⓑ Ⓒ Ⓓ   10 Ⓐ Ⓑ Ⓒ Ⓓ   14 Ⓐ Ⓑ Ⓒ Ⓓ

3 Ⓐ Ⓑ Ⓒ Ⓓ   7 Ⓐ Ⓑ Ⓒ Ⓓ   11 Ⓐ Ⓑ Ⓒ Ⓓ   15 Ⓐ Ⓑ Ⓒ Ⓓ

4 Ⓐ Ⓑ Ⓒ Ⓓ   8 Ⓐ Ⓑ Ⓒ Ⓓ   12 Ⓐ Ⓑ Ⓒ Ⓓ

PART 5—NUMERICAL OPERATIONS

1 Ⓐ Ⓑ Ⓒ Ⓓ	11 Ⓐ Ⓑ Ⓒ Ⓓ	21 Ⓐ Ⓑ Ⓒ Ⓓ	31 Ⓐ Ⓑ Ⓒ Ⓓ	41 Ⓐ Ⓑ Ⓒ Ⓓ
2 Ⓐ Ⓑ Ⓒ Ⓓ	12 Ⓐ Ⓑ Ⓒ Ⓓ	22 Ⓐ Ⓑ Ⓒ Ⓓ	32 Ⓐ Ⓑ Ⓒ Ⓓ	42 Ⓐ Ⓑ Ⓒ Ⓓ
3 Ⓐ Ⓑ Ⓒ Ⓓ	13 Ⓐ Ⓑ Ⓒ Ⓓ	23 Ⓐ Ⓑ Ⓒ Ⓓ	33 Ⓐ Ⓑ Ⓒ Ⓓ	43 Ⓐ Ⓑ Ⓒ Ⓓ
4 Ⓐ Ⓑ Ⓒ Ⓓ	14 Ⓐ Ⓑ Ⓒ Ⓓ	24 Ⓐ Ⓑ Ⓒ Ⓓ	34 Ⓐ Ⓑ Ⓒ Ⓓ	44 Ⓐ Ⓑ Ⓒ Ⓓ
5 Ⓐ Ⓑ Ⓒ Ⓓ	15 Ⓐ Ⓑ Ⓒ Ⓓ	25 Ⓐ Ⓑ Ⓒ Ⓓ	35 Ⓐ Ⓑ Ⓒ Ⓓ	45 Ⓐ Ⓑ Ⓒ Ⓓ
6 Ⓐ Ⓑ Ⓒ Ⓓ	16 Ⓐ Ⓑ Ⓒ Ⓓ	26 Ⓐ Ⓑ Ⓒ Ⓓ	36 Ⓐ Ⓑ Ⓒ Ⓓ	46 Ⓐ Ⓑ Ⓒ Ⓓ
7 Ⓐ Ⓑ Ⓒ Ⓓ	17 Ⓐ Ⓑ Ⓒ Ⓓ	27 Ⓐ Ⓑ Ⓒ Ⓓ	37 Ⓐ Ⓑ Ⓒ Ⓓ	47 Ⓐ Ⓑ Ⓒ Ⓓ
8 Ⓐ Ⓑ Ⓒ Ⓓ	18 Ⓐ Ⓑ Ⓒ Ⓓ	28 Ⓐ Ⓑ Ⓒ Ⓓ	38 Ⓐ Ⓑ Ⓒ Ⓓ	48 Ⓐ Ⓑ Ⓒ Ⓓ
9 Ⓐ Ⓑ Ⓒ Ⓓ	19 Ⓐ Ⓑ Ⓒ Ⓓ	29 Ⓐ Ⓑ Ⓒ Ⓓ	39 Ⓐ Ⓑ Ⓒ Ⓓ	49 Ⓐ Ⓑ Ⓒ Ⓓ
10 Ⓐ Ⓑ Ⓒ Ⓓ	20 Ⓐ Ⓑ Ⓒ Ⓓ	30 Ⓐ Ⓑ Ⓒ Ⓓ	40 Ⓐ Ⓑ Ⓒ Ⓓ	50 Ⓐ Ⓑ Ⓒ Ⓓ

PART 6—CODING SPEED

1 Ⓐ Ⓑ Ⓒ Ⓓ Ⓔ	15 Ⓐ Ⓑ Ⓒ Ⓓ Ⓔ	29 Ⓐ Ⓑ Ⓒ Ⓓ Ⓔ	43 Ⓐ Ⓑ Ⓒ Ⓓ Ⓔ	57 Ⓐ Ⓑ Ⓒ Ⓓ Ⓔ	71 Ⓐ Ⓑ Ⓒ Ⓓ Ⓔ
2 Ⓐ Ⓑ Ⓒ Ⓓ Ⓔ	16 Ⓐ Ⓑ Ⓒ Ⓓ Ⓔ	30 Ⓐ Ⓑ Ⓒ Ⓓ Ⓔ	44 Ⓐ Ⓑ Ⓒ Ⓓ Ⓔ	58 Ⓐ Ⓑ Ⓒ Ⓓ Ⓔ	72 Ⓐ Ⓑ Ⓒ Ⓓ Ⓔ
3 Ⓐ Ⓑ Ⓒ Ⓓ Ⓔ	17 Ⓐ Ⓑ Ⓒ Ⓓ Ⓔ	31 Ⓐ Ⓑ Ⓒ Ⓓ Ⓔ	45 Ⓐ Ⓑ Ⓒ Ⓓ Ⓔ	59 Ⓐ Ⓑ Ⓒ Ⓓ Ⓔ	73 Ⓐ Ⓑ Ⓒ Ⓓ Ⓔ
4 Ⓐ Ⓑ Ⓒ Ⓓ Ⓔ	18 Ⓐ Ⓑ Ⓒ Ⓓ Ⓔ	32 Ⓐ Ⓑ Ⓒ Ⓓ Ⓔ	46 Ⓐ Ⓑ Ⓒ Ⓓ Ⓔ	60 Ⓐ Ⓑ Ⓒ Ⓓ Ⓔ	74 Ⓐ Ⓑ Ⓒ Ⓓ Ⓔ
5 Ⓐ Ⓑ Ⓒ Ⓓ Ⓔ	19 Ⓐ Ⓑ Ⓒ Ⓓ Ⓔ	33 Ⓐ Ⓑ Ⓒ Ⓓ Ⓔ	47 Ⓐ Ⓑ Ⓒ Ⓓ Ⓔ	61 Ⓐ Ⓑ Ⓒ Ⓓ Ⓔ	75 Ⓐ Ⓑ Ⓒ Ⓓ Ⓔ
6 Ⓐ Ⓑ Ⓒ Ⓓ Ⓔ	20 Ⓐ Ⓑ Ⓒ Ⓓ Ⓔ	34 Ⓐ Ⓑ Ⓒ Ⓓ Ⓔ	48 Ⓐ Ⓑ Ⓒ Ⓓ Ⓔ	62 Ⓐ Ⓑ Ⓒ Ⓓ Ⓔ	76 Ⓐ Ⓑ Ⓒ Ⓓ Ⓔ
7 Ⓐ Ⓑ Ⓒ Ⓓ Ⓔ	21 Ⓐ Ⓑ Ⓒ Ⓓ Ⓔ	35 Ⓐ Ⓑ Ⓒ Ⓓ Ⓔ	49 Ⓐ Ⓑ Ⓒ Ⓓ Ⓔ	63 Ⓐ Ⓑ Ⓒ Ⓓ Ⓔ	77 Ⓐ Ⓑ Ⓒ Ⓓ Ⓔ
8 Ⓐ Ⓑ Ⓒ Ⓓ Ⓔ	22 Ⓐ Ⓑ Ⓒ Ⓓ Ⓔ	36 Ⓐ Ⓑ Ⓒ Ⓓ Ⓔ	50 Ⓐ Ⓑ Ⓒ Ⓓ Ⓔ	64 Ⓐ Ⓑ Ⓒ Ⓓ Ⓔ	78 Ⓐ Ⓑ Ⓒ Ⓓ Ⓔ
9 Ⓐ Ⓑ Ⓒ Ⓓ Ⓔ	23 Ⓐ Ⓑ Ⓒ Ⓓ Ⓔ	37 Ⓐ Ⓑ Ⓒ Ⓓ Ⓔ	51 Ⓐ Ⓑ Ⓒ Ⓓ Ⓔ	65 Ⓐ Ⓑ Ⓒ Ⓓ Ⓔ	79 Ⓐ Ⓑ Ⓒ Ⓓ Ⓔ
10 Ⓐ Ⓑ Ⓒ Ⓓ Ⓔ	24 Ⓐ Ⓑ Ⓒ Ⓓ Ⓔ	38 Ⓐ Ⓑ Ⓒ Ⓓ Ⓔ	52 Ⓐ Ⓑ Ⓒ Ⓓ Ⓔ	66 Ⓐ Ⓑ Ⓒ Ⓓ Ⓔ	80 Ⓐ Ⓑ Ⓒ Ⓓ Ⓔ
11 Ⓐ Ⓑ Ⓒ Ⓓ Ⓔ	25 Ⓐ Ⓑ Ⓒ Ⓓ Ⓔ	39 Ⓐ Ⓑ Ⓒ Ⓓ Ⓔ	53 Ⓐ Ⓑ Ⓒ Ⓓ Ⓔ	67 Ⓐ Ⓑ Ⓒ Ⓓ Ⓔ	81 Ⓐ Ⓑ Ⓒ Ⓓ Ⓔ
12 Ⓐ Ⓑ Ⓒ Ⓓ Ⓔ	26 Ⓐ Ⓑ Ⓒ Ⓓ Ⓔ	40 Ⓐ Ⓑ Ⓒ Ⓓ Ⓔ	54 Ⓐ Ⓑ Ⓒ Ⓓ Ⓔ	68 Ⓐ Ⓑ Ⓒ Ⓓ Ⓔ	82 Ⓐ Ⓑ Ⓒ Ⓓ Ⓔ
13 Ⓐ Ⓑ Ⓒ Ⓓ Ⓔ	27 Ⓐ Ⓑ Ⓒ Ⓓ Ⓔ	41 Ⓐ Ⓑ Ⓒ Ⓓ Ⓔ	55 Ⓐ Ⓑ Ⓒ Ⓓ Ⓔ	69 Ⓐ Ⓑ Ⓒ Ⓓ Ⓔ	83 Ⓐ Ⓑ Ⓒ Ⓓ Ⓔ
14 Ⓐ Ⓑ Ⓒ Ⓓ Ⓔ	28 Ⓐ Ⓑ Ⓒ Ⓓ Ⓔ	42 Ⓐ Ⓑ Ⓒ Ⓓ Ⓔ	56 Ⓐ Ⓑ Ⓒ Ⓓ Ⓔ	70 Ⓐ Ⓑ Ⓒ Ⓓ Ⓔ	84 Ⓐ Ⓑ Ⓒ Ⓓ Ⓔ

PART 7—AUTO & SHOP INFORMATION

1 Ⓐ Ⓑ Ⓒ Ⓓ	6 Ⓐ Ⓑ Ⓒ Ⓓ	11 Ⓐ Ⓑ Ⓒ Ⓓ	16 Ⓐ Ⓑ Ⓒ Ⓓ	21 Ⓐ Ⓑ Ⓒ Ⓓ
2 Ⓐ Ⓑ Ⓒ Ⓓ	7 Ⓐ Ⓑ Ⓒ Ⓓ	12 Ⓐ Ⓑ Ⓒ Ⓓ	17 Ⓐ Ⓑ Ⓒ Ⓓ	22 Ⓐ Ⓑ Ⓒ Ⓓ
3 Ⓐ Ⓑ Ⓒ Ⓓ	8 Ⓐ Ⓑ Ⓒ Ⓓ	13 Ⓐ Ⓑ Ⓒ Ⓓ	18 Ⓐ Ⓑ Ⓒ Ⓓ	23 Ⓐ Ⓑ Ⓒ Ⓓ
4 Ⓐ Ⓑ Ⓒ Ⓓ	9 Ⓐ Ⓑ Ⓒ Ⓓ	14 Ⓐ Ⓑ Ⓒ Ⓓ	19 Ⓐ Ⓑ Ⓒ Ⓓ	24 Ⓐ Ⓑ Ⓒ Ⓓ
5 Ⓐ Ⓑ Ⓒ Ⓓ	10 Ⓐ Ⓑ Ⓒ Ⓓ	15 Ⓐ Ⓑ Ⓒ Ⓓ	20 Ⓐ Ⓑ Ⓒ Ⓓ	25 Ⓐ Ⓑ Ⓒ Ⓓ

PART 8—MATHEMATICS KNOWLEDGE

1 Ⓐ Ⓑ Ⓒ Ⓓ	6 Ⓐ Ⓑ Ⓒ Ⓓ	11 Ⓐ Ⓑ Ⓒ Ⓓ	16 Ⓐ Ⓑ Ⓒ Ⓓ	21 Ⓐ Ⓑ Ⓒ Ⓓ
2 Ⓐ Ⓑ Ⓒ Ⓓ	7 Ⓐ Ⓑ Ⓒ Ⓓ	12 Ⓐ Ⓑ Ⓒ Ⓓ	17 Ⓐ Ⓑ Ⓒ Ⓓ	22 Ⓐ Ⓑ Ⓒ Ⓓ
3 Ⓐ Ⓑ Ⓒ Ⓓ	8 Ⓐ Ⓑ Ⓒ Ⓓ	13 Ⓐ Ⓑ Ⓒ Ⓓ	18 Ⓐ Ⓑ Ⓒ Ⓓ	23 Ⓐ Ⓑ Ⓒ Ⓓ
4 Ⓐ Ⓑ Ⓒ Ⓓ	9 Ⓐ Ⓑ Ⓒ Ⓓ	14 Ⓐ Ⓑ Ⓒ Ⓓ	19 Ⓐ Ⓑ Ⓒ Ⓓ	24 Ⓐ Ⓑ Ⓒ Ⓓ
5 Ⓐ Ⓑ Ⓒ Ⓓ	10 Ⓐ Ⓑ Ⓒ Ⓓ	15 Ⓐ Ⓑ Ⓒ Ⓓ	20 Ⓐ Ⓑ Ⓒ Ⓓ	25 Ⓐ Ⓑ Ⓒ Ⓓ

PART 9—MECHANICAL COMPREHENSION

1 Ⓐ Ⓑ Ⓒ Ⓓ	6 Ⓐ Ⓑ Ⓒ Ⓓ	11 Ⓐ Ⓑ Ⓒ Ⓓ	16 Ⓐ Ⓑ Ⓒ Ⓓ	21 Ⓐ Ⓑ Ⓒ Ⓓ
2 Ⓐ Ⓑ Ⓒ Ⓓ	7 Ⓐ Ⓑ Ⓒ Ⓓ	12 Ⓐ Ⓑ Ⓒ Ⓓ	17 Ⓐ Ⓑ Ⓒ Ⓓ	22 Ⓐ Ⓑ Ⓒ Ⓓ
3 Ⓐ Ⓑ Ⓒ Ⓓ	8 Ⓐ Ⓑ Ⓒ Ⓓ	13 Ⓐ Ⓑ Ⓒ Ⓓ	18 Ⓐ Ⓑ Ⓒ Ⓓ	23 Ⓐ Ⓑ Ⓒ Ⓓ
4 Ⓐ Ⓑ Ⓒ Ⓓ	9 Ⓐ Ⓑ Ⓒ Ⓓ	14 Ⓐ Ⓑ Ⓒ Ⓓ	19 Ⓐ Ⓑ Ⓒ Ⓓ	24 Ⓐ Ⓑ Ⓒ Ⓓ
5 Ⓐ Ⓑ Ⓒ Ⓓ	10 Ⓐ Ⓑ Ⓒ Ⓓ	15 Ⓐ Ⓑ Ⓒ Ⓓ	20 Ⓐ Ⓑ Ⓒ Ⓓ	25 Ⓐ Ⓑ Ⓒ Ⓓ

PART 10—ELECTRONICS INFORMATION

1 Ⓐ Ⓑ Ⓒ Ⓓ	6 Ⓐ Ⓑ Ⓒ Ⓓ	11 Ⓐ Ⓑ Ⓒ Ⓓ	16 Ⓐ Ⓑ Ⓒ Ⓓ
2 Ⓐ Ⓑ Ⓒ Ⓓ	7 Ⓐ Ⓑ Ⓒ Ⓓ	12 Ⓐ Ⓑ Ⓒ Ⓓ	17 Ⓐ Ⓑ Ⓒ Ⓓ
3 Ⓐ Ⓑ Ⓒ Ⓓ	8 Ⓐ Ⓑ Ⓒ Ⓓ	13 Ⓐ Ⓑ Ⓒ Ⓓ	18 Ⓐ Ⓑ Ⓒ Ⓓ
4 Ⓐ Ⓑ Ⓒ Ⓓ	9 Ⓐ Ⓑ Ⓒ Ⓓ	14 Ⓐ Ⓑ Ⓒ Ⓓ	19 Ⓐ Ⓑ Ⓒ Ⓓ
5 Ⓐ Ⓑ Ⓒ Ⓓ	10 Ⓐ Ⓑ Ⓒ Ⓓ	15 Ⓐ Ⓑ Ⓒ Ⓓ	20 Ⓐ Ⓑ Ⓒ Ⓓ

GENERAL SCIENCE

The general science part of your examination asks questions based upon the science you learned in high school. For each question there are four possible answers. Only one answer is correct. Choose the answer which you think is correct and mark the corresponding space on your answer sheet. Try these questions.

1. Of the following, the process which will result in water that is the most nearly chemically pure is

1-A   aeration
1-B   distillation
1-C   chlorination
1-D   filtration

1. Ⓐ Ⓑ Ⓒ Ⓓ

1-B DISTILLATION is the correct answer. Aeration (A) adds air to the water, but does nothing to purify it. Chlorination (B) may make water safe to drink, but it does so by adding chemicals, not by purifying the water. Filtration (D) removes solid matter from water, but does not make it chemically pure. Distilled water is made by evaporating water and collecting the water vapor. The vapor is then allowed to cool so that it becomes liquid again. Since the chemicals in water do not evaporate, they remain in the original container and the "new" water is chemically pure.

2. A child with extremely thin arms and legs and with a large, distended (swollen) belly is probably suffering from

2-A   tuberculosis
2-B   child abuse
2-C   malnutrition
2-D   measles

2. Ⓐ Ⓑ Ⓒ Ⓓ

2-C MALNUTRITION is the correct answer. The symptoms described are commonly seen in the children of war-torn nations which have experienced crop failures. An undernourished child is likely to be more susceptible to disease (A) and (D), but need not have a disease to display the symptoms. Child abuse (B) only occasionally takes the form of starving the child.

3. The *most common* bad health habit of the American people is

3-A   taking cold showers
3-B   dressing too warmly
3-C   overeating
3-D   drunken driving

3. Ⓐ Ⓑ Ⓒ Ⓓ

3-C OVEREATING is the correct answer. While drunken driving (D) is more dangerous, many more people are guilty of overeating. Overweight contributes to a great many diseases, most notably high blood pressure, diabetes and heart disease. Overdressing (B) is not a serious bad habit. Taking cold showers (A) may not be a bad habit at all.

DO NOT TURN THE PAGE UNTIL YOU ARE TOLD TO DO SO

GENERAL SCIENCE

TIME: 11 Minutes—25 Questions

1. Which one of the following is *not* a fruit?

   1-A potato
   1-B tomato
   1-C cucumber
   1-D green pepper

2. What temperature is shown on a Fahrenheit thermometer when a centigrade thermometer reads 0°?

   2-A −40°
   2-B −32°
   2-C 0°
   2-D +32°

3. The most likely reason why dinosaurs became extinct was that they

   3-A were killed by erupting volcanoes
   3-B were eaten as adults by the advancing mammalian groups
   3-C failed to adapt to a changing environment
   3-D killed each other in combat

4. You are most likely to develop hypothermia when

   4-A it is very hot and you have nothing to drink
   4-B you are bitten by a rabid dog
   4-C you fall asleep with a thermometer in your mouth
   4-D it is very cold and your clothes are wet

5. Alcoholic beverages contain

   5-A wood alcohol
   5-B isopropyl alcohol
   5-C glyceryl alcohol
   5-D grain alcohol

6. One-celled animals belong to the group of living things known as

   6-A protozoa
   6-B annelida
   6-C porifera
   6-D arthropoda

7. Of the following, a human blood disease which has been definitely shown to be due to a hereditary factor or factors is

   7-A pernicious anemia
   7-B polyscythemia
   7-C sickle cell anemia
   7-D leukemia

8. Ringworm is caused by a(n)

   8-A alga
   8-B fungus
   8-C bacterium
   8-D protozoan

9. Of the following, the lightest element known on earth is

   9-A hydrogen
   9-B oxygen
   9-C helium
   9-D air

10. Of the following, the gas which is needed for burning is

   10-A carbon dioxide
   10-B nitrogen
   10-C oxygen
   10-D argon

11. The vitamin which helps coagulation of the blood is

    11-A C
    11-B E
    11-C D
→ 11-D K

12. Of the following types of clouds, the ones which occur at the greatest height are called

    12-A cirrus
    12-B nimbus
    12-C cumulus
    12-D stratus

13. If all pork were thoroughly cooked before being eaten, there would be very few cases of

    13-A cancer
    13-B hookworm
    13-C trichinosis
⇒13-D ringworm

14. Which of the following minerals is restored to the soil by plants of the pea and bean family?

    14-A sulfates
    14-B carbonates
    14-C nitrates
→14-D phosphates

15. Radium is stored in lead containers because

    15-A the lead absorbs the harmful radiations
    15-B radium is a heavy substance
⇒ 15-C lead prevents the disintegration of the radium
    15-D lead is cheap

16. The presence of coal deposits in Alaska shows that at one time Alaska

    16-A had a tropical climate
    16-B was covered with ice
    16-C was connected to Asia
    16-D was formed by volcanic action

17. The cyclotron is used to

    17-A measure radioactivity
    17-B measure the speed of the earth's rotation
    17-C split atoms
    17-D store radioactive energy

18. The time that it takes for the earth to rotate 45° is

    18-A one hour
    18-B four hours
    18-C three hours
    18-D ten hours

19. Which of the following birds would most probably *not* be found in a wooded area?

    19-A thrush
    19-B green heron
    19-C barred owl
    19-D towhee

20. A volcanic eruption is caused by

    20-A sunspots
    20-B pressure inside the earth
    20-C nuclear fallout
    20-D boiling lava

21. Of the following planets, the one which has the shortest revolutionary period around the sun is

    21-A Earth
    21-B Jupiter
    21-C Mercury
    21-D Venus

22. Nitrogen-fixing bacteria are found in nodules on the roots of the

    22-A beet
    22-B potato
    22-C carrot
    22-D clover

23. All types of steel contain

    23-A carbon
    23-B chromium
    23-C nickel
    23-D tungsten

24. What is the name of the negative particle which circles the nucleus of the atom?

    24-A neutron
    24-B meson
    24-C proton
    24-D electron

25. A well-balanced meal would include peas, bread, milk and

    25-A fish
    25-B spaghetti
    25-C jello
    25-D string beans

STOP

IF YOU FINISH THIS PART BEFORE THE TIME IS UP, CHECK OVER YOUR WORK ON THIS PART ONLY. DO NOT GO ON UNTIL YOU ARE TOLD TO DO SO.

PART 2

ARITHMETIC REASONING

The arithmetic reasoning questions require careful thinking as well as arithmetic calculation. Some problems require more than one step for their solutions. You must decide exactly what the question asks; than you must determine the best method for finding the answer; finally you must work out the problem on your scratch paper. Be sure to mark the letter of the correct answer on your answer sheet. Try these questions:

1. If a plane travels 1,000 miles in 5 hours 30 minutes, what is its average speed in miles per hour?

1-A $181\frac{9}{11}$
1-B 200
1-C 215
1-D $192\frac{1}{2}$

1. Ⓐ Ⓑ Ⓒ Ⓓ

1-A 5 hours 30 minutes = $5\frac{1}{2}$ hours
1000 mph ÷ $5\frac{1}{2}$ hours
$= 1000 ÷ \frac{11}{2} = 1000 × \frac{2}{11} = 181\frac{9}{11}$ mph

2. A jacket that normally sells for $35 can be purchased on sale for 2,975 pennies. What is the rate of discount represented by the sale price?

2-A 5%
2-B 10%
2-C 15%
2-D 20%

2. Ⓐ Ⓑ Ⓒ Ⓓ

2-C 2,975 pennies = $29.75
$35.00 − $29.75 = $5.25 saved

Rate of discount $= \frac{5.25}{35} × 100 = .15 × 100$
$= 15\%$

3. In making a bracelet a girl uses three 10-inch strips of cord. How many bracelets can she make from a 5-yard roll of cord?

3-A 2
3-B 5
3-C 6
3-D 15

3. Ⓐ Ⓑ Ⓒ Ⓓ

3-C 10 inches × 3 strips = 30 inches per bracelet; 36 inches per yard × 5 yards of cord = 180 inches in the roll; 180 ÷ 30 = 6 bracelets can be made from the roll.

4. As an employee at a clothing store, you are entitled to a 10% discount on all purchases. When the store has a sale, employees are also entitled to the 20% discount offered to all customers. What would you have to pay for a $60 jacket bought on a sale day?

4-A $6
4-B $10.80
4-C $36
4-D $43.20

4. Ⓐ Ⓑ Ⓒ Ⓓ

4-D $60 × .10 = $6 (employee discount)
$60 − $6 = $54
$54 × .20 = $10.80 (sale discount)
$54 − $10.80 = $43.20

DO NOT TURN THE PAGE UNTIL YOU ARE TOLD TO DO SO

ARITHMETIC REASONING

TIME: 36 Minutes—30 Questions

1. If pencils are bought at 35 cents per dozen and sold at 3 for 10 cents the total profit on $5\frac{1}{2}$ dozen is

    1-A   25 cents
    1-B $27\frac{1}{2}$ cents
    1-C $28\frac{1}{2}$ cents
    1-D $31\frac{1}{2}$ cents

2. If a scow is towed at the rate of three miles an hour, it will need how many hours to go 28 miles?

    2-A   10 hrs. 30 min.
    2-B   9 hrs. 20 min.
    2-C   12 hrs.
    2-D   9 hrs. 15 min.

3. A pint of milk is what part of half a gallon?

    3-A $\frac{1}{8}$
    3-B $\frac{1}{4}$
    3-C $\frac{1}{2}$
    3-D $\frac{1}{16}$

4. A typist uses lengthwise a sheet of paper 9 inches by 12 inches. She leaves a 1-inch margin on each side and a $1\frac{1}{2}$-inch margin on top and bottom. What fractional part of the page is used for typing?

    4-A $\frac{21}{22}$
    4-B $\frac{7}{12}$
    4-C $\frac{5}{9}$
    4-D $\frac{3}{4}$

5. A dealer bought some bicycles for $4000. He sold them for $6200, making $50 on each bicycle. How many bicycles were there?

    5-A   40
    5-B   43

5-C   38
5-D   44

6. How many minutes are there in 1 day?

    6-A   60
    6-B   1440
    6-C   24
    6-D 1440×60

7. On a house plan on which 2 inches represents 5 feet, the length of a room measures $7\frac{1}{2}$ inches. The actual length of the room is

    7-A $12\frac{1}{2}$ feet
    7-B $17\frac{1}{2}$ feet
    7-C $15\frac{3}{4}$ feet
    7-D $18\frac{3}{4}$ feet

8. A stock clerk had 600 pads on hand. He then issued $\frac{3}{8}$ of his supply of pads to Division X, $\frac{1}{4}$ to Division Y, and $\frac{1}{6}$ to Division Z. The number of pads remaining in stock is

    8-A   48
    8-B   240
    8-C   125
    8-D   475

9. What is the greatest number of half-pint bottles that can be filled from a 10-gallon can of milk?

    9-A   160
    9-B   170
    9-C   16
    9-D   17

10. A piece of wood 35 feet, 6 inches long was used to make 4 shelves of equal length. The length of each shelf was

    10-A   9 feet, $1\frac{1}{2}$ inches
    10-B   8 feet, $10\frac{1}{2}$ inches

10-C 7 feet, 10$\frac{1}{2}$ inches

10-D 7 feet, 1$\frac{1}{2}$ inches

11. Two airmen traveled by bus from one point to another. The trip took 15 hours, and they left their point of origin at 8 A.M. What time did they arrive at their destination?

11-A 11 A.M.

11-B 10 P.M.

11-C 11 P.M.

11-D 12 A.M.

12. How much time is there between 8:30 a.m. today and 3:15 a.m. tomorrow?

12-A 17$\frac{3}{4}$ hrs.

12-B 18$\frac{2}{3}$ hrs.

12-C 18$\frac{1}{2}$ hrs.

12-D 18$\frac{3}{4}$ hrs.

13. A change purse contained 3 half dollars, 8 quarters, 7 dimes, 6 nickels and 9 pennies. Express in dollars and cents the total amount of money in the purse.

13-A $3.78

13-B $4.32

13-C $3.95

13-D $4.59

14. A shopper bought 4 pillow cases that cost $4.98 apiece, 2 fitted bottom sheets that cost $8.29 apiece, and 2 fitted top sheets that cost $8.09 apiece. What was her total bill?

14-A $52.58

14-B $51.68

14-C $52.68

14-D $21.36

15. A truck going at a rate of 20 miles an hour will reach a town 40 miles away in how many hours?

15-A 3 hrs.

15-B 4 hrs.

15-C 1 hr.

15-D 2 hrs.

16. Patty went to the store and bought a bottle of cologne, 2 tubes of lipstick, and 1 box of powder. The cologne cost $4.98 a bottle, lipstick $2.29 each, and the powder $1.89 a box. What was the amount Patty had to pay for these cosmetics?

16-A $9.16

16-B $9.45

16-C $11.45

16-D $11.89

17. The Youth Fellowship decided to have a hayride. Five girls and five boys went on the trip. The parents of two of the children went along as chaperons. How many children went on the trip?

17-A 12

17-B 10

17-C 8

17-D 14

18. If $1000 is the cost of repairing 100 square yards of pavement, the cost of repairing one square yard is

18-A $10

18-B $100

18-C $150

18-D $300

19. How many packages of candy, containing $\frac{3}{4}$ of a pound each can be filled from 15 pounds of candy?

19-A 10

19-B 20

19-C 15

19-D 25

20. A skier started a fire in the fireplace. Each log she put on burned for a half-hour. If she started with 10 logs, for how many hours could the fire burn?

20-A 5 hrs.

20-B 8$\frac{1}{2}$ hrs.

20-C 10 hrs.

20-D 7 hrs.

21. A man takes out a $5,000 life insurance policy at a yearly rate of $29.62 per $1,000. What is the semi-annual premium?

12-A $37.03
21-B $74.05
21-C $148.10
21-D $296.20

22. A woman bought a lamp for $37.50. She gave the clerk $40.00. How much change did she get?

22-A $3.50
22-B $2.50
22-C $2.75
22-D $3.25

23. If a boy had $15 and spent $13.72, how do you find how much money he had left?

23-A add
23-B divide
23-C multiply
23-D subtract

24. John bought 20 party favors for $66.00. What was the cost of each one?

24-A $3.35
24-B $3.30
24-C $2.45
24-D $3.50

25. In a 45 minute gym class, 30 boys want to play basketball. Only 10 can play at once. If each player is to play the same length of time, how many minutes should each play?

25-A 8
25-B 12
25-C 15
25-D 20

26. A boy sold $88.50 worth of stationery. If he received a $33\frac{1}{3}$% commission, what was the amount of his commission?

26-A $29.50
26-B $40.00
26-C $50.00
26-D $62.50

27. A pile of magazines is 4 feet high. If each magazine is $\frac{3}{4}$ of an inch thick, the number of magazines is

27-A 36
27-B 48
27-C 64
27-D 96

28. If $\frac{1}{2}$ cup of spinach contains 80 calories and the same amount of peas contains 300 calories, how many cups of spinach have the same caloric content as $\frac{2}{3}$ cup of peas?

28-A $\frac{2}{5}$
28-B $1\frac{1}{3}$
28-C 2
28-D $2\frac{1}{2}$

29. Don and Frank started from the same point and drove in opposite directions. Don's rate of speed was 50 miles per hour. Frank's rate of speed was 40 miles per hour. How many miles apart were they at the end of 2 hours?

29-A 90
29-B 160
29-C 140
29-D 180

30. A folding chair regularly sells for $29.50. How much money is saved if the chair is bought at a 20% discount?

30-A $4.80
30-B $5.90
30-C $6.20
30-D $7.40

END OF PART 2

IF YOU FINISH BEFORE THE TIME IS UP, CHECK TO BE CERTAIN THAT YOU HAVE MARKED ALL OF YOUR ANSWERS ON THE ANSWER SHEET. THEN CHECK OVER YOUR WORK ON THIS PART ONLY. DO NOT RETURN TO PART ONE. DO NOT GO ON TO THE NEXT PART UNTIL YOU ARE TOLD TO DO SO.

PART 3

WORD KNOWLEDGE

The questions in this part test how well you understand the meanings of words. Each question has an underlined word. Read all four possible answers and decide which one has a meaning closest to the meaning of the underlined word. On your answer sheet mark the letter of the answer you choose. Try these questions.

1. Exterminate most nearly means

   1-A destroy
   1-B classify
   1-C experiment with
   1-D drive away

1. Ⓐ Ⓑ Ⓒ Ⓓ

1-A DESTROY is the correct answer. *To exterminate* means *to get rid of by killing off*. *Driving away* (D) might be a way to get rid of, but it would not be extermination. (B) and (C) are wrong.

2. The military vehicles travelled in a convoy.

   2-A hearse
   2-B thunderstorm
   2-C jeep
   2-D group

2. Ⓐ Ⓑ Ⓒ Ⓓ

2-D GROUP is the correct answer. A *jeep* (C) may be part of a *convoy*. A *convoy* is a group travelling together for protection or convenience. You have probably seen *convoys* of military vehicles travelling single-file up the highway toward summer reserve camp. (A) and (B) are wrong.

3. Reservoir most nearly means

   3-A lake
   3-B water
   3-C storage place
   3-D dam

3. Ⓐ Ⓑ Ⓒ Ⓓ

3-C STORAGE PLACE is the correct answer. A *reservoir* need not be a place for *storing water* (B), though that is its most familiar use. A *reservoir* for *water* is often created by a *dam* (D) and takes the form of an artificial *lake* (A).

4. Penalty most nearly means

   4-A foul
   4-B mistake
   4-C punishment
   4-D fine

4. Ⓐ Ⓑ Ⓒ Ⓓ

4-C PUNISHMENT is the correct answer. A *penalty* may be imposed upon someone who commits a *foul* (A) in a sports contest or upon someone who makes a *mistake* (B). A *fine* (D) is only one kind of *penalty*.

5. Calculated most nearly means

   5-A multiplied
   5-B added
   5-C answered
   5-D figured out

5. Ⓐ Ⓑ Ⓒ Ⓓ

5-D FIGURED OUT is the best answer. *Calculating* may well include *multiplying* (A) or *adding* (B) in order to arrive at the *answer* (C), but not all *calculations* need be mathematical. Since the word *calculated* was not given to you in a sentence, the most general definition is the best answer.

DO NOT TURN THE PAGE UNTIL YOU ARE TOLD TO DO SO

WORD KNOWLEDGE

TIME: 11 Minutes—35 Questions

1. Superiority most nearly means

    1-A abundance
    1-B popularity
    1-C permanence
    1-D excellence

2. Convene most nearly means

    2-A meet
    2-B debate
    2-C agree
    2-D drink

3. Hollow most nearly means

    3-A empty
    3-B brittle
    3-C rough
    3-D smooth

4. Conscious most nearly means

    4-A surprised
    4-B afraid
    4-C disappointed
    4-D aware

5. I could not go to the party because I had a prior engagement.

    5-A personal
    5-B more urgent
    5-C more attractive
    5-D earlier

6. The carpenter was criticized for his slipshod work.

    6-A slow
    6-B careful
    6-C careless
    6-D original

7. Counterfeit most nearly means

    7-A mysterious
    7-B false
    7-C unreadable
    7-D priceless

8. The man survived his three sisters.

    8-A outlived
    8-B envied
    8-C excelled
    8-D destroyed

9. Fictitious most nearly means

    9-A imaginary
    9-B well-known
    9-C odd
    9-D easy to remember

10. Each morning the children pledge allegiance to the flag.

    10-A freedom
    10-B homeland
    10-C protection
    10-D loyalty

11. The territory is too large for one platoon to defend.

    11-A region
    11-B swamp
    11-C ranch
    11-D beach

12. To penetrate most nearly means

    12-A to enter into
    12-B to bounce off
    12-C to dent
    12-D to weaken

13. The driver <u>heeded</u> the traffic signals.

    13-A worried about
    13-B ignored
    13-C disagreed with
    13-D took notice of

14. All mail is to be <u>forwarded</u> to our new address.

    14-A sent
    14-B returned
    14-C canceled
    14-D received

15. <u>Punctual</u> most nearly means

    15-A polite
    15-B thoughtful
    15-C proper
    15-D prompt

16. The <u>severity</u> of their criticism upset us.

    16-A harshness
    16-B suddenness
    16-C method
    16-D unfairness

17. The cyclist pedaled at a <u>uniform</u> rate.

    17-A increasing
    17-B unchanging
    17-C unusual
    17-D very slow

18. <u>Unite</u> most nearly means

    18-A improve
    18-B serve
    18-C uphold
    18-D combine

19. <u>Gratitude</u> most nearly means

    19-A thankfulness
    19-B excitement
    19-C disappointment
    19-D sympathy

20. <u>Flexible</u> most nearly means

    20-A pliable
    20-B rigid
    20-C weak
    20-D athletic

21. <u>Assemble</u> most nearly means

    21-A bring together
    21-B examine carefully
    21-C locate
    21-D fill

22. <u>Bewildered</u> most nearly means

    22-A worried
    22-B offended
    22-C puzzled
    22-D delighted

23. The boy scouts were <u>commended</u> for their actions at the scene of the accident.

    23-A reprimanded
    23-B praised
    23-C promoted
    23-D blamed

24. The eagle has a <u>keen</u> eye.

    24-A bright
    24-B shiny
    24-C sharp
    24-D tiny

25. <u>Nonessential</u> most nearly means

    25-A damaged
    25-B unnecessary
    25-C expensive
    25-D foreign-made

26. The computer did not <u>function</u> yesterday.

    26-A finish
    26-B stop
    26-C operate
    26-D overheat

27. <u>Verdict</u> most nearly means

    27-A approval
    27-B decision
    27-C sentence
    27-D arrival

28. Penicillin is a <u>potent</u> drug when used correctly.

   28-A harmless
   28-B possible
   28-C effective
   28-D drinkable

29. The package will be <u>conveyed</u> by Greyhound bus.

   29-A carried
   29-B guarded
   29-C refused
   29-D damaged

30. <u>Insignificant</u> most nearly means

   30-A unimportant
   30-B unpleasant
   30-C secret
   30-D thrilling

31. <u>Fatal</u> most nearly means

   31-A accidental
   31-B deadly
   31-C dangerous
   31-D beautiful

32. <u>Obsolete</u> most nearly means

   32-A out-of-date
   32-B broken down
   32-C as good as new
   32-D improved

33. The door was left <u>ajar</u>.

   33-A blocked
   33-B locked
   33-C unlocked
   33-D open

34. <u>Vocation</u> most nearly means

   34-A school
   34-B examination
   34-C occupation
   34-D carpentry

35. The letter <u>emphasized</u> two important ideas.

   35-A introduced
   35-B overlooked
   35-C contrasted
   35-D stressed

END OF PART 3

IF YOU FINISH BEFORE TIME IS UP, CHECK YOUR WORK ON THIS PART ONLY. DO NOT GO BACK TO EITHER PREVIOUS PART. DO NOT GO ON TO THE NEXT PART UNTIL YOU ARE TOLD TO DO SO.

PART 4

PARAGRAPH COMPREHENSION

The paragraph comprehension part of your test battery requires concentration and attention to detail. First you must read and understand the paragraph. Then you must read and understand each of the answer choices, noticing the differences of meaning or emphasis that are imparted by little words. There is one question based upon each paragraph. You must answer that question on the basis of what is stated or implied in the passage, even if you know a better answer and even if you know the information in the paragraph to be false. In some cases more than one answer might be correct, but you must choose the BEST answer and mark its letter on your answer sheet. Try these questions.

1. At times it has been suggested that it is incongruous for the government to employ one lawyer to prosecute and another to defend the same prisoner. This is a superficial point of view, for it overlooks the principle that the government should be as anxious to shield the innocent as it is to punish the guilty.

The paragraph best supports the statement that

1-A it is not properly within the scope of the government to provide criminals with both prosecuting and defending lawyers

1-B a person held for a crime, if he be poor, need never fear that he will not be adequately defended, because the government makes provision for competent lawyers to aid him in his defense

1-C although sometimes criticized, it is governmental policy to shield the innocent by providing legal defense for indigent persons accused of crime

1-D it is an incongruous point of view that the government should concurrently shield the innocent and punish the guilty

1. Ⓐ Ⓑ Ⓒ Ⓓ

1-C The paragraph states the principle that the government must shield the innocent. Ordinarily this is done through the establishment of trial machinery whereby the accused may present his case to a jury of his peers. Since, under this principle, every accused is entitled to trial, the government provides counsel for indigent defen-

dents. Choice B is incorrect because the government does not guarantee the competence of the lawyers it provides. Choice D contradicts the paragraph. Choice A is incorrect, for the government provides prosecuting lawyers for its own benefit, not for the benefit of the accused.

2. The capacity of banks to grant loans depends, in the long run, on the amount of money deposited with them by the public. In the short run, however, it is a well known fact that banks not only can, but do lend more than is deposited with them. If such lending is carried to excess, it leads to inflation.

The paragraph best supports the statement that

2-A banks often indulge in the vicious practice of lending more than is deposited with them

2-B in the long run, a sound banking policy operates for the mutual advantage of the bankers and the public

2-C inflation is sometimes the result of excess lending by the banks

2-D bank lending is always in direct ratio with bank deposits

2. Ⓐ Ⓑ Ⓒ Ⓓ

2-C This is the best interpretation of the paragraph. While the paragraph is cautionary, it is not judgmental, so choice A is incorrect. Choice D is directly contradicted by the paragraph.

DO NOT TURN THE PAGE UNTIL YOU ARE TOLD TO DO SO

PARAGRAPH COMPREHENSION

TIME: 13 Minutes—15 Questions

1. Prior to the Civil War, the steamboat was the center of life in the thriving Mississippi towns. With the war came the railroads. River traffic dwindled and the white-painted vessels rotted at the wharves. During World War I, the government decided to relieve rail congestion by reviving the long-forgotten waterways. Today, steamers, diesels, and barges ply the Mississippi.

   The paragraph best supports the statement that

   1-A the volume of river transportation was greater than the volume of rail transportation during World War I
   1-B growth of river transportation greatly increased the congestion on the railroads
   1-C business found river transportation more profitable than railroad transportation during World War I
   1-D since the Civil War, the volume of transportation on the Mississippi has varied

2. Although rural crime reporting is spottier and less efficient than city and town reporting, sufficient data is collected to support the statement that rural crime rates are lower than those of urban communities.

   The paragraph best supports the statement that

   2-A better reporting of crime occurs in rural areas than in cities
   2-B there appears to be a lower proportion of crime in rural areas than in cities
   2-C cities have more crime than towns
   2-D no conclusions can be drawn regarding crime in rural areas because of inadequate reporting

3. There exists a false but popular idea that a clue is a mysterious fact that most people overlook but which some very keen investigator easily discovers and recognizes as having, in itself, a remarkable meaning. The clue is most often an ordinary fact that an observant person picks up—something that gains its significance when, after a long series of careful investigations, it is connected with a network of other clues.

   To be of value clues must be

   3-A discovered by skilled investigators
   3-B found under mysterious circumstances
   3-C connected with other facts
   3-D discovered soon after the crime

4. What gave this country the isolation it enjoyed in the 19th century was the statesmanship of Jefferson, Adams, Madison, and Monroe on this side of the Atlantic and of men like Canning on the other side. American independence of the European system did not exist in the two centuries before the Monroe Doctrine of 1823, and it has not existed in the century which began in 1914.

   The paragraph best supports the statement that

   4-A America enjoyed greater isolation from European affairs from 1823 to 1914 than before or after
   4-B the isolation of this country from European affairs was, prior to 1914, the result of our geographic position
   4-C Canning was a statesman living in the 20th century
   4-D America is less isolated today than it has ever been

5. Economy once in a while is just not enough. I expect to find it at every level of responsibility, from cabinet member to the newest and youngest recruit. Controlling waste is some-

thing like bailing a boat; you have to keep at it. I have no intention of easing up on my insistence on getting a dollar of value for each dollar we spend.

The paragraph best supports the statement that

5-A we need not be concerned about items which cost less than a dollar

5-B it is advisable to buy the cheaper of two items

5-C the responsibility of economy is greater at high levels than at low levels

5-D economy is a continuing responsibility

6. The location of a railway line is necessarily a compromise between the desire to build the line with as little expense as possible and the desire to construct it so that its route will cover that over which trade and commerce are likely to flow.

The route selected for a railway line

6-A should be the one over which the line can be built most cheaply

6-B determines the location of commercial centers

6-C should always cover the shortest possible distance between its terminals

6-D cannot always be the one involving the lowest construction costs

7. In almost every community, fortunately, there are certain men and women known to be public-spirited. Others, however, may be selfish and act only as their private interests seem to require.

The paragraph suggests that those citizens who disregard others are

7-A needed

7-B found only in small communities

7-C not known

7-D not public-spirited

8. Salt has always been important in our diet as a flavoring for food, but recently doctors have come to recognize it as an absolute necessity. Most living things contain salt and it is almost impossible to eat a normal diet without getting some. However, that "some" may not be enough. Now doctors recommend that those who normally use little salt step up their salt consumption in hot weather, when more than the usual salt intake is required.

The paragraph best supports the statement that

8-A salt is necessary if flavor is to be maintained

8-B people living on a normal diet have an intake of salt which is sufficient to maintain good blood pressure

8-C the body needs more salt in summer than in winter

8-D all organic life contains salt in one form or another

9. It is a common assumption that city directories are prepared and published by the cities concerned. However, the directory business is as much a private business as is the publishing of dictionaries and encyclopedias. The companies financing the publication make their profits through the sales of the directories themselves and through the advertising in them.

The paragraph best supports the statement that

9-A the publication of a city directory is a commercial enterprise

9-B the size of a city directory limits the space devoted to advertising

9-C many city directories are published by dictionary and encyclopedia concerns

9-D city directories are sold at cost to local residents and businessmen

10. Scientific judgments as opposed to legal judgments are more impartial, objective, and precise. They are more subject to verification by any competent observer.

Scientific judgments

10-A can be verified by competent observers

10-B can be tested by advanced laboratory methods

10-C accept no opinion until validated

10-D are usually propounded by experts in their fields

11. The labor required to produce a bushel of wheat in 1830 was three hours. Today it takes

less than ten minutes. Further, it has been estimated that fifty men, employing modern farm machinery and agricultural methods, can do the work of five hundred peasants toiling under the conditions of the eighteenth century.

On the basis of the facts presented above, one could best conclude that

11-A the increase of efficiency in agriculture is almost as great as that in manufacturing

11-B modern farm machinery has resulted in serious unemployment among farmers

11-C more than 18 times as much wheat is produced today than in 1830

11-D modern farm machinery is labor-saving

12. The coloration of textile fabrics composed of cotton and wool generally requires two processes, as the process used in dyeing wool is seldom capable of fixing the color upon cotton. The usual method is to immerse the fabric in the requisite baths to dye the wool and then to test the partially dyed material in the manner found suitable for cotton.

The dyeing of textile fabrics composed of cotton and wool

12-A is more successful when the material contains more cotton than wool

12-B is not satisfactory when solid colors are desired

12-C is restricted to two colors for any one fabric

12-D is based upon the methods required for dyeing the different materials

13. The increasing size of business organizations has resulted in less personal contact between superior and subordinate. Consequently, business executives today depend more upon records and reports to secure information and exercise control over the operations of various departments.

The increasing size of business organizations

13-A has caused a complete cleavage between employer and employee

13-B has resulted in less personal contact between superior and subordinate

13-C has tended toward class distinctions in large organizations

13-D has resulted in a better means of controlling the operations of various departments

14. Certain chemical changes, such as fermentation, are due to the action of innumerable living micro-organisms known as bacteria. Bacteria also cause the decomposition of sewage.

Certain chemical changes are due to

14-A bacteria
14-B oxidation
14-C fermentation
14-D decomposition

15. Any business not provided with capable substitutes to fill all important positions is a weak business. Therefore, a foreman should train each man not only to perform his own particular duties but also to do those of two or three positions.

The paragraph best supports the statement that

15-A dependence on substitutes is a sign of a weak organization

15-B training will improve the strongest organization

15-C the foreman should be the most expert at any particular job under him

15-D vacancies in vital positions should be provided for in advance

END OF PART 4

IF YOU FINISH BEFORE TIME IS UP, CHECK OVER YOUR WORK ON THIS PART ONLY. DO NOT GO BACK TO ANY PREVIOUS PART. DO NOT GO ON UNTIL YOU ARE TOLD TO DO SO.

PART 5

NUMERICAL OPERATIONS

The numerical operations part of your test battery consists of fifty very simple arithmetic questions which must be answered in only three minutes. Obviously, speed is a very important factor. You should not attempt to compute these answers using pencil and scratch paper. Instead, solve each problem in your head, then choose the correct answer from among the four choices and mark the letter of the correct answer on your answer sheet. If you are not sure of an answer, guess and go on to the next question. Do not skip any questions. You will most certainly not have time to go back to fill in. Since a wrong answer will not count against you, it cannot hurt to guess. Many people cannot complete all fifty questions in the three minutes allowed. Do not be upset if you cannot finish. Just answer as many questions as you can. Try these questions.

1. $4 + 6 =$

    1-A 8
    1-B 2
    1-C 10
    1-D 12

    1. Ⓐ Ⓑ Ⓒ Ⓓ

1-C $4 + 6 = 10$

2. $12 \div 2 =$

    2-A 4
    2-B 6
    2-C 8
    2-D 10

    2. Ⓐ Ⓑ Ⓒ Ⓓ

2-B $12 \div 2 = 6$

3. $6 + 6 =$

    3-A 0
    3-B 1
    3-C 8
    3-D 12

    3. Ⓐ Ⓑ Ⓒ Ⓓ

3-D $6 + 6 = 12$

4. $9 - 1 =$

    4-A 10
    4-B 9
    4-C 8
    4-D 0

    4. Ⓐ Ⓑ Ⓒ Ⓓ

4-C $9 - 1 = 8$

5. $16 \div 4 =$

    5-A 12
    5-B 10
    5-C 4
    5-D 2

    5. Ⓐ Ⓑ Ⓒ Ⓓ

5-C $16 \div 4 = 4$

6. $3 \times 2 =$

    6-A 6
    6-B 4
    6-C 1
    6-D 5

    6. Ⓐ Ⓑ Ⓒ Ⓓ

6-A $3 \times 2 = 6$

DO NOT TURN THE PAGE UNTIL YOU ARE TOLD TO DO SO

NUMERICAL OPERATIONS

TIME: 3 Minutes—50 Questions

1. 2 + 5 =

1-A 3
1-B 7
1-C 9
1-D 10

2. 18 ÷ 2 =

2-A 3
2-B 6
2-C 9
2-D 11

3. 10 − 8 =

3-A 2
3-B 9
3-C 16
3-D 18

4. 3 × 3 =

4-A 6
4-B 9
4-C 30
4-D 33

5. 1 + 8 =

5-A 18
5-B 80
5-C 7
5-D 9

6. 9 × 8 =

6-A 56
6-B 64
6-C 72
6-D 76

7. 4 × 5 =

7-A 20
7-B 24
7-C 28
7-D 30

8. 3 + 7 =

8-A 37
8-B 21
8-C 10
8-D 4

9. 9 − 5 =

9-A 7
9-B 14
9-C 12
9-D 4

10. 3 + 9 =

10-A 3
10-B 6
10-C 12
10-D 15

11. 9 × 3 =

11-A 21
11-B 25
11-C 27
11-D 29

12. 3 + 4 =

12-A 1
12-B 7
12-C 9
12-D 11

13. 10 − 6 =

13-A 4
13-B 8
13-C 14
13-D 16

14. 1 + 5 =

14-A 0
14-B 4
14-C 5
14-D 6

15. 4 × 2 =

15-A 6
15-B 16
15-C 12
15-D 8

16. 49 ÷ 7 =

16-A 6
16-B 7
16-C 8
16-D 9

17. 3 × 10 =

17-A 7
17-B 13
17-C 15
17-D 30

18. 8 + 0 =

18-A 8
18-B 0
18-C 1
18-D 80

19. 5 + 8 =

19-A 11
19-B 12
19-C 13
19-D 15

20. 7 − 6 =

20-A 5
20-B 1
20-C 11
20-D 13

21. 9 × 1 =

21-A 10
21-B 11
21-C 9
21-D 8

22. 4 + 8 =

22-A 32
22-B 24
22-C 12
22-D 4

23. 5 − 1 =

23-A 4
23-B 5
23-C 6
23-D 15

24. 9 + 3 =

24-A 3
24-B 6
24-C 12
24-D 15

25. 4 × 6 =

25-A 21
25-B 24
25-C 26
25-D 28

26. 7 + 2 =

26-A 3
26-B 5
26-C 9
26-D 14

27. 8 + 8 =

27-A 0
27-B 1
27-C 8
27-D 16

28. 15 ÷ 3 =

28-A   5
28-B   3
28-C   12
28-D   45

29. 2 × 8 =

29-A   6
29-B   16
29-C   18
29-D   36

30. 1 + 6 =

30-A   16
30-B   12
30-C   7
30-D   6

31. 7 + 9 =

31-A   12
31-B   15
31-C   16
31-D   17

32. 5 − 4 =

32-A   9
32-B   20
32-C   3
32-D   1

33. 4 + 4 =

33-A   1
33-B   4
33-C   8
33-D   16

34. 10 − 5 =

34-A   50
34-B   15
34-C   9
34-D   5

35. 7 × 4 =

35-A   21
35-B   28
35-C   36
35-D   42

36. 36 ÷ 6 =

36-A   11
36-B   9
36-C   10
36-D   6

37. 8 × 3 =

37-A   24
37-B   21
37-C   29
37-D   32

38. 2 + 4 =

38-A   6
38-B   2
38-C   16
38-D   8

39. 8 − 1 =

39-A   9
39-B   8
39-C   7
39-D   6

40. 1 + 5 =

40-A   6
40-B   5
40-C   4
40-D   1

41. 4 − 0 =

41-A   0
41-B   4
41-C   1
41-D   5

42. 1 + 2 =

42-A   1
42-B   2
42-C   3
42-D   4

43. $16 \div 4 =$

43-A 4
43-B 8
43-C 12
43-D 20

44. $9 \times 9 =$

44-A 99
44-B 0
44-C 72
44-D 81

45. $5 + 7 =$

45-A 11
45-B 2
45-C 12
45-D 13

46. $10 - 4 =$

46-A 4
46-B 6
46-C 8
46-D 14

47. $4 + 7 =$

47-A 3
47-B 21
47-C 12
47-D 11

48. $9 \times 5 =$

48-A 45
48-B 47
48-C 55
48-D 36

49. $20 \div 2 =$

49-A 40
49-B 22
49-C 18
49-D 10

50. $8 - 7 =$

50-A 56
50-B 15
50-C 5
50-D 1

END OF PART 5

DO NOT GO ON UNTIL YOU ARE TOLD TO DO SO

CODING SPEED

The coding part of your exam is different from all other parts of the exam. Nothing that you have learned enters into your answering of these questions. Coding is a test of your memory, your eye-hand coordination and your working speed.

Before each set of questions you will find a "key." The key consists of ten words listed in alphabetical order. Each word has a four-digit code number assigned to it.

In the set of questions you will find the same ten words, scrambled and sometimes repeated. Following each word in the test are *five* answer choices in columns labelled "A" to "E." Each answer choice is a four-digit number. The answer choices are in ascending order; that is, the lowest number is always in column A, the next higher number is in column B, and so on to the highest number in column E. You must look at the word, find the correct code number among the choices and mark on your answer sheet the letter of the column in which you found the correct code number.

On the actual examination you must work very quickly. You have only seven minutes in which to try to answer eighty-four questions. Use the sample questions that follow to develop a system that works for you—memorization, some sort of word-number association, a mathematical formula or any private method that helps you work up speed and accuracy. Many people cannot finish this part in the time allowed. Do not be upset if you cannot finish. Just do your best. Try these questions.

Key

bee 8176	fish 5921	moon 3672
cattle 4238	gloves 4970	nose 6482
diet 1910	lake 2286	rail 7657
	ledge 1152	

Answers

		A	B	C	D	E	
1.	diet	1910	1152	4970	6482	7657	1. Ⓐ Ⓑ Ⓒ Ⓓ Ⓔ
2.	rail	2286	5921	6482	7657	8176	2. Ⓐ Ⓑ Ⓒ Ⓓ Ⓔ
3.	fish	1152	1910	4238	5921	6482	3. Ⓐ Ⓑ Ⓒ Ⓓ Ⓔ
4.	nose	2286	4238	4970	5921	6482	4. Ⓐ Ⓑ Ⓒ Ⓓ Ⓔ
5.	gloves	4238	4970	5921	7657	8176	5. Ⓐ Ⓑ Ⓒ Ⓓ Ⓔ
6.	lake	2286	3672	4970	6482	7657	6. Ⓐ Ⓑ Ⓒ Ⓓ Ⓔ
7.	bee	1910	4238	6482	7657	8176	7. Ⓐ Ⓑ Ⓒ Ⓓ Ⓔ
8.	ledge	1152	2286	3672	4238	5921	8. Ⓐ Ⓑ Ⓒ Ⓓ Ⓔ
9.	cattle	1152	1910	3672	4238	6482	9. Ⓐ Ⓑ Ⓒ Ⓓ Ⓔ
10.	gloves	1910	4970	5921	6482	8176	10. Ⓐ Ⓑ Ⓒ Ⓓ Ⓔ
11.	moon	2286	3672	4238	4970	6482	11. Ⓐ Ⓑ Ⓒ Ⓓ Ⓔ
12.	fish	1152	1910	3672	4238	5921	12. Ⓐ Ⓑ Ⓒ Ⓓ Ⓔ

The correct answers are:

1-A	4-E	7-E	10-B
2-D	5-B	8-A	11-B
3-D	6-A	9-D	12-E

Key

arrow 7813	deed 4957	noon 8695
bride 1012	gray 5858	nun 9486
cave 6590	infant 1212	pig 2342
	junk 3666	

Answers

		A	B	C	D	E	
13.	gray	2342	3666	5858	6590	9486	13. Ⓐ Ⓑ Ⓒ Ⓓ Ⓔ
14.	infant	1012	1212	3666	5858	8695	14. Ⓐ Ⓑ Ⓒ Ⓓ Ⓔ
15.	nun	2342	4957	6590	8695	9486	15. Ⓐ Ⓑ Ⓒ Ⓓ Ⓔ
16.	junk	1212	2342	3666	4957	8695	16. Ⓐ Ⓑ Ⓒ Ⓓ Ⓔ
17.	arrow	1012	3666	5858	7813	9486	17. Ⓐ Ⓑ Ⓒ Ⓓ Ⓔ
18.	cave	1212	2342	6590	7813	8695	18. Ⓐ Ⓑ Ⓒ Ⓓ Ⓔ
19.	pig	2342	3666	4957	6590	7813	19. Ⓐ Ⓑ Ⓒ Ⓓ Ⓔ
20.	deed	4957	5858	6590	7813	8695	20. Ⓐ Ⓑ Ⓒ Ⓓ Ⓔ
21.	cave	1012	1212	3666	4957	6590	21. Ⓐ Ⓑ Ⓒ Ⓓ Ⓔ
22.	noon	1212	2342	4957	7813	8695	22. Ⓐ Ⓑ Ⓒ Ⓓ Ⓔ
23.	bride	1012	1212	2342	4957	5858	23. Ⓐ Ⓑ Ⓒ Ⓓ Ⓔ
24.	junk	1212	3666	4957	5858	6590	24. Ⓐ Ⓑ Ⓒ Ⓓ Ⓔ

The correct answers are:

13-C	16-C	19-A	22-E
14-B	17-D	20-A	23-A
15-E	18-C	21-E	24-B

DO NOT TURN THE PAGE UNTIL YOU ARE TOLD TO DO SO

CODING SPEED

TIME: 7 Minutes—84 Questions

Key

apron 4341	date 2024	jet 7699
bridge 3636	earth 9229	knot 6157
canoe 1936	face 5678	lizard 5163
	germ 8606	

Answers

		A	B	C	D	E
1.	lizard	2024	3636	4341	5163	7699
2.	jet	1936	5163	5678	6157	7699
3.	bridge	1936	3636	4341	7699	8606
4.	face	5678	6157	7699	8606	9229
5.	knot	1936	2024	4341	5163	6157
6.	apron	2024	4341	5163	6157	9229
7.	canoe	1936	3636	4341	5163	5678
8.	date	2024	5163	6157	7699	8606
9.	germ	2024	3636	6157	7699	8606
10.	earth	1936	4341	5163	6157	9229
11.	face	2024	3636	4341	5163	5678
12.	knot	1936	4341	6157	8606	9229

Key

axle 5614	guitar 4379	noose 7867
baby 9846	lamp 6686	trip 8968
club 1090	mop 2545	waste 4886
	muffin 3939	

Answers

		A	B	C	D	E
13.	guitar	3939	4379	4886	6686	7867
14.	waste	1090	2545	3939	4379	4886
15.	axle	4379	4886	5614	6686	8968
16.	mop	1090	2545	4379	7867	9846
17.	trip	3939	4886	6686	8968	9846
18.	lamp	2545	3939	4886	5614	6686
19.	club	1090	4379	4886	5614	7867
20.	muffin	2545	3939	4379	7867	8968
21.	noose	4379	5614	7867	8968	9846
22.	lamp	1090	3939	4886	6686	8968
23.	baby	4379	4886	6686	7867	9846
24.	noose	1090	6686	7867	8968	9846

Key

ant	4848	fog	6848	queen	7512
bus	9735	house	2345	tree	8864
drama	1981	laugh	5005	zoo	4584
		note	3689		

Answers

		A	B	C	D	E
25.	laugh	2345	4584	4848	5005	8864
26.	queen	1981	2345	3689	6848	7512
27.	ant	2345	4584	4848	6848	8864
28.	drama	1981	2345	3689	7512	9735
29.	note	1981	3689	4584	8864	9735
30.	fog	3689	4584	4848	6848	8864
31.	tree	4584	4848	6848	8864	9735
32.	bus	1981	2345	3689	7512	9735
33.	house	2345	3689	4584	5005	7512
34.	zoo	2345	4584	4848	6848	8864
35.	note	3689	4848	5005	7512	9735
36.	laugh	2345	3689	5005	6848	7512

Key

author	6509	card	7074	pin	8768
blood	3348	fire	1886	shore	5135
cake	2988	frog	9492	time	6852
		hunter	4141		

Answers

		A	B	C	D	E
37.	hunter	1886	2988	4141	5135	8768
38.	shore	2988	3348	5135	6509	7074
39.	frog	3348	4141	6852	8768	9492
40.	author	2988	5135	6509	6852	8768
41.	blood	1886	3348	4141	6852	7074
42.	cake	2988	3348	5135	6509	6852
43.	card	1886	4141	7074	8768	9492
44.	pin	2988	3348	5135	6852	8768
45.	fire	1886	2988	4141	6509	7074
46.	time	3348	4141	5135	6509	6852
47.	author	1886	3348	4141	6509	6852
48.	shore	5135	6509	6852	7074	9492

Key

bed 4814	elbow 5511	index 6904
coat 3765	fence 2026	kick 7546
doll 9086	gift 1683	lump 2826
	girl 8797	

Answers

		A	B	C	D	E
49.	index	2026	2826	3765	6904	9086
50.	coat	1683	3765	4814	5511	7546
51.	lump	2826	3765	6904	7546	8797
52.	fence	1683	2026	4814	5511	6904
53.	kick	1683	3765	6904	7546	8797
54.	doll	2026	2826	6904	8797	9086
55.	bed	4814	5511	7546	8797	9086
56.	elbow	1683	4814	5511	6904	7546
57.	gift	1683	2026	3765	4814	6904
58.	girl	2826	3765	6904	7546	8797
59.	coat	1683	2026	2826	3765	4814
60.	kick	2026	2826	3765	4814	7546

Key

apple 6080	devil 4598	roof 7503
bud 2722	drum 5489	shoe 9890
cone 1787	ear 3343	train 4672
	frown 8932	

Answers

		A	B	C	D	E
61.	devil	4598	4672	5489	8932	9890
62.	ear	1787	2722	3343	5489	6080
63.	frown	2722	4598	5489	7503	8932
64.	drum	3343	4598	4672	5489	9890
65.	bud	1787	2722	4672	6080	7503
66.	roof	1787	2722	5489	7503	8932
67.	train	4598	4672	5489	6080	8932
68.	cone	1787	3343	4598	5489	9890
69.	apple	2722	5489	6080	7503	9890
70.	bud	1787	2722	3343	4598	8932
71.	drum	2722	4598	5489	6080	7503
72.	frown	1787	3343	5489	8932	9890

Key

acorn	 4745	desk	 7621	star	 5704
bear	 1086	ego	 2190	steak	 6667
camel	 8808	fly	 9266	wax	 7512
		halo	 3835		

Answers

		A	B	C	D	E
73.	steak	3835	4745	5704	6667	7621
74.	ego	2190	5704	7512	7621	8808
75.	halo	1086	2190	3835	4745	6667
76.	fly	4745	5704	7512	8808	9266
77.	wax	3835	4745	5704	7512	7621
78.	camel	1086	2190	5704	6667	8808
79.	bear	1086	2190	6667	8808	9266
80.	desk	4745	5704	6667	7512	7621
81.	acorn	3835	4745	5704	7621	9266
82.	star	1086	2190	3835	4745	5704
83.	camel	2190	3835	6667	8808	9266
84.	steak	4745	5704	6667	7512	7621

END OF PART 6

IF YOU FINISH BEFORE TIME IS UP, CHECK TO BE SURE THAT YOUR ANSWERS ARE CLEARLY MARKED. DO NOT GO BACK TO ANY PREVIOUS PART. DO NOT GO ON UNTIL YOU ARE TOLD TO DO SO.

PART 7

AUTO & SHOP INFORMATION

The auto and shop information questions test your knowledge and understanding of automobiles and of tools and shop practices. The answers to many questions come straight from your life experience. However, if this is not your area of interest, there will be questions to which you do not know the answer. Make the most sensible guess. Answer all questions. Mark the letter of your choice on your answer sheet. Try these questions.

1. The function of the generator or alternator is to

1-A start the engine
1-B carry electricity from the battery to the engine
1-C keep the battery charged
1-D control production of hydrocarbons

1. Ⓐ Ⓑ Ⓒ Ⓓ

1-C The GENERATOR or ALTERNATOR is operated by the car's engine. It produces electricity which flows to the battery and keeps the battery charged.

2. The main advantage of four-wheel drive is

2-A higher speed
2-B better traction
2-C better gas mileage
2-D greater durability of the vehicle

2. Ⓐ Ⓑ Ⓒ Ⓓ

2-B Since power from the engine is transmitted to both the front wheels and the back wheels, a four-wheel drive vehicle has much BETTER TRACTION. Four-wheel drive is especially useful in mud, sand and very uneven terrain. While four-wheel drive tends to be a feature of durable vehicles (D), like jeeps, it is not the four-wheel drive that makes them durable.

3.

```
 STEEL POCKET RULE
 |  1  |  2  |  3  |  4  |  5  |  6
```

It would be most appropriate to use the tool above to

3-A measure a living room for carpeting
3-B pry open a tight can of paint
3-C measure the distance between exposed terminals on a live switchboard
3-D draw straight lines on a poster

3. Ⓐ Ⓑ Ⓒ Ⓓ

3-D The short straight edge would be fine for drawing straight lines on cardboard or paper. The measurements of a room (A), if taken with a six inch rule, would be highly inaccurate. A pocket rule is not sturdy enough to pry open a paint can (B) and the ruler would be damaged besides. Using a steel ruler when working with electricity (C) is very dangerous.

4. The solvent that should be used to clean a brush immediately after it was used to apply rubber base paint is

4-A turpentine
4-B mineral oil
4-C alcohol
4-D warm water

4. Ⓐ Ⓑ Ⓒ Ⓓ

4-D Clean-up for latex or rubber based paint is plain water. Turpentine (A) is a solvent for oil paints. Alcohol (C) is used for shellac base paint.

DO NOT TURN THE PAGE UNTIL YOU ARE TOLD TO DO SO

AUTO & SHOP INFORMATION

TIME: 11 Minutes—25 Questions

1. Burned engine bearings are caused by

   1-A lack of oil in the engine
   1-B lack of water in the engine
   1-C too much oil in the engine
   1-D too much water in the engine

2. In the four stroke cycle gasoline engine, the sequence of the steps in each cylinder to complete a cycle is which one of the following?

   2-A Intake stroke, power stroke, compression stroke, exhaust stroke
   2-B Intake stroke, compression stroke, exhaust stroke, power stroke
   2-C Intake stroke, exhaust stroke, compression stroke, power stroke
   2-D Intake stroke, compression stroke, power stroke, exhaust stroke

3. The function of the rotor is to

   3-A open and close the distributor points
   3-B rotate the distributor cam
   3-C distribute electricity to the spark plugs
   3-D rotate the distributor shaft

4. What happens if cylinder head torquing is not done in proper sequence?

   4-A It warps the piston rings.
   4-B It cracks the intake manifold.
   4-C It distorts the head.
   4-D It reduces valve clearance.

5. After brakes have been severely overheated, what should be checked for?

   5-A water condensation in brake fluid
   5-B glazed brake shoes
   5-C wheels out of alignment
   5-D crystallized wheel bearings

6. A wood screw that can be tightened by a wrench is known as a

   6-A lag screw
   6-B carriage screw
   6-C Philips screw
   6-D monkey screw

7.

   The tool shown above is a

   7-A punch
   7-B drill holder
   7-C Philips-type screwdriver
   7-D socket wrench

8.

   The tool shown above is

   8-A an offset wrench
   8-B a box wrench
   8-C a spanner wrench
   8-D an open end wrench

9. The purpose of flashing on roofs is to

   9-A secure roofing materials to the roof
   9-B make it easier to lay the roofing
   9-C prevent leaks
   9-D insulate the roof from excessive heat

10. End grain of wood should be sanded

10-A   crosswise
10-B   with the grain
10-C   obliquely
10-D   with a circular motion

11.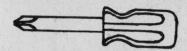

The tool shown above is used to

11-A   ream holes in wood
11-B   countersink holes in soft metals
11-C   turn Philips-head screws
11-D   drill holes in concrete

12. The tool that is best suited for use with a wood chisel is

12-A

12-B

12-C

12-D

13. A method that can be used to prevent the forming of "skin" on a partially used can of oil paint is to

13-A   turn the can upside down every few months
13-B   pour a thin layer of solvent over the top of the paint
13-C   store the paint in a well ventilated room
13-D   avoid shaking the can after it has been sealed

14. If the "charge and discharge" indicator, whether a meter or a light, suddenly indicates "discharge" while a car is in normal operation, it is best that the car be

14-A   stopped immediately and then be towed in for repairs
14-B   stopped immediately and have a new battery installed on the spot
14-C   driven as usual and the incident ignored
14-D   driven to the nearest garage for inspection and repair

15. When reference is made to the "Compression Ratio" of an automotive gasoline engine, this is best described to be the

15-A   volume above the piston at top dead center
15-B   displacement volume as the piston moves down to bottom dead center
15-C   total volume of a cylinder divided by its clearance volume
15-D   displacement volume of a cylinder divided by its clearance volume

16. An engine starts, but stalls as it warms up. Which of the following most likely causes this condition?

16-A   the battery is run down
16-B   the ignition timing is off
16-C   the choke valve sticks closed
16-D   the throttle valve does not open freely

17. The most probable cause of a complete loss of oil pressure while driving is

17-A a crankcase oil level which is too low
17-B a crankcase oil level which is too high
17-C the use of too thick an oil
17-D dirty oil

18. Water in the cooling system should be

18-A alkaline
18-B acid
18-C salty
18-D neutral

19. What is used to fasten ceramic tiles to walls?

19-A putty
19-B caulking
19-C plaster of paris
19-D mastic

20. With which of these screw heads do you use an "Allen" wrench?

20-A (−)

20-B (+)

20-C (hex)

20-D (*)

21. A lathe would normally be used in making which of the following items?

21-A a hockey stick
21-B a picture frame
21-C a bookcase
21-D a baseball bat

22. The plane to use in shaping a curved edge on wood is known as

22-A jack
22-B spoke shave
22-C smooth
22-D rabbet

23. If the intake manifold of a gasoline engine is warped to the extent that it leaks, the engine will most likely tend to

23-A check out with a vacuum gauge as running on a rich mixture
23-B miss on one cylinder
23-C perform better on acceleration
23-D have a fast idle

24. Lacquer thinner would most likely be used to

24-A clean oil paint from a brush immediately after use
24-B rinse a new paint brush before using it
24-C clean a paint brush upon which paint has hardened
24-D remove paint from the hands

25. A squeegee is a tool that is used in

25-A drying windows after washing
25-B cleaning inside boiler surfaces
25-C the central vacuum cleaning system
25-D clearing stoppages in waste lines

END OF PART 7

IF YOU FINISH BEFORE TIME IS UP, CHECK OVER YOUR WORK ON THIS PART ONLY. DO NOT RETURN TO ANY PREVIOUS PART. DO NOT GO ON UNTIL YOU ARE TOLD TO DO SO.

PART 8

MATHEMATICS KNOWLEDGE

To solve the problems in this part, you must draw upon your knowledge of high school mathematics. The problems require you to use simple algebra and geometry along with arithmetic skills and reasoning power. Some questions can be answered in your head. Others will require the use of scratch paper. If you use scratch paper for your calculations, be sure to mark the letter of the correct answer on your answer sheet. Try these questions.

1. A section of pavement which is 10 feet long and 8 feet wide contains how many square feet?

1-A 80 sq. ft.
1-B 92 sq. ft.
1-C 800 sq. ft.
1-D 18 sq. ft.

1. Ⓐ Ⓑ Ⓒ Ⓓ

1-A Area equals Length times Width
$A = L \times W$
$A = 10 \text{ ft.} \times 8 \text{ ft.}$
$A = 80 \text{ sq. ft.}$

2. A square has an area of 49 sq. in. The number of inches in its perimeter is

2-A 7
2-B 28
2-C 14
2-D 98

2. Ⓐ Ⓑ Ⓒ Ⓓ

2-B Area of a square $= s^2$

$49 = 7^2$
one side $= 7$ inches
$P = 4s$
$P = 4'' \times 7'' = 28$ inches

3. 42 divided by .06 =

3-A 7
3-B 70
3-C 700
3-D .7

3. Ⓐ Ⓑ Ⓒ Ⓓ

3-C To divide by a decimal, convert the divisor to a whole number by moving the decimal point to the right. Move the decimal point of the dividend the same number of spaces to the right. Place the decimal point of the quotient directly above the new location of the decimal point of the dividend.

$$.06\,\overline{)4\,2.0\,0}\quad 7\,0\,0.$$

4. When one-fifth is added to one-third the sum is

4-A $\frac{1}{4}$
4-B $\frac{1}{8}$
4-C eight-fifteenths
4-D one-fifteenth

4. Ⓐ Ⓑ Ⓒ Ⓓ

4-C First find the lowest common denominator, in this case 15. Then change each fraction to a fraction with 15 as its denominator by multiplying the numerator and the denominator by the same number. Then add.

$$\begin{array}{r} 1/5 = 3/15 \\ + \; 1/3 = 5/15 \\ \hline 8/15 \end{array}$$

DO NOT TURN THE PAGE UNTIL YOU ARE TOLD TO DO SO

MATHEMATICS KNOWLEDGE

TIME: 24 Minutes—25 Questions

1. If two numbers are multiplied together, the result is 3752. If one of the two numbers is 56, the other number is

1-A   41
1-B   15
1-C   67
1-D   76

2.

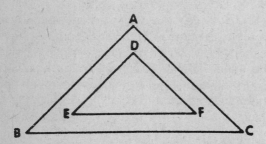

In the figure above, the sides of △ABC are respectively parallel to the sides of triangle DEF. If the complement of A is 40°, then the complement of D is

2-A   20°
2-B   50°
2-C   40°
2-D   60°

3. 150 is what percent of 30?

3-A   50
3-B   150
3-C   180
3-D   500

4. R is what percent of 1000?

4-A   .001R
4-B   1R
4-C   .01R
4-D   .1R

5. If 6 + x + y = 20, and x + y = k, then 20 − k =

5-A   6
5-B   0
5-C   14
5-D   20

6.

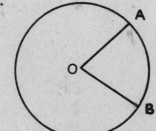

In the figure above, ∠AOB = 60°. If O is the center of the circle, then minor arc AB is what part of the circumference of the circle?

6-A $\frac{1}{2}$
6-B $\frac{1}{3}$
6-C $\frac{1}{6}$
6-D $\frac{1}{8}$

7. When 2x + 3 is multiplied by 10, the result is 55. What is the value of x?

7-A $1\frac{1}{4}$
7-B   4
7-C   2
7-D   3

8. (6 + 8) − (21 − 4) =

8-A   14 × 17
8-B   14 − 3
8-C   14 + 17
8-D   14 − 17

9. 25.726 × .04 =

9-A 102.904
9-B 10.2904
9-C .0102904
9-D 1.02904

10. If $\frac{3}{8}$ of a number is 96, the number is

10-A 132
10-B 36
10-C 256
10-D 156

11. If x = y, find the value of 8 + 5(x − y).

11-A 8 + 5x − 5y
11-B 8 + 5xy
11-C 13x − 13y
11-D 8

12. $\sqrt{\frac{9}{64} + \frac{16}{64}}$ =

12-A $\frac{5}{8}$
12-B $\frac{7}{64}$
12-C $\frac{5}{64}$
12-D $\frac{25}{64}$

13. If $\frac{2}{3}$ of a jar is filled with water in one minute, how many minutes longer will it take to fill the jar?

13-A $\frac{1}{4}$
13-B $\frac{1}{3}$
13-C $\frac{1}{2}$
13-D $\frac{2}{3}$

14. If .10 is divided by 50, the result is

14-A .002
14-B .02
14-C .2
14-D 2.

15. A group left on a trip at 8:50 A.M. and reached its destination at 3:30 P.M. How long, in hours and minutes, did the trip take?

15-A 3 hours 10 minutes
15-B 4 hours 40 minutes
15-C 5 hours 10 minutes
15-D 6 hours 40 minutes

16. A square is changed into a rectangle by increasing its length 10% and decreasing its width 10%. Its area

16-A remains the same
16-B decreases by 10%
16-C increases by 1%
16-D decreases by 1%

17. A prime number is a number that can be divided only by itself and one. Which is *not* a prime number?

17-A 23
17-B 37
17-C 87
17-D 53

18. In the diagram below, chord TU =

18-A (TY + UY)^2
18-B $\sqrt{TY + TU}$
18-C $\sqrt{TY^2 + UY^2}$
18-D $\dfrac{TY \times UY}{2}$

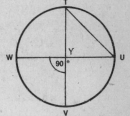

19. If $\frac{5}{4}x = \frac{5}{4}$, then 1 − x =

19-A $-\frac{5}{4}$
19-B 1
19-C 0
19-D −1

20. A desk was listed at $90.00 and was bought for $75.00. What was the rate of discount?

20-A 15%
20-B 16$\frac{2}{3}$%
20-C 18%
20-D 20%

21. 10 to the fifth power may correctly be expressed as

21-A 10 × 5
21-B 5^{10}
21-C 5$\sqrt{10}$
21-D 10 × 10 × 10 × 10 × 10

22. 2.2 × .00001 =

    22-A .0022
    22-B .00022
    22-C .000022
    22-D .0000022

23. If psychological studies of college students show K percent to be emotionally unstable, the number of college students not emotionally unstable per one hundred college students is

    23-A 100 minus K
    23-B 1 minus K
    23-C K minus 1
    23-D 100 ÷ K

24. 8! = 8 × 7 × 6 × 5 × 4 × 3 × 2 × 1
4! =

    24-A 4^4
    24-B 32
    24-C 4^2
    24-D 24

25. 75% of 4 is the same as what percent of 9?

    25-A 36
    25-B 25
    25-C 40
    25-D $33\frac{1}{3}$

END OF PART 8

IF YOU FINISH BEFORE TIME IS UP, MAKE CERTAIN THAT YOU HAVE MARKED ALL YOUR ANSWERS ON THE ANSWER SHEET. THEN CHECK OVER YOUR WORK ON THIS PART ONLY. DO NOT RETURN TO ANY PREVIOUS PART. DO NOT GO ON TO THE NEXT PART UNTIL YOU ARE TOLD TO DO SO.

PART 9

MECHANICAL COMPREHENSION

Part 9 consists of questions about your understanding of general mechanical and physical principles. Your understanding of these principles will come from your own observations, from experience in working with mechanical devices and from your reading and school courses. Answer all the questions as best you can, marking the letter of your choice on your answer sheet. Try these questions.

1.

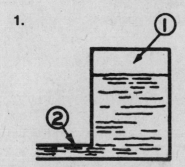

The figure above represents an enclosed water chamber, partially filled with water. The number 1 indicates air in the chamber and 2 indicates a pipe by which water enters the chamber. If the water pressure in the pipe, 2, increases then the

1-A water pressure in the chamber will be decreased
1-B water level in the chamber will fall
1-C air in the chamber will be compressed
1-D air in the chamber will expand

1. Ⓐ Ⓑ Ⓒ Ⓓ

1-C If water pressure in the pipe is increased, more water will flow into the water chamber. Since the chamber is enclosed, the air will be unable

to escape. As more water enters the chamber, the existing air must be compressed into a smaller space.

2.

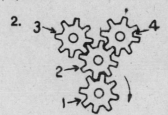

The figure above shows four gears. If gear 1 turns as shown, then the gears turning in the same direction are

2-A 2, 3 and 4
2-B 2 and 4
2-C 2 and 3
2-D 3 and 4

2. Ⓐ Ⓑ Ⓒ Ⓓ

2-D A turning gear always turns the gear with which it interlocks in the opposite direction. If gear 1 turns clockwise, then gear 2 must turn counterclockwise. In turn, gears 3 and 4, since they are both turned by gear 2, must both turn clockwise.

DO NOT TURN THE PAGE UNTIL YOU ARE TOLD TO DO SO

MECHANICAL COMPREHENSION

TIME: 19 Minutes—25 Questions

1.

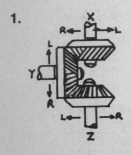

Which of the following is correct if gear Z is turned to the right (R)?

1-A   Gear Y turns L, and gear X turns R.
1-B   Gear Y turns R, and gear X turns R.
1-C   Gear Y turns L, and gear X turns L.
1-D   Gear Y turns R, and gear X turns L.

2.

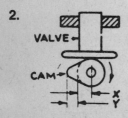

The figure above shows a cam and a valve. For each cam revolution, the vertical valve rise equals distance

2-A   Y
2-B   X
2-C   X plus Y
2-D   twice X

3.

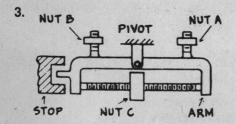

The arm in the figure at 3 is exactly balanced as shown. If nut "A" is removed entirely then, in order to rebalance the arm, it will be necessary to turn

3-A   nut "C" toward the right
3-B   nut "C" toward the left
3-C   nut "B" up
3-D   nut "B" down

4.

What is the function of A and B in the crankshaft shown in the drawing?

4-A   They strengthen the crankshaft by increasing its weight.
4-B   They make it easier to remove the crankshaft for repairs.
4-C   They are necessary to maintain the proper balance of the crankshaft.
4-D   They hold grease for continuous lubrication of the crankshaft.

5.

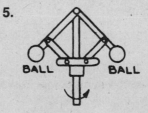

The figure above shows a governor on a rotating shaft. As the shaft speeds up, the governor balls will

5-A   move down
5-B   move upward and inward
5-C   move upward
5-D   move inward

6.

The figure above shows a brass and an iron strip continuously riveted together. High temperatures would probably

6-A have no effect at all
6-B bend the strips
6-C separate the strips
6-D shorten the strips

7.

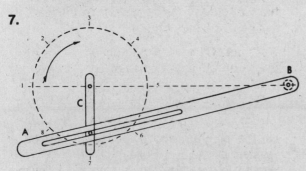

In the diagram above, crank arm "C" revolves at a constant speed of 400 RPM and drives the lever "AB". When lever "AB" is moving the fastest, arm "C" will be in position

7-A 1
7-B 6
7-C 5
7-D 7

8.

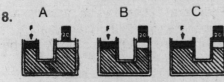

Which hydraulic press requires the least force to lift the weight?

8-A A
8-B B
8-C C
8-D All three require the same force.

9.

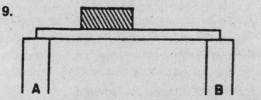

In the figure above, which upright supports the greater part of the load?

9-A upright A
9-B upright B
9-C they support it equally
9-D it cannot be determined

10.

The reading shown on the gage is

10-A 10.35
10-B 13.5
10-C 10.7
10-D 17.0

11.

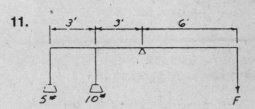

The force F needed to balance the lever is, in lbs., most nearly

11-A 7.5
11-B 12.5
11-C 10
11-D 15

12.

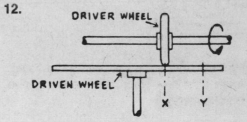

When the driver wheel is moved from location X to location Y, the driven wheel will

12-A reverse its direction of rotation
12-B turn slower
12-C not change its speed of rotation
12-D turn faster

13. The main purpose of a float in a flush tank is to regulate the

13-A water pressure
13-B water velocity

13-C   rate of discharge
13-D   water supply

14. The main purpose of baffle plates in a furnace is to

14-A   change the direction of flow of heated gases
14-B   retard the burning of gases
14-C   increase combustion rate of the fuel
14-D   prevent escape of flue gases through furnace openings

15.

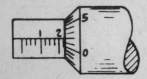

The micrometer above reads

15-A   .2270
15-B   .2120
15-C   .2252
15-D   .2020

16.

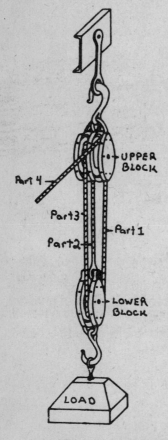

Determine which part of the rope is fastened directly to the block.

16-A   Part 1
16-B   Part 3
16-C   Part 2
16-D   Part 4

17.

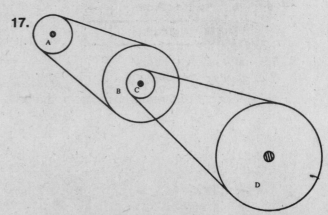

In the diagram above, pulley "A" drives a system of pulleys. Pulleys "B" and "C" are keyed to the same shaft. Use the following diameters in your computations: A = 1 inch; B = 2 inches; C = $\frac{1}{2}$ inch; and D = 4 inches. When pulley "A" runs at an RPM of 2000, pulley "D" will make

17-A   125 RPM
17-B   500 RPM
17-C   250 RPM
17-D   8000 RPM

18.

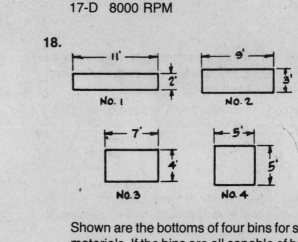

Shown are the bottoms of four bins for storing materials. If the bins are all capable of holding the same amount of any particular material, then you would expect the bin with the least height of sides to be the one whose bottom is shown as

18-A   No. 1
18-B   No. 3
18-C   No. 2
18-D   No. 4

19.

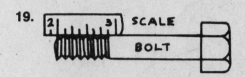

The number of threads per inch on the bolt is:

19-A   16
19-B   8
19-C   10
19-D   7

20.

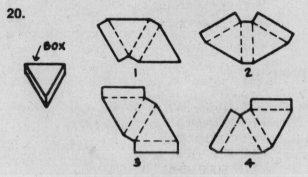

The flat sheet metal pattern which can be bent along the dotted lines to form the completely closed triangular box is

20-A   1
20-B   3
20-C   2
20-D   4

21. At atmospheric pressure, water changes to steam at _____ degrees F.

21-A   100
21-B   183
21-C   212
21-D   237

22.

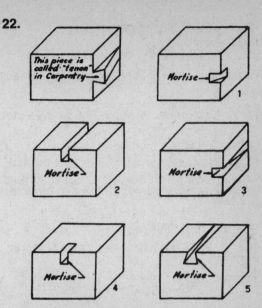

Examine the tenon and the numbered mortises previously shown. The tenon best fits into the mortise numbered

22-A   1
22-B   3
22-C   2
22-D   5

23.

If all of these are the same temperature, which will feel coldest?

23-A   A
23-B   B
23-C   C
23-D   D

24.

— film of water in loop

— printed page

— copper wire

The print looked at through the film of water will

24-A be too blurred to read
24-B look the same as the surrounding print
24-C be enlarged
24-D appear smaller

25.

20 teeth   10 teeth

There are twenty teeth on the front sprocket and ten teeth on the rear sprocket on the bicycle above. Each time the pedals go around, the rear wheel will

25-A go half way around
25-B go around once
25-C go around twice
25-D go around four times

END OF PART 9

IF YOU FINISH BEFORE TIME IS UP, CHECK OVER YOUR WORK ON THIS PART ONLY. DO NOT RETURN TO ANY PREVIOUS PART. DO NOT GO ON UNTIL YOU ARE TOLD TO DO SO.

PART 10

ELECTRONICS INFORMATION

The questions in this part test your knowledge and understanding of electricity, radio and electronics. To answer some of the questions all you need is common sense. Other questions can be answered on the basis of experience, courses and reading. Answer all the questions. Mark the letter of your answer on the answer sheet. Try these questions.

1. If a co-worker is not breathing after receiving an electric shock but is no longer in contact with the electricity, it is most important for you to

    1-A wrap the victim in a blanket
    1-B force him to take hot liquids
    1-C start artificial respiration promptly
    1-D avoid moving him

    1. Ⓐ Ⓑ Ⓒ Ⓓ

1-C Once a victim of electric shock is no longer in contact with the electricity, whether from a turn-off of the current or from falling or being thrown from the source of the shock, it is no longer dangerous to come into contact with that person. Breathing is absolutely essential to life. The oxygen starved person will die within minutes. Therefore, if a person is not breathing, you must start artificial respiration IMMEDIATELY, no matter what the weather or the extent of his other injuries.

2. Light fixtures suspended from chains should be wired so that the

    2-A wires do not support the fixture
    2-B wires help support the fixture
    2-C chains have an insulated link
    2-D chain is not grounded to prevent short circuits

    2. Ⓐ Ⓑ Ⓒ Ⓓ

2-A The answer to this question is pure common sense. Electrical wires should serve only one purpose—to supply electricity. If electrical wires are required to support weight there is danger of breakage in the wires and of damage to the fixture itself caused by tension at the connections.

3. A completely short circuited heater resistance will be

    3-A hotter than normal
    3-B cooler than normal
    3-C inoperative
    3-D white hot

    3. Ⓐ Ⓑ Ⓒ Ⓓ

3-C A complete short circuit means no circuit at all. If there is no circuit then the heater resistance will be inoperative.

4. Safety regulations prohibit testing even a 20-volt light socket with the fingers to see whether the socket is alive. The main reason for this prohibition is that

    4-A such action can become a bad working habit
    4-B sockets usually have sharp edges
    4-C a 20-volt shock is often fatal
    4-D the skin will become less sensitive to higher voltages

    4. Ⓐ Ⓑ Ⓒ Ⓓ

4-A It is hard to break a bad habit, far more sensible to not develop the bad habit in the first place. Sticking a finger into a socket, any socket, to find out if it is live is foolish.

DO NOT TURN THE PAGE UNTIL YOU ARE TOLD TO DO SO

ELECTRONICS INFORMATION

TIME: 9 Minutes—20 Questions

1. Boxes and fittings intended for outdoor use should be of

   1-A weatherproof type
   1-B stamped steel of not less than No. 16
   1-C standard gauge
   1-D stamped steel plated with cadmium

2. When working on live 600-volt equipment where rubber gloves might be damaged, an electrician should

   2-A work without gloves
   2-B carry a spare pair of rubber gloves
   2-C reinforce the fingers of the rubber gloves with rubber tape
   2-D wear leather gloves over the rubber gloves

3. If the radio tubes of a certain receiver are to be operated with their filaments (or heaters) in series, it is most important that their ratings be the same with respect to filament or heater

   3-A voltage
   3-B current
   3-C power
   3-D temperature

4. When working near lead acid storage batteries extreme care should be taken to guard against sparks, essentially to avoid

   4-A overheating the electrolyte
   4-B an electric shock
   4-C a short circuit
   4-D an explosion

5. If a fuse of higher than the required current rating is used in an electrical circuit

   5-A better protection will be afforded

   5-B the fuse will blow more often since it carries more current
   5-C serious damage may result to the circuit from overload
   5-D maintenance of the large fuse will be higher

6. The standard colors of the outer coverings of wires used in series lighting circuits are

   6-A Positive—black; Negative—white; Series—red
   6-B Positive—black; Negative—red; Series—white
   6-C Positive—white; Negative—black; Series—red
   6-D Positive—red; Negative—white; Series—black

7. Receptacles in a house-lighting system are regularly connected in

   7-A parallel
   7-B series
   7-C diagonal
   7-D perpendicular

8.

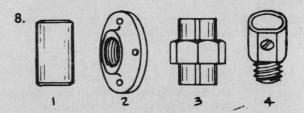

The standard coupling for rigid electrical conduit is

   8-A 1
   8-B 2

8-C 3
8-D 4

9.

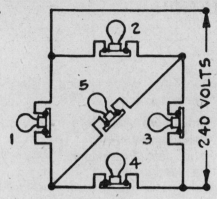

The five lamps shown are each rated at 120-volts, 60-watts. If all are good lamps, lamp no. 5 will be

9-A much brighter than normal
9-B about its normal brightness
9-C much dimmer than normal
9-D completely dark

10. If a condenser is connected across the make-and-break contact of an ordinary electric bell, the effect will be to

10-A speed up the action of the clapper
10-B reduce the amount of arcing at the contact
10-C slow down the action of the clapper
10-D reduce the load on the bell transformer or battery

11. The purpose of having a rheostat in the field circuit of a d.c. shunt motor is to

11-A control the speed of the motor
11-B minimize the starting current
11-C limit the field current to a safe value
11-D reduce sparking at the brushes

12. Is it proper procedure to ground the frame of a portable motor?

12-A No
12-B No, if it is A.C.

12-C Yes, unless the tool is specifically designed for use without a ground
12-D Yes, if the operation takes place at less than 150 volts

13. Silver is a better conductor of electricity than copper; however copper is generally used for electrical conductors. The main reason for using copper instead of silver is its

13-A cost
13-B weight
13-C strength
13-D melting point

14. Commutators are found on

14-A mercury rectifiers
14-B D.C. motors
14-C circuit breakers
14-D alternators

15. In a house bell circuit, the push button for ringing the bell is generally connected in the secondary of the transformer feeding the bell. One reason for doing this is to

15-A save power
15-B keep line voltage out of the push button circuit
15-C prevent the bell from burning out
15-D prevent arcing of the vibrator contact points in the bell

16. Operating an incandescent electric light bulb at less than its rated voltage will result in

16-A shorter life and brighter light
16-B brighter light and longer life
16-C longer life and dimmer light
16-D dimmer light and shorter life

17.

The fitting shown is used in electrical construction to

17-A clamp two adjacent junction boxes together

17-B act as a ground clamp for the conduit system
17-C attach flexible metallic conduit to a junction box
17-D protect exposed wires where they pass through a wall

18. The *least* likely result of a severe electric shock is

18-A unconsciousness
18-B a burn
18-C clenched muscles
18-D heavy breathing

19. A circular mil is a measure of electrical conductor

19-A length
19-B area
19-C volume
19-D weight

20. The letters RIWP when applied to electrical wire indicate the wire

20-A has a solid conductor
20-B has rubber insulation
20-C is insulated with paper
20-D has lead sheath

END OF EXAMINATION

IF YOU FINISH BEFORE TIME IS UP, CHECK OVER YOUR WORK ON THIS PART ONLY. DO NOT GO BACK TO ANY PREVIOUS PART.

CORRECT ANSWERS—FIRST MODEL EXAM

PART 1—GENERAL SCIENCE

1. A	5. D	8. B	11. D	14. C	17. C	20. B	23. A
2. D	6. A	9. A	12. A	15. A	18. C	21. C	24. D
3. C	7. C	10. C	13. C	16. A	19. B	22. D	25. A
4. D							

PART 2—ARITHMETIC REASONING

1. B	5. D	9. A	13. D	17. B	21. B	25. C	28. D
2. B	6. B	10. B	14. C	18. A	22. B	26. A	29. D
3. B	7. D	11. C	15. D	19. B	23. D	27. C	30. B
4. B	8. C	12. D	16. C	20. A	24. B		

PART 3—WORD KNOWLEDGE

1. D	6. C	11. A	16. A	20. A	24. C	28. C	32. A
2. A	7. B	12. A	17. B	21. A	25. B	29. A	33. D
3. A	8. A	13. D	18. D	22. C	26. C	30. A	34. C
4. D	9. A	14. A	19. A	23. B	27. B	31. B	35. D
5. D	10. D	15. D					

PART 4—PARAGRAPH COMPREHENSION

1. D	3. C	5. D	7. D	9. A	11. D	13. B	15. D
2. B	4. A	6. D	8. C	10. A	12. D	14. A	

PART 5—NUMERICAL OPERATIONS

1. B	8. C	15. D	21. C	27. D	33. C	39. C	45. C
2. C	9. D	16. B	22. C	28. A	34. D	40. A	46. B
3. A	10. C	17. D	23. A	29. B	35. B	41. B	47. D
4. B	11. C	18. A	24. C	30. C	36. D	42. C	48. A
5. D	12. B	19. C	25. B	31. C	37. A	43. A	49. D
6. C	13. A	20. B	26. C	32. D	38. A	44. D	50. D
7. A	14. D						

PART 6—CODING SPEED

1. D	12. C	23. E	34. B	45. A	55. A	65. B	75. C
2. E	13. B	24. C	35. A	46. E	56. C	66. D	76. E
3. B	14. E	25. D	36. C	47. D	57. A	67. B	77. D
4. A	15. C	26. E	37. C	48. A	58. E	68. A	78. E
5. E	16. B	27. C	38. C	49. D	59. D	69. C	79. A
6. B	17. D	28. A	39. E	50. B	60. E	70. B	80. E
7. A	18. E	29. B	40. C	51. A	61. A	71. C	81. B
8. A	19. A	30. D	41. B	52. B	62. C	72. D	82. E
9. E	20. B	31. D	42. A	53. D	63. E	73. D	83. D
10. E	21. C	32. E	43. C	54. E	64. D	74. A	84. C
11. E	22. D	33. A	44. E				

PART 7—AUTO & SHOP INFORMATION

1. A	5. B	8. D	11. C	14. D	17. A	20. C	23. D
2. D	6. A	9. C	12. D	15. C	18. D	21. D	24. C
3. C	7. D	10. A	13. B	16. C	19. D	22. B	25. A
4. C							

PART 8—MATHEMATICS KNOWLEDGE

1. C	5. A	8. D	11. D	14. A	17. C	20. B	23. A
2. C	6. C	9. D	12. A	15. D	18. C	21. D	24. D
3. D	7. A	10. C	13. C	16. D	19. C	22. C	25. D
4. D							

PART 9—MECHANICAL COMPREHENSION

1. A	5. C	8. A	11. C	14. A	17. A	20. B	23. D
2. A	6. B	9. A	12. B	15. A	18. B	21. C	24. C
3. A	7. C	10. D	13. D	16. C	19. B	22. D	25. C
4. C							

PART 10—ELECTRONICS INFORMATION

1. A	4. D	7. A	10. B	13. A	15. B	17. C	19. B
2. D	5. C	8. A	11. A	14. B	16. C	18. D	20. B
3. B	6. A	9. D	12. C				

SCORE SHEET—FIRST MODEL EXAM

Now that you have taken and corrected your first exam, you will want to figure out your score on each part and on the exam as a whole. By converting each score into a percent, you can immediately see where your strengths lie and where you may want to do extra work to bring up your score. And, after you complete the book, you will be able to see the progress you have made after experience with all these questions.

The scores you convert to percents will be very useful to you. The actual exam, however, is *not* scored in percents. The ASVAB raw scores (number right) are converted to standard scores expressed within a rough range of 20 to 70. The formula by which the scores are converted is not available, nor would it be very useful to you. You should, however, be aware that the combined scores required for guaranteed admission to the training school of your choice are neither combined raw scores nor combined percents. The services combine standard scores when they determine your eligibility for each area.

PART	NUMBER CORRECT		NUMBER OF QUESTIONS		
GENERAL SCIENCE	_____	÷ 25 =	_____	× 100 =	_____ %
ARITHMETIC REASONING	_____	÷ 30 =	_____	× 100 =	_____ %
WORD KNOWLEDGE	_____	÷ 35 =	_____	× 100 =	_____ %
PARAGRAPH COMPREHENSION	_____	÷ 15 =	_____	× 100 =	_____ %
NUMERICAL OPERATIONS	_____	÷ 50 =	_____	× 100 =	_____ %
CODING SPEED	_____	÷ 84 =	_____	× 100 =	_____ %
AUTO & SHOP INFORMATION	_____	÷ 25 =	_____	× 100 =	_____ %
MATHEMATICS KNOWLEDGE	_____	÷ 25 =	_____	× 100 =	_____ %
MECHANICAL COMPREHENSION	_____	÷ 25 =	_____	× 100 =	_____ %
ELECTRONICS INFORMATION	_____	÷ 20 =	_____	× 100 =	_____ %
TOTAL	_____	÷ 334 =	_____	× 100 =	_____ %

STEPS TO TAKE AFTER THE FIRST MODEL EXAM

You have taken the first model exam. You have scored yourself and have before you your score on each part of the exam. Now you want to know what you can do to improve, to raise your marks and to qualify for the training program of your choice.

To a large extent, your learning experiences of the last eighteen or so years are the determining factors in how you perform on this exam. If you have been a "reader," then you probably have an extensive vocabulary and probably do well when you must answer questions based upon reading passages. If your favorite activities have taken place in a "shop," then chances are you will earn your best scores in "Auto and Shop Information," "Mechanical Comprehension" and "Electronics Information." If science has always fascinated you, then you are more likely to have gathered more information in that area and will have a high mark in "General Science." And if you have always liked math and done well in it, you probably will do well in "Arithmetic Reasoning," "Numerical Operations" and "Mathematics Knowledge."

Some parts of the exam really do not lend themselves to any further instruction at this time. Improvement on the two heavily speeded parts can be gained only through practice. If you have time after you have completed this book, go back and do over the "Numerical Operations" and "Coding Speed" parts of all the exams. Your answer sheets will be filled, but you can get good practice writing your letter answers on a blank piece of paper. You are unlikely to remember any of these answers, so doing the tests again will give you valuable practice and will help your speed. You will find some helpful hints for "Numerical Operations" in the math refresher course which follows, but for the most part, repeating the questions will do you the most good.

If it has been a few years since you last took math in school, you may well have forgotten some basic rules, formulas and methods. A brush-up can be very helpful to you, especially for the "Arithmetic Reasoning" and "Mathematics Knowledge" parts of your exam. The next chapter should *not*, however, be considered a comprehensive mathematics course. Many topics have been omitted altogether. We have purposefully kept the math refresher course short and have limited it to formulas, concepts and procedures which you are most likely to need most often. The course is short enough so that you can master it before you take your exam.

The next chapter, which you should find helpful, deals with the verbal parts of the exam—"Word Knowledge" and "Paragraph Comprehension." This chapter gives you help in preparing for these parts of the exam and valuable suggestions for answering verbal questions.

"General Science" is a vast field. There is so much information included under the heading "general science" that it would be impossible to give you a cram course at this time. Where your knowledge is lacking, you must rely on common sense and calculated guesses. Similarly, there is little that can be taught on an "instant" basis in the area of "Shop Information."

The short chapter on "Electrical Theory and Work" will, in four brief pages, fill you in on some basic definitions and facts to supplement your knowledge and common sense in answering "Electronics Information" questions.

MATHEMATICS REFRESHER COURSE

Before we begin a systematic discussion of mathematics necessary to Arithmetic Reasoning and Mathematics Knowledge, let us quickly list a few basic rules which must be mastered for speed and accuracy in performing Numerical Operations. You should memorize these rules:

Any number multiplied by 0 = 0.
   $5 \times 0 = 0$.
Any number divided by 0 = 0.
   $2 \div 0 = 0$
If 0 is added to any number, the number does not change.
   $7 + 0 = 7$
If 0 is subtracted from any number, that number does not change.
   $4 - 0 = 4$
If a number is multiplied by 1, that number does not change.
   $3 \times 1 = 3$
If a number is divided by 1, that number does not change.
   $6 \div 1 = 6$
A number added to itself is doubled.
   $4 + 4 = 8$
If a number is subtracted from itself, the answer is 0.
   $9 - 9 = 0$
If a number is divided by itself, the answer is 1.
   $8 \div 8 = 1$

If you have memorized these rules, you should be able to write the answers to the questions in the following exercise as fast as you can read the questions.

Exercise 1. Answers appear on page 99.

1. $1 - 1 =$
2. $3 \div 1 =$
3. $6 \times 0 =$
4. $6 - 0 =$
5. $8 \div 0 =$
6. $9 \times 1 =$

7. $5 + 0 =$
8. $4 - 0 =$
9. $2 \div 1 =$
10. $7 - 7 =$
11. $8 \times 0 =$
12. $4 \div 0 =$

13. $1 + 0 =$

14. $3 - 0 =$

15. $5 \times 1 =$

16. $9 \div 1 =$

17. $6 + 6 =$

18. $4 - 4 =$

19. $5 \div 5 =$

20. $6 \times 1 =$

The more rules, procedures and formulas you are able to memorize, the easier it will be to solve mathematical problems on your exam and throughout life. Become thoroughly familiar with the following rules and try to commit to memory as many as possible.

When multiplying a number by 10, 100, 1000, etc., move the decimal point to the right a number of spaces equal to the number of zeros in the multiplier. If the number being multiplied is a whole number, push the decimal point to the *right* by inserting the appropriate number of zeros.

$$.36 \times 100 = 36.$$
$$1.2 \times 10 = 12.$$
$$5. \times 10 = 50.$$
$$60.423 \times 100 = 6042.3$$

When dividing a number by 10, 100, 1000, etc., again count the zeros, but this time move the decimal point to the *left*.

$$123. \div 100 = 1.23$$
$$352.8 \div 10 = 35.28$$
$$16. \div 100 = .16$$
$$7. \div 1000 = .007$$

Exercise 2.

1. $18 \times 10 =$

2. $5 \div 100 =$

3. $1.3 \times 1000 =$

4. $3.62 \times 10 =$

5. $9.86 \div 10 =$

6. $.12 \div 100 =$

7. $4.5 \times 10 =$

8. $83.28 \div 1000 =$

9. $761 \times 100 =$

10. $68.86 \div 10 =$

When adding or subtracting decimals, it is most important to keep the decimal points in line. Once the decimal points are aligned, proceed with the problem in exactly the same way as with whole numbers, simply maintaining the location of the decimal point.

36.08	If you find it easier,	036.0800
745.	you may fill in the	745.0000
+ 4.362	spaces with zeros.	+ 004.3620
58.6	The answer will be	058.6000
.0061	unchanged.	000.0061
844.0481		844.0481

$$\begin{array}{r} 82.1 \\ - 7.928 \\ \hline 74.172 \end{array} \qquad \begin{array}{r} 82.100 \\ - 7.928 \\ \hline 74.172 \end{array}$$

Exercise 3.

1. 1.52 + .389 + 42.9 =
2. .6831 + .01 + 4.26 + 98 =
3. 84 − 1.9 =
4. 3.25 + 5.66 + 9.1 =
5. 17 − 12.81 =

6. 46.33 − 12.1 =
7. 51 + 7.86 + 42.003 =
8. 35.4 − 18.21 =
9. .85 − .16 =
10. 7.6 + .32 + 830 =

When multiplying decimals, you can ignore the decimal points until you reach the product. Then the placement of the decimal point is dependent upon the sum of the places to the right of the decimal point in both the multiplier and number being multiplied.

$$\begin{array}{r} 1.482 \\ \times .16 \\ \hline 8892 \\ 14820 \\ \hline .23712 \end{array}$$ (3 places to right of decimal point)
(2 places to right of decimal point)

(5 places to right of decimal point)

You cannot divide by a decimal. If the divisor is a decimal, you must move the decimal point to the right until the divisor becomes a whole number, an integer. Count the number of spaces by which you moved the decimal point to the right and move the decimal point in the dividend (the number being divided) the same number of spaces to the right. The decimal point in the answer should be directly above the decimal point in the dividend.

$$.06\overline{)4.21.2}\begin{array}{l}7\ 0.2\end{array}$$ Decimal point moves two spaces to the right.

Exercise 4.

1. 3.62 × 5.6 =
2. 92 × .11 =
3. 18 ÷ .3 =
4. 1.5 × .9 =
5. 7.55 ÷ 5 =

6. 6.42 ÷ 2.14 =
7. 12.01 × 3 =
8. 24.82 ÷ 7.3 =
9. .486 ÷ .2 =
10. .21 × 12 =

When fractions are to be added or subtracted they must have the same denominator, a *common denominator*. The common denominator is a number into which the denominators of all the fractions in the problem can be divided without a remainder. The common denominator of $\frac{3}{8}$, $\frac{5}{6}$, $\frac{1}{4}$, and $\frac{2}{3}$ is 24. If you want to add these fractions, they must all be converted to fractions with the denominator 24. Convert each fraction by dividing 24 by the denominator and multiplying the numerator by the quotient.

$$\frac{3}{8} = \frac{(24 \div 8) \times 3}{24} = \frac{3 \times 3}{24} = \frac{9}{24}$$

$$\frac{5}{6} = \frac{(24 \div 6) \times 5}{24} = \frac{4 \times 5}{24} = \frac{20}{24}$$

$$\frac{1}{4} = \frac{(24 \div 4) \times 1}{24} = \frac{6 \times 1}{24} = \frac{6}{24}$$

$$\frac{2}{3} = \frac{(24 \div 3) \times 2}{24} = \frac{8 \times 2}{24} = \frac{16}{24}$$

Now you can add the fractions:

$$\frac{3}{8} = \frac{9}{24}$$

$$\frac{5}{6} = \frac{20}{24}$$

$$\frac{1}{4} = \frac{6}{24}$$

$$\frac{2}{3} = \frac{16}{24}$$

$$\overline{\phantom{\frac{2}{3}}\frac{51}{24}}$$

The answer, $\frac{51}{24}$, is an improper fraction; that is, its numerator is greater than its denominator. To convert the answer to a mixed number, divide the numerator by the denominator and express the remainder as a fraction.

$$\frac{51}{24} = 51 \div 24 = 2\frac{3}{24} = 2\frac{1}{8}$$

Exercise 5. Express your answers as simple mixed numbers.

1. $\frac{2}{4} + \frac{3}{5} + \frac{1}{2} =$ 6. $\frac{1}{2} + \frac{1}{4} + \frac{2}{3} =$

2. $\frac{6}{8} - \frac{2}{4} =$ 7. $\frac{5}{6} - \frac{1}{2} =$

3. $\frac{1}{3} + \frac{1}{2} =$ 8. $\frac{5}{8} - \frac{1}{3} =$

4. $\frac{4}{5} - \frac{3}{5} =$ 9. $\frac{5}{12} + \frac{3}{4} =$

5. $\frac{7}{8} + \frac{3}{4} + \frac{1}{3} =$ 10. $\frac{8}{9} - \frac{2}{3} =$

When multiplying fractions, multiply numerators by numerators and denominators by denominators.

$$\frac{3}{5} \cdot \frac{4}{7} \cdot \frac{1}{5} = \frac{3 \times 4 \times 1}{5 \times 7 \times 5} = \frac{12}{175}$$

In multiplying fractions, try to work with numbers that are as small as possible. You can make numbers smaller by *cancelling*. Cancel by dividing the numerator of any one fraction and the denominator of any one fraction by the same number.

$$\frac{\overset{1}{\cancel{3}}}{\underset{2}{\cancel{4}}} \cdot \frac{\overset{1}{\cancel{2}}}{\underset{3}{\cancel{9}}} = \frac{1 \times 1}{2 \times 3} = \frac{1}{6}$$

In this case the numerator of the first fraction and the denominator of the other fraction were divided by 3, while the denominator of the first fraction and the numerator of the other fraction were divided by 2.

To divide by a fraction, invert the fraction following the division sign and multiply.

$$\frac{3}{16} \div \frac{1}{8} = \frac{3}{\cancel{16}} \times \frac{\cancel{8}}{1} = \frac{3}{2} = 1\frac{1}{2}$$

Exercise 6. Cancel wherever possible and express your answer in the simplest terms possible.

1. $\frac{4}{5} \cdot \frac{3}{6} =$

2. $\frac{2}{4} \cdot \frac{8}{12} \cdot \frac{7}{1} =$

3. $\frac{3}{4} \div \frac{3}{8} =$

4. $\frac{5}{2} \div \frac{3}{6} =$

5. $\frac{8}{9} \cdot \frac{3}{4} \cdot \frac{1}{2} =$

6. $\frac{7}{8} \div \frac{2}{3} =$

7. $\frac{4}{6} \cdot \frac{8}{12} \cdot \frac{10}{3} =$

8. $\frac{1}{6} \cdot \frac{7}{6} \cdot \frac{12}{3} =$

9. $\frac{3}{7} \div \frac{9}{4} =$

10. $\frac{2}{3} \div \frac{2}{3} =$

The line in a fraction means "divided by." To change a fraction to a decimal follow through on the division.

$$\tfrac{4}{5} = 4 \div 5 = .8$$

To change a decimal to a percent, move the decimal point two places to the right and add a percent sign.

$$.8 = 80\%$$

Exercise 7. Change each fraction first to a decimal to three places and then to a percent.

1. $\frac{2}{4}$ $2 \div 4 = .5 = 50\%$

2. $\frac{7}{8}$ $7 \div 8 = 875\%$

3. $\frac{5}{6}$ $5 \div 6 =$

4. $\frac{6}{8}$

5. $\frac{3}{4}$

6. $\frac{2}{3}$

7. $\frac{3}{5}$

8. $\frac{4}{10}$

9. $\frac{1}{4}$

10. $\frac{2}{5}$

To find a percent of a number, change the percent to a decimal and multiply the number by it.

$$5\% \text{ of } 80 = 80 \times .05 = 4$$

To find out what a number is when a percent of it is given, change the percent to a decimal and divide the given number by it.

5 is 10% of what number?

$$5 \div .10 = 50$$

To find what percent one number is of another number, create a fraction by putting the part over the whole. Reduce the fraction if possible, then convert it to a decimal (remember: the line means *divided by*, so divide the numerator by the denominator) and change to a percent by multiplying by 100, moving the decimal point two places to the right.

4 is what percent of 80?

$$\frac{4}{80} = \frac{1}{20} = .05 = 5\%$$

Exercise 8.

1. 10% of 32 = $32 \times .10 = 3.2$

2. 8 is 25% of what number?

$8 \div .25 = 32$

3. 12 is what percent of 24? $\frac{12}{24} = \frac{1}{2} = 50$

4. 20% of 360 is

$20 \times 360 = 72$

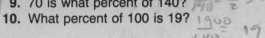

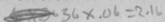

5. 5 is what percent of 60?   **8.** 25 is 5% of what number?
6. 12 is 8% of what number? $12 \div .8 = 1.4$ **9.** 70 is what percent of 140?
7. 6% of 36 =   **10.** What percent of 100 is 19?

$36 \times .06 = 2.16$

An equation is an equality. The values on either side of the equals sign in an equation must be equal. In order to learn the value of an unknown in an equation, do the same thing to both sides of the equation so as to leave the unknown on one side of the equal sign and its value on the other side.

$$X - 2 = 8$$
Add 2 to both sides of the equation.
$$X - 2 + 2 = 8 + 2; X = 10$$

$$5X = 25$$
Divide both sides of the equation by 5.
$$\frac{\overset{1}{\cancel{5}}X}{\underset{1}{\cancel{5}}} = \frac{25}{5}; X = 5$$

$$Y + 9 = 15$$
Subtract 9 from both sides of the equation.
$$Y + 9 - 9 = 15 - 9; Y = 6$$

$$A \div 4 = 48$$
Multiply both sides of the equation by 4.
$$\frac{\overset{1}{\cancel{4}}A}{\underset{1}{\cancel{4}}} = 48 \times 4; A = 192$$

Sometimes more than one step is required to solve an equation.
$$6A \div 4 = 48$$
First, multiply both sides of the equation by 4.
$$\frac{6A}{\underset{1}{\cancel{4}}} \times \frac{\overset{1}{\cancel{4}}}{1} = 48 \times 4; 6A = 192$$

Then divide both sides of the equation by 6.
$$\frac{\overset{1}{\cancel{6}}A}{\underset{1}{\cancel{6}}} = \frac{192}{6}; A = 32$$

Exercise 9. Solve for X.

1. X + 13 = 25   **3.** X − 5 = 28
2. 4X = 84   **4.** X ÷ 9 = 4

5. $3X + 2 = 14$

6. $\dfrac{X}{4} - 2 = 4$

7. $10X - 27 = 73$

8. $2X \div 4 = 13$

9. $8X + 9 = 81$

10. $2X \div 11 = 6$

Area is the space enclosed by a plane (flat) figure. A rectangle is a plane figure with four right angles. Opposite sides of a rectangle are of equal length and are parallel to each other. To find the area of a rectangle, multiply the length of the base of the rectangle by the length of its height. Area is *always* expressed in square units.

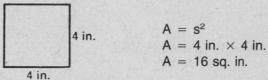

3 ft

9 ft

$A = bh$
$A = 9 \text{ ft.} \times 3 \text{ ft.}$
$A = 27 \text{ sq. ft.}$

A square is a rectangle in which all four sides are the same length. The area of a rectangle is found by squaring the length of one side, which is exactly the same as multiplying the square's length by its width.

4 in.

4 in.

$A = s^2$
$A = 4 \text{ in.} \times 4 \text{ in.}$
$A = 16 \text{ sq. in.}$

A triangle is a three-sided plane figure. The area of a triangle is found by multiplying the base by the altitude (height) and dividing by two.

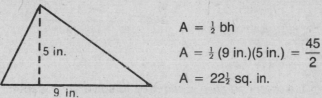

5 in.

9 in.

$A = \frac{1}{2} bh$
$A = \frac{1}{2} (9 \text{ in.})(5 \text{ in.}) = \dfrac{45}{2}$
$A = 22\frac{1}{2} \text{ sq. in.}$

A circle is a perfectly round plane figure. The distance from the center of a circle to its rim is its radius. The distance from one edge to the other through the center is its diameter. The diameter is twice the length of the radius.

Pi (π) is a mathematical value equal to approximately 3.14 or $\dfrac{22}{7}$. Pi is frequently used in calculations involving circles. The area of a circle is found by squaring the radius and multiplying it by π.

4 cm

$A = \pi r^2$
$A = \pi (4 \text{ cm.})^2$
$A = 16\pi \text{ sq. cm.}$
You may leave the area in terms of pi unless you are told what value to assign π.

Exercise 10. Find the area.

1.
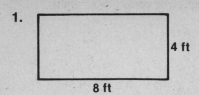
4 ft
8 ft

2.
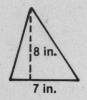
8 in.
7 in.

3.
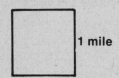
1 mile

4.
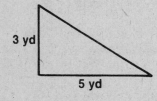
3 yd
5 yd

5.

2 cm

6.
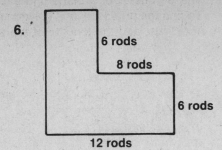
6 rods
8 rods
6 rods
12 rods

7.
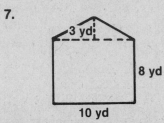
3 yd
8 yd
10 yd

8.
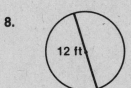
12 ft

9.
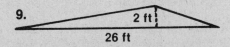
2 ft
26 ft

10.
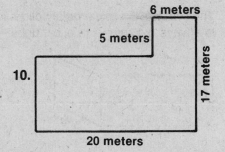
6 meters
5 meters
17 meters
20 meters

The perimeter of a plane figure is the distance around the outside. To find the perimeter of a polygon (a plane figure bounded by straight lines) just add the lengths of the sides.

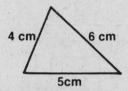

P = 3 in. + 5 in. + 3 in. + 5 in.
 = 16 in.

P = 4 cm. + 6 cm. + 5 cm.
 = 15 cm.

The perimeter of a circle is called the *circumference*. The formula for the circumference of a circle is πd or 2πr, which are both, of course, the same thing.

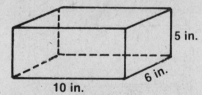

$C = 2 \cdot 3 \cdot \pi = 6\pi$

The volume of a solid figure is the measure of the space within. To figure the volume of a solid figure, multiply the area by the height or depth.

The volume of a rectangular solid is length × width × height. Volume is always expressed in cubic units.

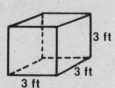

V = lwh

V = (10 in.)(6 in.)(5 in.)

V = 300 cu. in.

The volume of a cube is the cube of one side.

$V = s^3$

$V = (3 \text{ ft.})^3$

V = 27 cu. ft.

The volume of a cylinder is π times the square of the radius of the base times the height.

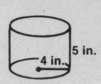

$$V = \pi r^2 h$$

$$V = \pi (4 \text{ in.})^2 (5 \text{ in.})$$

$$V = \pi (16)(5) = 80\pi \text{ cu. in.}$$

Exercise 11.

1. Find the perimeter.

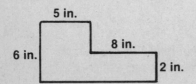

2. Find the volume.

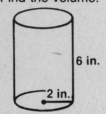

3. Find the circumference.

4. Find the volume.

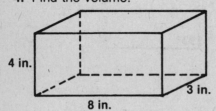

5. Find the volume.

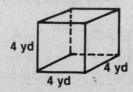

6. Find the perimeter.

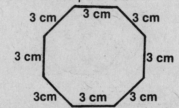

7. Find the perimeter.

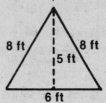

8. Find the perimeter.

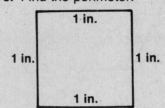

The sum of the angles of a straight line is 180°.

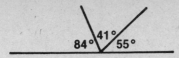

The sum of the angles of a triangle is 180°.

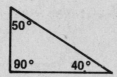

The sum of the angles of a rectangle is 360°.

```
90°              90°



90°              90°
```

The sum of the angles of a circle is 360°.

The sum of the angles of a polygon of n sides is (n − 2)180°.

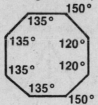

(8 − 2)(180°)
6·180° = 1080°

Exercise 12. What is the size of the unlabelled angle?

1.

3.

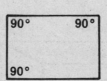

2.

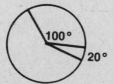

4.

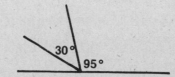

5.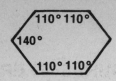

7.

6.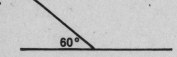

8.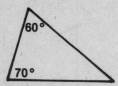

ANSWERS TO MATH REFRESHER COURSE EXERCISES

Exercise 1.

1. 0
2. 3
3. 0
4. 6
5. 0
6. 9
7. 5
8. 4
9. 2
10. 0

11. 0
12. 0
13. 1
14. 3
15. 5
16. 9
17. 12
18. 0
19. 1
20. 6

Exercise 2.

1. 180
2. .05
3. 1300
4. 36.2
5. .986

6. .0012
7. 45
8. .08328
9. 76100
10. 6.886

Exercise 3.

1. 44.809
2. 102.9531
3. 82.1
4. 18.01
5. 4.19

6. 34.23
7. 100.863
8. 17.19
9. .69
10. 837.92

Exercise 4.

1. 20.272
2. 10.12
3. 60
4. 1.35
5. 1.51

6. 3
7. 36.03
8. 3.4
9. 2.43
10. 2.52

Exercise 5.

1. $\frac{32}{20} = 1\frac{12}{20} = 1\frac{3}{5}$

2. $\frac{2}{8} = \frac{1}{4}$

3. $\frac{5}{6}$

4. $\frac{1}{5}$

5. $\frac{47}{24} = 1\frac{23}{24}$

6. $\frac{17}{12} = 1\frac{5}{12}$

7. $\frac{2}{6} = \frac{1}{3}$

8. $\frac{7}{24}$

9. $\frac{14}{12} = 1\frac{2}{12} = 1\frac{1}{6}$

10. $\frac{2}{9}$

Exercise 6.

1. $\frac{2}{5}$

2. $2\frac{1}{3}$

3. 2

4. $\frac{15}{3} = 5$

5. $\frac{1}{3}$

6. $\frac{21}{16} = 1\frac{5}{16}$

7. $1\frac{13}{27}$

8. $\frac{7}{9}$

9. $\frac{4}{21}$

10. 1

Exercise 7.

1. $.50 = 50\%$
2. $.875 = 87\frac{1}{2}\%$
3. $.833 = 83\frac{1}{3}\%$
4. $.75 = 75\%$
5. $.75 = 75\%$

6. $.666 = 66\frac{2}{3}\%$
7. $.60 = 60\%$
8. $.40 = 40\%$
9. $.25 = 25\%$
10. $.40 = 40\%$

Exercise 8.

1. $32 \times .10 = 3.2$
2. $8 \div .25 = 32$
3. $\frac{12}{24} = \frac{1}{2} = .50 = 50\%$
4. $360 \times .20 = 72$
5. $\frac{5}{60} = \frac{1}{12} = .0833 = 8\frac{1}{3}\%$

6. $12 \div .08 = 150$
7. $36 \times .06 = 2.16$
8. $25 \div .05 = 500$
9. $\frac{70}{140} = \frac{1}{2} = .50 = 50\%$
10. $\frac{19}{100} = .19 = 19\%$

Exercise 9.

1. $X = 12$
2. $X = 21$
3. $X = 33$
4. $X = 36$
5. $X = 4$

6. $X = 24$
7. $X = 10$
8. $X = 26$
9. $X = 9$
10. $X = 33$

Exercise 10

1. $A = bh$
   $A = 8 \times 4 = 32$ sq. ft.
2. $A = \frac{1}{2}bh$
   $A = \frac{1}{2}(7 \times 8)$
   $A = \frac{1}{2}(56) = 28$ sq. in.
3. $A = s^2$
   $A = 1^2 = 1$ sq. mile
4. $A = \frac{1}{2}bh$
   $A = \frac{1}{2}(5 \times 3)$
   $A = \frac{1}{2}(15) = 7\frac{1}{2}$ sq. yds.
5. $A = \pi r^2$
   $A = \pi 2^2$
   $A = 4\pi$ sq. cm.
6. $A = bh$
   $A = 12 \times 6 + (12 - 8) \times 6$
   $A = 12 \times 6 + 4 \times 6$
   $A = 72 + 24 = 96$ sq. rd.

7. $A = bh$
   $A = 10 \times 8 = 80$ sq. yds.

   $A = \frac{1}{2}bh$
   $A = \frac{1}{2}(10 \times 3) = \frac{1}{2}(30)$
   $A = 15$ sq. yds.

   $80 + 15 = 95$ sq. yds.
8. $A = \pi r^2$
   $A = \pi 6^2$
   $A = 36\pi$ sq. ft.
9. $A = \frac{1}{2}bh$
   $A = \frac{1}{2}(26 \times 2) = \frac{1}{2}(52)$
   $A = 26$ sq. ft.
10. $A = bh$
    $A = 6 \times 5 + 20 \times (17 - 5)$
    $A = 6 \times 5 + 20 \times 12$
    $A = 30 + 240 = 270$ sq. meters

Exercise 11.

1. $P = 6 + 5 + (6 - 2) + 8 + 2 + (8 + 5) = 38$ in.
2. $V = \pi r^2 h$
   $V = \pi \times 2^2 \times 6$
   $V = \pi \times 4 \times 6$
   $V = 24\pi$ cu. in.
3. $C = 2\pi r$
   $C = 2 \times \pi \times 7$
   $C = 14\pi$ cm.
4. $V = lwh$
   $V = 8 \times 3 \times 4$
   $V = 96$ cu. in.

5. $V = s^3$
   $V = 4^3 = 4 \times 4 \times 4$
   $V = 64$ cu. yd.
6. $P = 3 + 3 + 3 + 3 + 3 + 3 + 3 + 3$
   $P = 24$ cm.
7. $P = 8 + 8 + 6 = 22$ ft.
8. $P = 1 + 1 + 1 + 1 = 4$ in.

Exercise 12.

1. $80°$
2. $240°$
3. $90°$
4. $55°$

5. $140°$
6. $120°$
7. $180°$
8. $50°$

HELP WITH THE VERBAL QUESTIONS

The Verbal questions of your exam are found in two parts, Word Knowledge and Paragraph Comprehension.

WORD KNOWLEDGE

The "Word Knowledge" questions test your understanding of words. In these questions, you are given a word and asked to choose another word which has the same meaning or most nearly the same meaning as the given word. This is a test of synonyms.

Sometimes the given word is presented in a sentence. If the given word is in a sentence, you should always try substituting the choices in the place of the underlined word. This procedure may help you to find the answer. Consider:

The surface of the <u>placid</u> lake was as smooth as glass.

   A cold
   B muddy
   C deep
   D calm

Any one of the choices might be substituted for the word *placid,* and the sentence would still be entirely sensible. However, if the surface of the lake was as smooth as glass, the water would have had to be very *calm.* Thus, while a cold, muddy or deep lake could have a smooth surface, it is most reasonable to assume, on the basis of the sentence, that *placid* means *calm.*

Or, consider the following question:

The camel is sometimes called the ship of the <u>desert</u>.

   A abandon
   B ice cream
   C sandy wasteland
   D leave

Here the sentence is absolutely necessary to the definition of the word. Without the sentence, you would not know whether the word *desert* is to be pronounced *de·sert'*, which means *to leave* or *to abandon*, or *de'sert*, which means a *sandy wasteland.* If you are not sure of your spelling, the sentence can also spare you the confusion of *desert* with *dessert*, which is the last course of a meal.

On the other hand, the sentence may be of no use at all:

The robbery suspect had a <u>sallow</u> complexion.

    A ruddy
    B pale
    C pock-marked
    D freckled

The sentence shows you a use of the word *sallow*, that it is used to describe a complexion, but it gives no clue that *sallow* means *pale.* You either know the meaning of the word or you must guess.

If the given word is not part of a sentence, or if the sentence is of no use in defining the word, you must rely on other clues. Perhaps you have seen the word used but were never sure what it meant. Look carefully. Can you see any part of a word of which you do know the meaning? An example:

<u>Remedial</u> most nearly means

    A reading
    B slow
    C corrective
    D special

Your association is probably "remedial reading." Be careful. *Remedial* does not mean *reading. Remedial* is an adjective, *reading* the noun it modifies. Slow readers may receive remedial reading instruction in special classes. The *remedial* reading classes are intended to *correct* bad reading practices. Do you see the word *remedy* in *remedial*? You know that a *remedy* is a *cure* or a *correction* for an ailment. If you combine all the information you now have, you can choose *corrective* as the word which most nearly means *remedial.*

Sometimes you can figure the meaning of a word by combining your knowledge with elimination of wrong answers. For instance:

<u>Infamous</u> most nearly means

    A well-known
    B poor
    C disgraceful
    D young

The first word you see when you look at *infamous* is *famous. Famous,* of course, means *well-known.* Since the prefix *in* often means *not,* you will eliminate (A) as the answer. A person who is not well-known might be poor, but not necessarily. *Poor* should not be eliminated as a possible answer, but you should carefully consider the other choices before choosing *poor.* Since *in* meaning *not* is a negative prefix, you should be looking for a negative word as the meaning of *infamous.*

There is no choice meaning *not famous,* so you must look for negative fame. *Disgrace* is a negative kind of *fame.* A person who behaves *disgracefully* is well-known for his bad behavior; he is *infamous.* If you had chosen *young* as your answer, you would have mistakenly seen *infant* in *infamous.* You must be careful and thorough when figuring out the meanings of words.

In the past few paragraphs we have given you suggestions for figuring out the meanings of words when there is any possibility for doing so. Many "Word Knowledge" questions give you no such possibility. Often, you simply must know the meaning of the word. Since this is so often the case, we will here repeat the advice we gave you in Chapter 1, How To Use This Book.

Work with a dictionary. Look up words you meet in anything you read. Look up *every* unfamiliar word in this book. If you run across a word you do not know while doing the exams, circle the word and look it up later. Look up words you find in the reading passages, new words from among answer choices, words you find in the explanations, words you meet in the study chapters. Looking up words for yourself is the best way to learn them. If you understand every word used in this book, you are well on your way toward a broad-based vocabulary and should be able to handle Word Knowledge and Paragraph Comprehension.

PARAGRAPH COMPREHENSION

"Paragraph Comprehension" questions test not only how well you understand what you read, but also how well you can interpret the meaning of the passage and the intent of the author. Reading speed is vital for success with "Paragraph Comprehension" questions. You cannot even attempt to answer questions based upon a paragraph if you have not had time to read it.

The best way to increase your reading speed is to read. Read everything in sight between now and the exam. Newspaper reading is an especially good way to improve your reading skills. Don't be satisfied with just the opening paragraph of each article. Push yourself to read the whole story and give it your full attention as you read. If your mind wanders, you will not comprehend what you read.

To read with understanding your eyes must fixate (stop). Most people fixate on each word because that is the way reading is taught in the early grades. For adults, this method wastes a great deal of time. The key to increasing your reading speed is to take in more words each time your eyes stop. If a line has ten words in it and you are able to read the line by stopping only twice instead of ten times, you would be reading five times as fast as you do now. Try to train yourself.

Don't *subvocalize.* If you can hear every word you read, you are subvocalizing. No matter how fast you can talk, you can read faster if you stop subvocalizing. Some people have found that putting pebbles in their mouths or chewing on pencils helps them to stop subvocalizing. For others, awareness of the possibility is enough to help them to correct this bad habit.

In building up reading speed try using your hand. When you read, move your hand or pencil underneath the line you are reading. Because your eyes tend to move as quickly as your pencil, you will not stop on every word, you will not regress (look back) and you probably will not subvocalize. However, what you may do is concentrate on your pencil and not on the reading passage. This is why you must practice this technique before using it on your test. Start your hand or your pencil at the second or third word in the line and stop it before the last word in the line. Your peripheral vision (what you see at the edges) will pick up the first and last words in the lines and you will save time by not having to focus on them.

Become more aware of words. "Word Knowledge" and "Paragraph Comprehension" are tied together to yield a "Verbal" score because they are so closely interrelated. You cannot have a large vocabulary without reading. You cannot understand what you read without an understanding of the words. When you look up words, study the roots, prefixes and suffixes so that you can apply all that you know whenever you meet unfamiliar words.

HOW TO ANSWER READING COMPREHENSION QUESTIONS

1. Skim the paragraph to get a general idea of the subject matter and of the point that is being made.
2. Reread the paragraph, giving attention to details and point of view. Be alert for the author's hints as to what he or she thinks is important. Phrases such as "Note that . . .", "Of importance is . . ." and "Do not overlook . . ." give clues to what the writer is stressing.
3. If the author has quoted material from another source, be sure that you understand the purpose of the quote. Does the author agree or disagree?
4. Carefully read the question or incomplete statement. Determine exactly what is being asked. Watch for negatives or all-inclusive words, such as "always," "never," "all," "only," "every," "absolutely," "completely," "none," "entirely," "no." These words can affect your choice of answer.
5. Read all four answer choices. Do not rush to choose the first answer that might be correct. Eliminate those choices that are obviously incorrect. Reread the remaining choices and refer to the paragraph, if necessary, to determine the *best* answer.
6. Avoid inserting your own judgments into your answers. Even if you disagree with the author or even if you spot a factual error in the paragraph, you must answer on the basis of what is stated or implied in the paragraph.
7. Do not allow yourself to spend too much time on any one question. If looking back at the paragraph does not help you to find or figure out the answer, choose from among the answers remaining after you eliminate the obviously wrong answers, and go on to the next paragraph.

ELECTRICAL THEORY
AND WORK

Definition of Electricity. Electricity is an invisible force which we only know about through the effects it produces. While the exact nature of electricity is not known, the laws governing electrical phenomena are clearly understood and defined, just as the laws of gravitation are known, although we cannot define the nature of gravity.

The Movement of Electricity. In many ways electricity in motion is like flowing water, and electrical phenomena can be more easily understood if this analogy is borne in mind. In dealing with the flow of electricity and the flow of water, we consider three factors: (a) Current (Flow of electricity, usually along a conductor); (b) Pressure (that which causes the current to flow); (c) Resistance (that which regulates the flow of current).

Electrical Current or Flow. If we want to know about the flow of water in a pipe, we would determine how many gallons of water flow through the pipe in a second. In exactly the same way, the electrician determines the number of *coulombs* of electricity that flow through a wire in a second. Just as the gallon is a measure of the quantity of water, the coulomb is a measure of the quantity of electricity. There is an abbreviated method of describing the flow of electrical current. The electrician speaks of the *ampere,* which means one coulomb per second, and is thus saved the trouble of saying "per second" every time he wants to describe the current flow.

Electrical Pressure. Water pressure is measured in pounds per square inch. There is also a measure of electrical pressure. This electrical pressure has a definite effect upon the number of amperes flowing along a wire. The electrical unit of pressure is the volt. A volt means the same thing in speaking of a current of electricity that a pound-per-square-inch pressure does in speaking of a current of water. Just as a higher pressure is required to force the same current of water through a small pipe than through a large pipe, so a higher electrical pressure is required to force the same current of electricity through a small wire than through a large wire. The voltage (pressure) between two points in an electric circuit is sometimes spoken of as the difference in potential, or the drop in potential, or merely the "drop" between those two points.

The distinction between amperes and volts should now be plain. The amperes represent the amount of the current flowing through a circuit; the volts represent the pressure causing it to flow.

Electrical Resistance. The electrical unit of resistance is the ohm. We say a wire has one ohm resistance when a pressure of one volt forces a current of one ampere through it.

Ohm's Law. In any circuit through which a current is flowing, the three following factors are present: (1) The pressure or potential difference, expressed in volts, causing the current to flow; (2) the opposition or resistance of the circuit, expressed in ohms, which must be overcome; (3) the current strength, expressed in amperes, which is maintained in the circuit as a result of the pressure overcoming the resistance. A definite and exact relation exists between three factors; pressure, current strength, and resistance in any circuit, whereby the value of any one factor may always be calculated when the values of the other two factors are known. This relation, known as Ohm's Law, is very important, since it forms the basis for all calculations in electrical engineering. It may be summarized as follows:

The current in any electric circuit is equal to the electromotive force applied to the circuit, divided by the resistance of the circuit.

Let E = E. M. F. or available pressure, expressed in volts, applied to any circuit.
  R = resistance of the circuit, expressed in ohms,
  I = current strength, expressed in amperes, to be maintained through circuit.

Then, by the above statement of Ohm's Law,

$$\text{Current} = \frac{\text{(Pressure)}}{\text{Resistance}} \text{ or}$$

$$\text{Amperes} = \frac{\text{volts}}{\text{ohms}} \quad \text{or } I = \frac{E}{R}$$

The Circuit. Electricity is not as simple as water in that it can not be piped from one point to another. In order to flow, electricity must be sent along a closed circuit. Except through a generator or a battery cell, electricity always flows from a higher to a lower level. The higher level, or positive, is marked +, and the lower level, or negative, is marked −, in order to indicate the direction in which the current is flowing. A given point is + to all points below its level, and − to all points above its level.

If any of the wires leading from the + to the − terminal is broken, the current cannot flow, for the circuit has been interrupted and is incomplete.

Measuring Electrical Current. In order to find out how much current is flowing through an electric circuit, we insert a current meter into the circuit so that all the current which we wish to measure flows through the meter. Since an instrument which measures an electric current must read in amperes, such a current meter is called an ammeter. The ammeter must be of very low resistance in order not to hinder the current. Such an instrument is very delicate and must be handled carefully.

Measurement of Electrical Pressure. When it is necessary to measure the pressure which is causing an electric current to flow through a circuit, the terminals of a *voltmeter* are tapped on to that circuit in such a way that the voltmeter is made to register not current but pressure. The method of attaching a voltmeter is different from that used in attaching an ammeter. The ammeter becomes a part of the circuit. The voltmeter does not become a part of the circuit.

Measurement of Electrical Resistance. In order to find the resistance of an electrical piece, the voltmeter reading is divided by the ammeter reading.

Regulating and Controlling Electrical Current. The usual method of regulating and controlling the current required for various electrical purposes is by inserting or removing resistance from a circuit. An adjustable resistance, or any apparatus for changing the resistance without opening the circuit, is called a rheostat. The function of a rheostat is to absorb electrical energy; and this energy, which appears as heat, is wasted instead of performing any useful work. A rheostat may be constructed of coils of iron wire, iron plates or strips; of carbon, either pulverized in tubes or in the form of solid rods or disks; German silver, platinoid, or wires of other alloys wound on spools; columns of liquids, as water and mercury, etc. The cross-sectional area of the material must be sufficient to carry the current without excessive heating. In rheostats used for regulating the current in commercial electrical circuits no great degree of accuracy of the resistance coils is required, as is the case with laboratory rheostats.

The Effects of a Current. A current of electricity is believed to be a transfer of electrons through a circuit, and since these carriers are so minute, a direct measurement of them is impractical. Consequently, an electric current is measured by the effects it produces, all of which are commercially utilized. The effects manifested by a current of electricity are: Heating Effect, Magnetic Effect, Chemical Effect, and Physiological Effect.

Heating Effect. Every wire which conducts a current of electricity becomes heated to some extent as a result of the current, because the best conductors offer some opposition (resistance) to the flow of the current, and it is in overcoming this resistance that the heat is developed. If the wire is large in cross-sectional area and the current small, the heat developed will be so small in amount as not to be recognized by the touch; nevertheless, the wire releases some heat energy. On the other hand, with a small wire and a large current, it becomes quite hot.

Magnetic Effect. A wire carrying a current of electricity deflects a magnetic needle. When the wire is insulated and coiled around an iron core, the current magnetizes the core.

Chemical Effect. Electrical current is capable of decomposing certain chemical compounds when it is passed through them, breaking up the compounds into their constituent parts. In the production of electrical energy by a simple primary cell, electrolytic decomposition takes place inside the cell when the current is flowing. Electroplating, or the art of depositing a coating of metal upon any object, is based upon the principles of electrolytic decomposition.

Physiological Effect. A current of electricity passed through the body produces muscular contractions which are due to the physiological effects of an electrical current. Electrotherapeutics deals with the study of this effect.

Direct and Alternating Current. A direct or continuous current flows always in the same direction. In many cases it has a constant strength for definite periods of time. A pulsating current has a uniform direction, but the current strength varies. Most direct current generators furnish pulsating current; but since the pulsations are very small, the current is practically constant.

An alternating current of electricity is one that changes its direction of flow at regular intervals of time. These intervals are usually much shorter than one second. During an interval, the current strength is capable of varying in any way. In practice, the strength rises and then falls smoothly. Most electricity today comes in the form of alternating current. This is so because high voltage can more easily be obtained with alternating current than with direct current. High voltages, of course, are much more cheaply transmitted over power lines than are low voltages.

The Dynamo and Electromagnetic Induction. The electrical generator and the electric motor are intimately related. The term dynamo is applied to machines which convert either mechanical energy into electrical energy or electrical energy into mechanical energy by utilizing the principles of electromagnetic induction. A dynamo is called a generator when mechanical energy supplied in the form of rotation is converted into electrical energy. When the energy conversion takes place in the reverse order the dynamo is called a motor. Thus a dynamo is a reversible machine capable of operation as a generator or motor as desired.

The generator consists fundamentally of a number of loops of insulated wires revolving in a strong magnetic field in such a way that these wires cut across the lines of magnetic force. This cutting of the lines of force sets up an electromotive force along the wires.

We have shown that wherever there is an electric current present, there is also present a magnetic field. It is not true that wherever a magnetic field exists, there also exists an electric current, in the ordinary sense; but we can say that wherever a conductor moves in a magnetic field in such a way as to cut lines of force, an electromotive force is set up. It is on this principle that the electric generator works.

SECOND MODEL EXAM

ANSWER SHEET—SECOND MODEL EXAM

PART 1—GENERAL SCIENCE

1 Ⓐ Ⓑ Ⓒ Ⓓ   6 Ⓐ Ⓑ Ⓒ Ⓓ   11 Ⓐ Ⓑ Ⓒ Ⓓ   16 Ⓐ Ⓑ Ⓒ Ⓓ   21 Ⓐ Ⓑ Ⓒ Ⓓ
2 Ⓐ Ⓑ Ⓒ Ⓓ   7 Ⓐ Ⓑ Ⓒ Ⓓ   12 Ⓐ Ⓑ Ⓒ Ⓓ   17 Ⓐ Ⓑ Ⓒ Ⓓ   22 Ⓐ Ⓑ Ⓒ Ⓓ
3 Ⓐ Ⓑ Ⓒ Ⓓ   8 Ⓐ Ⓑ Ⓒ Ⓓ   13 Ⓐ Ⓑ Ⓒ Ⓓ   18 Ⓐ Ⓑ Ⓒ Ⓓ   23 Ⓐ Ⓑ Ⓒ Ⓓ
4 Ⓐ Ⓑ Ⓒ Ⓓ   9 Ⓐ Ⓑ Ⓒ Ⓓ   14 Ⓐ Ⓑ Ⓒ Ⓓ   19 Ⓐ Ⓑ Ⓒ Ⓓ   24 Ⓐ Ⓑ Ⓒ Ⓓ
5 Ⓐ Ⓑ Ⓒ Ⓓ   10 Ⓐ Ⓑ Ⓒ Ⓓ   15 Ⓐ Ⓑ Ⓒ Ⓓ   20 Ⓐ Ⓑ Ⓒ Ⓓ   25 Ⓐ Ⓑ Ⓒ Ⓓ

PART 2—ARITHMETIC REASONING

1 Ⓐ Ⓑ Ⓒ Ⓓ   7 Ⓐ Ⓑ Ⓒ Ⓓ   13 Ⓐ Ⓑ Ⓒ Ⓓ   19 Ⓐ Ⓑ Ⓒ Ⓓ   25 Ⓐ Ⓑ Ⓒ Ⓓ
2 Ⓐ Ⓑ Ⓒ Ⓓ   8 Ⓐ Ⓑ Ⓒ Ⓓ   14 Ⓐ Ⓑ Ⓒ Ⓓ   20 Ⓐ Ⓑ Ⓒ Ⓓ   26 Ⓐ Ⓑ Ⓒ Ⓓ
3 Ⓐ Ⓑ Ⓒ Ⓓ   9 Ⓐ Ⓑ Ⓒ Ⓓ   15 Ⓐ Ⓑ Ⓒ Ⓓ   21 Ⓐ Ⓑ Ⓒ Ⓓ   27 Ⓐ Ⓑ Ⓒ Ⓓ
4 Ⓐ Ⓑ Ⓒ Ⓓ   10 Ⓐ Ⓑ Ⓒ Ⓓ   16 Ⓐ Ⓑ Ⓒ Ⓓ   22 Ⓐ Ⓑ Ⓒ Ⓓ   28 Ⓐ Ⓑ Ⓒ Ⓓ
5 Ⓐ Ⓑ Ⓒ Ⓓ   11 Ⓐ Ⓑ Ⓒ Ⓓ   17 Ⓐ Ⓑ Ⓒ Ⓓ   23 Ⓐ Ⓑ Ⓒ Ⓓ   29 Ⓐ Ⓑ Ⓒ Ⓓ
6 Ⓐ Ⓑ Ⓒ Ⓓ   12 Ⓐ Ⓑ Ⓒ Ⓓ   18 Ⓐ Ⓑ Ⓒ Ⓓ   24 Ⓐ Ⓑ Ⓒ Ⓓ   30 Ⓐ Ⓑ Ⓒ Ⓓ

PART 3—WORD KNOWLEDGE

1 Ⓐ Ⓑ Ⓒ Ⓓ   8 Ⓐ Ⓑ Ⓒ Ⓓ   15 Ⓐ Ⓑ Ⓒ Ⓓ   22 Ⓐ Ⓑ Ⓒ Ⓓ   29 Ⓐ Ⓑ Ⓒ Ⓓ
2 Ⓐ Ⓑ Ⓒ Ⓓ   9 Ⓐ Ⓑ Ⓒ Ⓓ   16 Ⓐ Ⓑ Ⓒ Ⓓ   23 Ⓐ Ⓑ Ⓒ Ⓓ   30 Ⓐ Ⓑ Ⓒ Ⓓ
3 Ⓐ Ⓑ Ⓒ Ⓓ   10 Ⓐ Ⓑ Ⓒ Ⓓ   17 Ⓐ Ⓑ Ⓒ Ⓓ   24 Ⓐ Ⓑ Ⓒ Ⓓ   31 Ⓐ Ⓑ Ⓒ Ⓓ
4 Ⓐ Ⓑ Ⓒ Ⓓ   11 Ⓐ Ⓑ Ⓒ Ⓓ   18 Ⓐ Ⓑ Ⓒ Ⓓ   25 Ⓐ Ⓑ Ⓒ Ⓓ   32 Ⓐ Ⓑ Ⓒ Ⓓ
5 Ⓐ Ⓑ Ⓒ Ⓓ   12 Ⓐ Ⓑ Ⓒ Ⓓ   19 Ⓐ Ⓑ Ⓒ Ⓓ   26 Ⓐ Ⓑ Ⓒ Ⓓ   33 Ⓐ Ⓑ Ⓒ Ⓓ
6 Ⓐ Ⓑ Ⓒ Ⓓ   13 Ⓐ Ⓑ Ⓒ Ⓓ   20 Ⓐ Ⓑ Ⓒ Ⓓ   27 Ⓐ Ⓑ Ⓒ Ⓓ   34 Ⓐ Ⓑ Ⓒ Ⓓ
7 Ⓐ Ⓑ Ⓒ Ⓓ   14 Ⓐ Ⓑ Ⓒ Ⓓ   21 Ⓐ Ⓑ Ⓒ Ⓓ   28 Ⓐ Ⓑ Ⓒ Ⓓ   35 Ⓐ Ⓑ Ⓒ Ⓓ

PART 4—PARAGRAPH COMPREHENSION

1 Ⓐ Ⓑ Ⓒ Ⓓ   5 Ⓐ Ⓑ Ⓒ Ⓓ   9 Ⓐ Ⓑ Ⓒ Ⓓ   13 Ⓐ Ⓑ Ⓒ Ⓓ
2 Ⓐ Ⓑ Ⓒ Ⓓ   6 Ⓐ Ⓑ Ⓒ Ⓓ   10 Ⓐ Ⓑ Ⓒ Ⓓ   14 Ⓐ Ⓑ Ⓒ Ⓓ
3 Ⓐ Ⓑ Ⓒ Ⓓ   7 Ⓐ Ⓑ Ⓒ Ⓓ   11 Ⓐ Ⓑ Ⓒ Ⓓ   15 Ⓐ Ⓑ Ⓒ Ⓓ
4 Ⓐ Ⓑ Ⓒ Ⓓ   8 Ⓐ Ⓑ Ⓒ Ⓓ   12 Ⓐ Ⓑ Ⓒ Ⓓ

PART 5—NUMERICAL OPERATIONS

1 Ⓐ Ⓑ Ⓒ Ⓓ	11 Ⓐ Ⓑ Ⓒ Ⓓ	21 Ⓐ Ⓑ Ⓒ Ⓓ	31 Ⓐ Ⓑ Ⓒ Ⓓ	41 Ⓐ Ⓑ Ⓒ Ⓓ
2 Ⓐ Ⓑ Ⓒ Ⓓ	12 Ⓐ Ⓑ Ⓒ Ⓓ	22 Ⓐ Ⓑ Ⓒ Ⓓ	32 Ⓐ Ⓑ Ⓒ Ⓓ	42 Ⓐ Ⓑ Ⓒ Ⓓ
3 Ⓐ Ⓑ Ⓒ Ⓓ	13 Ⓐ Ⓑ Ⓒ Ⓓ	23 Ⓐ Ⓑ Ⓒ Ⓓ	33 Ⓐ Ⓑ Ⓒ Ⓓ	43 Ⓐ Ⓑ Ⓒ Ⓓ
4 Ⓐ Ⓑ Ⓒ Ⓓ	14 Ⓐ Ⓑ Ⓒ Ⓓ	24 Ⓐ Ⓑ Ⓒ Ⓓ	34 Ⓐ Ⓑ Ⓒ Ⓓ	44 Ⓐ Ⓑ Ⓒ Ⓓ
5 Ⓐ Ⓑ Ⓒ Ⓓ	15 Ⓐ Ⓑ Ⓒ Ⓓ	25 Ⓐ Ⓑ Ⓒ Ⓓ	35 Ⓐ Ⓑ Ⓒ Ⓓ	45 Ⓐ Ⓑ Ⓒ Ⓓ
6 Ⓐ Ⓑ Ⓒ Ⓓ	16 Ⓐ Ⓑ Ⓒ Ⓓ	26 Ⓐ Ⓑ Ⓒ Ⓓ	36 Ⓐ Ⓑ Ⓒ Ⓓ	46 Ⓐ Ⓑ Ⓒ Ⓓ
7 Ⓐ Ⓑ Ⓒ Ⓓ	17 Ⓐ Ⓑ Ⓒ Ⓓ	27 Ⓐ Ⓑ Ⓒ Ⓓ	37 Ⓐ Ⓑ Ⓒ Ⓓ	47 Ⓐ Ⓑ Ⓒ Ⓓ
8 Ⓐ Ⓑ Ⓒ Ⓓ	18 Ⓐ Ⓑ Ⓒ Ⓓ	28 Ⓐ Ⓑ Ⓒ Ⓓ	38 Ⓐ Ⓑ Ⓒ Ⓓ	48 Ⓐ Ⓑ Ⓒ Ⓓ
9 Ⓐ Ⓑ Ⓒ Ⓓ	19 Ⓐ Ⓑ Ⓒ Ⓓ	29 Ⓐ Ⓑ Ⓒ Ⓓ	39 Ⓐ Ⓑ Ⓒ Ⓓ	49 Ⓐ Ⓑ Ⓒ Ⓓ
10 Ⓐ Ⓑ Ⓒ Ⓓ	20 Ⓐ Ⓑ Ⓒ Ⓓ	30 Ⓐ Ⓑ Ⓒ Ⓓ	40 Ⓐ Ⓑ Ⓒ Ⓓ	50 Ⓐ Ⓑ Ⓒ Ⓓ

PART 6—CODING SPEED

1 Ⓐ Ⓑ Ⓒ Ⓓ Ⓔ	15 Ⓐ Ⓑ Ⓒ Ⓓ Ⓔ	29 Ⓐ Ⓑ Ⓒ Ⓓ Ⓔ	43 Ⓐ Ⓑ Ⓒ Ⓓ Ⓔ	57 Ⓐ Ⓑ Ⓒ Ⓓ Ⓔ	71 Ⓐ Ⓑ Ⓒ Ⓓ Ⓔ
2 Ⓐ Ⓑ Ⓒ Ⓓ Ⓔ	16 Ⓐ Ⓑ Ⓒ Ⓓ Ⓔ	30 Ⓐ Ⓑ Ⓒ Ⓓ Ⓔ	44 Ⓐ Ⓑ Ⓒ Ⓓ Ⓔ	58 Ⓐ Ⓑ Ⓒ Ⓓ Ⓔ	72 Ⓐ Ⓑ Ⓒ Ⓓ Ⓔ
3 Ⓐ Ⓑ Ⓒ Ⓓ Ⓔ	17 Ⓐ Ⓑ Ⓒ Ⓓ Ⓔ	31 Ⓐ Ⓑ Ⓒ Ⓓ Ⓔ	45 Ⓐ Ⓑ Ⓒ Ⓓ Ⓔ	59 Ⓐ Ⓑ Ⓒ Ⓓ Ⓔ	73 Ⓐ Ⓑ Ⓒ Ⓓ Ⓔ
4 Ⓐ Ⓑ Ⓒ Ⓓ Ⓔ	18 Ⓐ Ⓑ Ⓒ Ⓓ Ⓔ	32 Ⓐ Ⓑ Ⓒ Ⓓ Ⓔ	46 Ⓐ Ⓑ Ⓒ Ⓓ Ⓔ	60 Ⓐ Ⓑ Ⓒ Ⓓ Ⓔ	74 Ⓐ Ⓑ Ⓒ Ⓓ Ⓔ
5 Ⓐ Ⓑ Ⓒ Ⓓ Ⓔ	19 Ⓐ Ⓑ Ⓒ Ⓓ Ⓔ	33 Ⓐ Ⓑ Ⓒ Ⓓ Ⓔ	47 Ⓐ Ⓑ Ⓒ Ⓓ Ⓔ	61 Ⓐ Ⓑ Ⓒ Ⓓ Ⓔ	75 Ⓐ Ⓑ Ⓒ Ⓓ Ⓔ
6 Ⓐ Ⓑ Ⓒ Ⓓ Ⓔ	20 Ⓐ Ⓑ Ⓒ Ⓓ Ⓔ	34 Ⓐ Ⓑ Ⓒ Ⓓ Ⓔ	48 Ⓐ Ⓑ Ⓒ Ⓓ Ⓔ	62 Ⓐ Ⓑ Ⓒ Ⓓ Ⓔ	76 Ⓐ Ⓑ Ⓒ Ⓓ Ⓔ
7 Ⓐ Ⓑ Ⓒ Ⓓ Ⓔ	21 Ⓐ Ⓑ Ⓒ Ⓓ Ⓔ	35 Ⓐ Ⓑ Ⓒ Ⓓ Ⓔ	49 Ⓐ Ⓑ Ⓒ Ⓓ Ⓔ	63 Ⓐ Ⓑ Ⓒ Ⓓ Ⓔ	77 Ⓐ Ⓑ Ⓒ Ⓓ Ⓔ
8 Ⓐ Ⓑ Ⓒ Ⓓ Ⓔ	22 Ⓐ Ⓑ Ⓒ Ⓓ Ⓔ	36 Ⓐ Ⓑ Ⓒ Ⓓ Ⓔ	50 Ⓐ Ⓑ Ⓒ Ⓓ Ⓔ	64 Ⓐ Ⓑ Ⓒ Ⓓ Ⓔ	78 Ⓐ Ⓑ Ⓒ Ⓓ Ⓔ
9 Ⓐ Ⓑ Ⓒ Ⓓ Ⓔ	23 Ⓐ Ⓑ Ⓒ Ⓓ Ⓔ	37 Ⓐ Ⓑ Ⓒ Ⓓ Ⓔ	51 Ⓐ Ⓑ Ⓒ Ⓓ Ⓔ	65 Ⓐ Ⓑ Ⓒ Ⓓ Ⓔ	79 Ⓐ Ⓑ Ⓒ Ⓓ Ⓔ
10 Ⓐ Ⓑ Ⓒ Ⓓ Ⓔ	24 Ⓐ Ⓑ Ⓒ Ⓓ Ⓔ	38 Ⓐ Ⓑ Ⓒ Ⓓ Ⓔ	52 Ⓐ Ⓑ Ⓒ Ⓓ Ⓔ	66 Ⓐ Ⓑ Ⓒ Ⓓ Ⓔ	80 Ⓐ Ⓑ Ⓒ Ⓓ Ⓔ
11 Ⓐ Ⓑ Ⓒ Ⓓ Ⓔ	25 Ⓐ Ⓑ Ⓒ Ⓓ Ⓔ	39 Ⓐ Ⓑ Ⓒ Ⓓ Ⓔ	53 Ⓐ Ⓑ Ⓒ Ⓓ Ⓔ	67 Ⓐ Ⓑ Ⓒ Ⓓ Ⓔ	81 Ⓐ Ⓑ Ⓒ Ⓓ Ⓔ
12 Ⓐ Ⓑ Ⓒ Ⓓ Ⓔ	26 Ⓐ Ⓑ Ⓒ Ⓓ Ⓔ	40 Ⓐ Ⓑ Ⓒ Ⓓ Ⓔ	54 Ⓐ Ⓑ Ⓒ Ⓓ Ⓔ	68 Ⓐ Ⓑ Ⓒ Ⓓ Ⓔ	82 Ⓐ Ⓑ Ⓒ Ⓓ Ⓔ
13 Ⓐ Ⓑ Ⓒ Ⓓ Ⓔ	27 Ⓐ Ⓑ Ⓒ Ⓓ Ⓔ	41 Ⓐ Ⓑ Ⓒ Ⓓ Ⓔ	55 Ⓐ Ⓑ Ⓒ Ⓓ Ⓔ	69 Ⓐ Ⓑ Ⓒ Ⓓ Ⓔ	83 Ⓐ Ⓑ Ⓒ Ⓓ Ⓔ
14 Ⓐ Ⓑ Ⓒ Ⓓ Ⓔ	28 Ⓐ Ⓑ Ⓒ Ⓓ Ⓔ	42 Ⓐ Ⓑ Ⓒ Ⓓ Ⓔ	56 Ⓐ Ⓑ Ⓒ Ⓓ Ⓔ	70 Ⓐ Ⓑ Ⓒ Ⓓ Ⓔ	84 Ⓐ Ⓑ Ⓒ Ⓓ Ⓔ

PART 7—AUTO & SHOP INFORMATION

1 Ⓐ Ⓑ Ⓒ Ⓓ	6 Ⓐ Ⓑ Ⓒ Ⓓ	11 Ⓐ Ⓑ Ⓒ Ⓓ	16 Ⓐ Ⓑ Ⓒ Ⓓ	21 Ⓐ Ⓑ Ⓒ Ⓓ
2 Ⓐ Ⓑ Ⓒ Ⓓ	7 Ⓐ Ⓑ Ⓒ Ⓓ	12 Ⓐ Ⓑ Ⓒ Ⓓ	17 Ⓐ Ⓑ Ⓒ Ⓓ	22 Ⓐ Ⓑ Ⓒ Ⓓ
3 Ⓐ Ⓑ Ⓒ Ⓓ	8 Ⓐ Ⓑ Ⓒ Ⓓ	13 Ⓐ Ⓑ Ⓒ Ⓓ	18 Ⓐ Ⓑ Ⓒ Ⓓ	23 Ⓐ Ⓑ Ⓒ Ⓓ
4 Ⓐ Ⓑ Ⓒ Ⓓ	9 Ⓐ Ⓑ Ⓒ Ⓓ	14 Ⓐ Ⓑ Ⓒ Ⓓ	19 Ⓐ Ⓑ Ⓒ Ⓓ	24 Ⓐ Ⓑ Ⓒ Ⓓ
5 Ⓐ Ⓑ Ⓒ Ⓓ	10 Ⓐ Ⓑ Ⓒ Ⓓ	15 Ⓐ Ⓑ Ⓒ Ⓓ	20 Ⓐ Ⓑ Ⓒ Ⓓ	25 Ⓐ Ⓑ Ⓒ Ⓓ

PART 8—MATHEMATICS KNOWLEDGE

1 Ⓐ Ⓑ Ⓒ Ⓓ	6 Ⓐ Ⓑ Ⓒ Ⓓ	11 Ⓐ Ⓑ Ⓒ Ⓓ	16 Ⓐ Ⓑ Ⓒ Ⓓ	21 Ⓐ Ⓑ Ⓒ Ⓓ
2 Ⓐ Ⓑ Ⓒ Ⓓ	7 Ⓐ Ⓑ Ⓒ Ⓓ	12 Ⓐ Ⓑ Ⓒ Ⓓ	17 Ⓐ Ⓑ Ⓒ Ⓓ	22 Ⓐ Ⓑ Ⓒ Ⓓ
3 Ⓐ Ⓑ Ⓒ Ⓓ	8 Ⓐ Ⓑ Ⓒ Ⓓ	13 Ⓐ Ⓑ Ⓒ Ⓓ	18 Ⓐ Ⓑ Ⓒ Ⓓ	23 Ⓐ Ⓑ Ⓒ Ⓓ
4 Ⓐ Ⓑ Ⓒ Ⓓ	9 Ⓐ Ⓑ Ⓒ Ⓓ	14 Ⓐ Ⓑ Ⓒ Ⓓ	19 Ⓐ Ⓑ Ⓒ Ⓓ	24 Ⓐ Ⓑ Ⓒ Ⓓ
5 Ⓐ Ⓑ Ⓒ Ⓓ	10 Ⓐ Ⓑ Ⓒ Ⓓ	15 Ⓐ Ⓑ Ⓒ Ⓓ	20 Ⓐ Ⓑ Ⓒ Ⓓ	25 Ⓐ Ⓑ Ⓒ Ⓓ

PART 9—MECHANICAL COMPREHENSION

1 Ⓐ Ⓑ Ⓒ Ⓓ	6 Ⓐ Ⓑ Ⓒ Ⓓ	11 Ⓐ Ⓑ Ⓒ Ⓓ	16 Ⓐ Ⓑ Ⓒ Ⓓ	21 Ⓐ Ⓑ Ⓒ Ⓓ
2 Ⓐ Ⓑ Ⓒ Ⓓ	7 Ⓐ Ⓑ Ⓒ Ⓓ	12 Ⓐ Ⓑ Ⓒ Ⓓ	17 Ⓐ Ⓑ Ⓒ Ⓓ	22 Ⓐ Ⓑ Ⓒ Ⓓ
3 Ⓐ Ⓑ Ⓒ Ⓓ	8 Ⓐ Ⓑ Ⓒ Ⓓ	13 Ⓐ Ⓑ Ⓒ Ⓓ	18 Ⓐ Ⓑ Ⓒ Ⓓ	23 Ⓐ Ⓑ Ⓒ Ⓓ
4 Ⓐ Ⓑ Ⓒ Ⓓ	9 Ⓐ Ⓑ Ⓒ Ⓓ	14 Ⓐ Ⓑ Ⓒ Ⓓ	19 Ⓐ Ⓑ Ⓒ Ⓓ	24 Ⓐ Ⓑ Ⓒ Ⓓ
5 Ⓐ Ⓑ Ⓒ Ⓓ	10 Ⓐ Ⓑ Ⓒ Ⓓ	15 Ⓐ Ⓑ Ⓒ Ⓓ	20 Ⓐ Ⓑ Ⓒ Ⓓ	25 Ⓐ Ⓑ Ⓒ Ⓓ

PART 10—ELECTRONICS INFORMATION

1 Ⓐ Ⓑ Ⓒ Ⓓ	6 Ⓐ Ⓑ Ⓒ Ⓓ	11 Ⓐ Ⓑ Ⓒ Ⓓ	16 Ⓐ Ⓑ Ⓒ Ⓓ
2 Ⓐ Ⓑ Ⓒ Ⓓ	7 Ⓐ Ⓑ Ⓒ Ⓓ	12 Ⓐ Ⓑ Ⓒ Ⓓ	17 Ⓐ Ⓑ Ⓒ Ⓓ
3 Ⓐ Ⓑ Ⓒ Ⓓ	8 Ⓐ Ⓑ Ⓒ Ⓓ	13 Ⓐ Ⓑ Ⓒ Ⓓ	18 Ⓐ Ⓑ Ⓒ Ⓓ
4 Ⓐ Ⓑ Ⓒ Ⓓ	9 Ⓐ Ⓑ Ⓒ Ⓓ	14 Ⓐ Ⓑ Ⓒ Ⓓ	19 Ⓐ Ⓑ Ⓒ Ⓓ
5 Ⓐ Ⓑ Ⓒ Ⓓ	10 Ⓐ Ⓑ Ⓒ Ⓓ	15 Ⓐ Ⓑ Ⓒ Ⓓ	20 Ⓐ Ⓑ Ⓒ Ⓓ

PART 1

GENERAL SCIENCE

The general science part of your examination asks questions based upon the science you learned in high school. For each question there are four possible answers. Only one answer is correct. Choose the answer which you think is correct and mark the corresponding space on your answer sheet. Try these questions.

1. Of the following methods, the one which is correct to use in converting a steel knitting needle into a permanent magnet is

1-A heating
1-B jarring
1-C stroking with a magnet
1-D passing electricity through it

1. Ⓐ Ⓑ Ⓒ Ⓓ

1-C STROKING WITH A MAGNET is the correct answer. A permanent magnet may be created by stroking a steel needle with a magnet, always in one direction. This action organizes the electrons in the needle so that they concentrate themselves at one end. That end is the negative pole of the needle. The other end is positive. Heating (A) and jarring (B) both lead to disorganization of the electrons and might destroy the magnet. Passing electricity through a wire which is wound around a steel needle creates an electromagnet (D). An electromagnet is not a permanent magnet. When the electricity is cut off, the magnetism disappears.

2. Of the following, the one which is *not* characteristic of poison ivy is that it has

2-A milky juice
2-B three leaflet clusters
2-C shiny leaves
2-D white berries

2. Ⓐ Ⓑ Ⓒ Ⓓ

2-A MILKY JUICE is the correct answer. Poison ivy has shiny leaves (C) in three leaflet clusters (B) and may have white berries (D). If you see such a plant, do *not* try to break a stem to check for milky juice. Poison ivy does not have milky juice, but if you handle poison ivy you are likely to get a painful rash.

3. Cloud-seeding is of limited usefulness in drought management because

3-A dry ice is very expensive
3-B a special type of airplane is required
3-C the water from seeded clouds is not as wet as natural rain water
3-D sufficient quantity of the right kind of clouds must be present in the right place

3. Ⓐ Ⓑ Ⓒ Ⓓ

3-D There *must* be enough clouds in the drought-stricken area if cloud-seeding is to be of any use. Unfortunately, this is not usually the case. Many kinds of airplanes (B) can be used to drop the pellets of dry ice (A) which are relatively cheap. The water produced by this method (C) is just as acceptable as natural rain water, but there is not enough of it.

DO NOT TURN THE PAGE UNTIL YOU ARE TOLD TO DO SO

GENERAL SCIENCE

TIME: 11 Minutes—25 Questions

1. Under natural conditions large quantities of organic matter decay after each year's plant growth has been completed. As a result of such conditions

 1-A many animals are deprived of adequate food supplies
 1-B soil erosion is accelerated
 1-C soils maintain their fertility
 1-D earthworms are added to the soil

2. The hammer, anvil, and stirrup bones lie in the

 2-A knee
 2-B hip
 2-C ear
 2-D elbow

3. The major chemical constituent of a cell (by weight) is

 3-A protein
 3-B ash
 3-C water
 3-D carbohydrates

4. Which of the following is a chemical change?

 4-A magnetizing a rod of iron
 4-B burning one pound of coal
 4-C mixing flake graphite with oil
 4-D vaporizing one gram of mercury in a vacuum

5. If you are caught away from home during a thunderstorm, the safest place to be is

 5-A in a car
 5-B under a tree
 5-C in an open field
 5-D at the top of a small hill

6. Water is composed mostly of:

 6-A carbon
 6-B nitrogen
 6-C hydrogen
 6-D oxygen

7. Spiders can be distinguished from insects by the fact that spiders have

 7-A hard outer coverings
 7-B large abdomens
 7-C four pairs of legs
 7-D biting mouth parts

8. The number of degrees on the Fahrenheit thermometer between the freezing point and the boiling point of water is

 8-A 100 degrees
 8-B 212 degrees
 8-C 180 degrees
 8-D 273 degrees

9. Among the following, the invertebrate is the

 9-A dinosaur
 9-B python
 9-C pigeon
 9-D starfish

10. Of the following gases in the air, the most plentiful is

 10-A argon
 10-B oxygen

10-C   nitrogen

10-D   carbon dioxide

11. Of the following, the only safe blood transfusion would be

11-A   Group A blood into a Group O person

11-B   Group B blood into a Group A person

11-C   Group O blood into a Group AB person

11-D   Group AB blood into a Group B person

12. Of the following, the part of a ship which gives it stability by lowering the center of gravity is the

12-A   bulkhead

12-B   keel

12-C   anchor

12-D   prow

13. A new drug for treatment of tuberculosis was being tested in a hospital. Patients in Group A actually received doses of the new drug; those in Group B were given only sugar pills. Group B represents

13-A   a scientific experiment

13-B   a scientific method

13-C   an experimental error

13-D   an experimental control

14. Narcotics may be dangerous if used without supervision, but they are useful in medicine because they

14-A   increase production of red blood cells

14-B   kill bacteria

14-C   relieve pain

14-D   stimulate the heart

15. In the production of sounds, the greater the number of vibrations per second

15-A   the greater the volume

15-B   the higher the tone

15-C   the lower the volume

15-D   the lower the tone

16. A boy examining his finger under a microscope could see no epidermal cells because

16-A   these cells are located under the skin

16-B   the nail blocked his view

16-C   each single cell is larger than the area of the microscope field

16-D   a finger is about one-half-inch thick

17. If a person has been injured in an accident and damage to the back and neck is suspected, it is best to

17-A   roll the person over so that he does not lie on his back

17-B   rush the person to the nearest hospital

17-C   force the person to drink water to replace body fluids

17-D   wait for professional help

18. In four hours the earth rotates

18-A   20 degrees

18-B   60 degrees

18-C   40 degrees

18-D   120 degrees

19. Of the following glands, the one which regulates the metabolic rate is the

19-A   adrenal

19-B   thyroid

19-C   salivary

19-D   thymus

20. Of the following phases of the moon, the invisible one is called

20-A   crescent

20-B   new moon

20-C   full moon

20-D   waxing and waning

21. The vitamin manufactured by the skin with the help of the sun is

21-A   A

21-B B_6

21-C B_{12}

21-D   D

22. A popular shrub that produces bell-shaped, yellow flowers in early spring is the

22-A tulip
22-B forsythia
22-C azalea
22-D flowering dogwood

23. The vascular system of the body is concerned with:

23-A respiration
23-B sense of touch
23-C circulation of blood
23-D enzymes

24. The *most important* provision for a hike in hot, dry countryside is

24-A dried meat
24-B raisins
24-C fresh fruit
24-D water

25. Which of the following rocks can be dissolved with a weak acid?

25-A sandstone
25-B gneiss
25-C granite
25-D limestone

STOP

IF YOU FINISH THIS PART BEFORE THE TIME IS UP, CHECK OVER YOUR WORK ON THIS PART ONLY. DO NOT GO ON UNTIL YOU ARE TOLD TO DO SO.

PART 2

ARITHMETIC REASONING

The arithmetic reasoning questions require careful thinking as well as arithmetic calculation. Some problems require more than one step for their solutions. You must decide exactly what the question asks; then you must determine the best method for finding the answer; finally, you must work out the problem on your scratch paper. Be sure to mark the letter of the correct answer on your answer sheet. Try these questions.

1. A recipe for 6 quarts of punch calls for $\frac{3}{4}$ cups of sugar. How much sugar is needed for 9 quarts of punch?

   1-A five-eighths of a cup
   1-B seven-eighths of a cup
   1-C $1\frac{1}{8}$ cups
   1-D $2\frac{1}{4}$ cups

   1. Ⓐ Ⓑ Ⓒ Ⓓ

1-C First find out how much sugar is needed for one quart of punch.

$$\frac{3}{4} \text{ cups} \div 6 = \frac{3}{4} \times \frac{1}{6} = \frac{\overset{1}{\cancel{3}}}{4} \times \frac{1}{\underset{2}{\cancel{6}}} = \frac{1}{8}$$

For 9 quarts of punch: $9 \times \frac{1}{8} = \frac{9}{8} = 1\frac{1}{8}$

2. How many yards of ribbon will it take to make 45 badges if each badge uses 4 inches of ribbon?

   2-A 5
   2-B 9
   2-C 11
   2-D 15

   2. Ⓐ Ⓑ Ⓒ Ⓓ

2-A 45 badges × 4 inches each = 180 inches needed
There are 36 inches in one yard.
180 inches ÷ 36 = 5 yards of ribbon needed

3. A stock clerk has on hand the following items:

  500 pads worth four cents each

  130 pencils worth three cents each
  50 dozen rubber bands worth two cents per dozen

If, from this stock, he issues 125 pads, 45 pencils, and 48 rubber bands, the value of the remaining stock would be

   3-A $6.43
   3-B $8.95
   3-C $17.63
   3-D $18.47

   3. Ⓐ Ⓑ Ⓒ Ⓓ

3-D 500 − 125 = 375 pads @ $.04 = $15.00
130 − 45 = 85 pencils @ $.03 = $ 2.55
50 dozen − 4 dozen = 46 dozen rubber bands @ $.02 = $.92
$15 + $2.55 + $.92 = $18.47

4. The net profits of a department store decreased from $650,000 to $400,000 in five years. What was the average decrease in net profit?

   4-A $5000
   4-B $25,000
   4-C $50,000
   4-D $200,000

   4. Ⓐ Ⓑ Ⓒ Ⓓ

4-C $650,000 − $400,000 = $250,000 decrease in profit over 5 years. $250,000 ÷ 5 = $50,000 per year.

DO NOT TURN THE PAGE UNTIL YOU ARE TOLD TO DO SO

ARITHMETIC REASONING

TIME: 36 Minutes—30 Questions

1. If a man invests $1,000 at an annual rate of 5%, how much money will the man have after one year?

   1-A $20
   1-B $50
   1-C $1020
   1-D $1050

2. A certain type of siding for a house costs $10.50 per square yard. What does it cost for the siding for a wall 4 yards wide and 60 feet long?

   2-A $800
   2-B $840
   2-C $2520
   2-D $3240

3. If a fire truck is 60 feet away from a hydrant, it is how many feet nearer to the hydrant than a truck that is 100 feet away?

   3-A 60 ft.
   3-B 50 ft.
   3-C 40 ft.
   3-D 20 ft.

4. At the rate of four peaches for a quarter, 20 peaches will cost

   4-A 80¢
   4-B $1.00
   4-C $1.20
   4-D $1.25

5. A carpenter needs four boards, each 2 feet, 9 inches long. If wood is sold only by the foot, how many feet must he buy?

   5-A 9
   5-B 10
   5-C 11
   5-D 12

6. Twelve clerks are assigned to enter certain data on index cards. This number of clerks could perform the task in 18 days. After these clerks have worked on this assignment for 6 days, 4 more clerks are added to the staff to do this work. Assuming that all the clerks work at the same rate of speed, the entire task, instead of taking 18 days, will be performed in

   6-A 15 days
   6-B 17 days
   6-C 12 days
   6-D 16 days

7. One year the postage rate for sending 1 ounce of mail first class was increased from 3 cents to 4 cents. What was the percent of increase in the postage rate?

   7-A $12\frac{1}{2}\%$
   7-B 15%
   7-C $33\frac{1}{3}$
   7-D 40%

8. A girl earns twice as much in December as in each of the other months. What part of her entire year's earnings does she earn in December?

   8-A $\frac{2}{11}$
   8-B $\frac{2}{13}$
   8-C $\frac{3}{14}$
   8-D $\frac{1}{6}$

9. The local music shop had a record sale. The records normally cost $6.98 each. The sale price was $12.50 for 2 records. Pete bought

4 records at the sale price. How much money did Pete save by buying the records at the sale price?

9-A $2.98
9-B $2.92
9-C $2.50
9-D $1.46

10. If six girls can paint a fence in two days, how many girls, working at the same uniform rate, can finish it in one day?

10-A 2
10-B 3
10-C 12
10-D 4

11. A team won 2 games and lost 10. The fraction of its games won is correctly expressed as

11-A 1/6
11-B 1/5
11-C 4/5
11-D 5/6

12. Gary went to the store and bought a toy harmonica for $1.95 and an instruction booklet for $.35. He gave the clerk $2.50. How much change did Gary get?

12-A $.20
12-B $.25
12-C $.30
12-D $.15

13. A clerk is requested to file 800 cards. If he can file cards at the rate of 80 cards an hour, the number of cards remaining to be filed after 7 hours of work is

13-A 140
13-B 240
13-C 250
13-D 260

14. How much does a salesperson earn for selling $68 worth of writing paper if she is paid a commission of 40% on her sales?

14-A $20.40
14-B $25.60
14-C $22.80
14-D $27.20

15. After an employer figures out an employee's weekly salary of $190.57, he deducts $13.05 for social security and $5.68 for pension. What is the amount of the check after these deductions?

15-A $171.84
15-B $171.92
15-C $172.84
15-D $172.99

16. If a barrel has a capacity of 100 gallons, it will contain how many gallons when it is two-fifths full?

16-A 20 gal.
16-B 40 gal.
16-C 60 gal.
16-D 80 gal.

17. A man had $25.00. He saw some ties that cost $4.95 apiece. How many of these ties could he buy?

17-A Six
17-B Seven
17-C Five
17-D Three

18. A student was planning a trip to Europe. She had a total of $700 available for expenses. If the plane ticket cost $372 how much money did she have left?

18-A $338.00
18-B $248.00
18-C $438.00
18-D $328.00

19. If a man's base pay is $23,000 and it is increased by a bonus of $500 and a seniority increment of $1,350, his total salary is

19-A $24,850
19-B $23,500
19-C $25,850
19-D $24,500

20. A champion runner ran the 100-yard dash in three track meets. The first time he ran it in 10.2 seconds; the second in 10.4 seconds; and the third in 10 seconds. What was his average time?

20-A 10.2 seconds
20-B 10.3 seconds
20-C 10.35 seconds
20-D 10.4 seconds

21. To go from Poughkeepsie, New York, to West Palm Beach, Florida, you must travel 1,400 miles. If you can average a driving speed of 50 miles an hour, how many hours must you drive to make this trip?

21-A 25
21-B 28
21-C 30
21-D $27\frac{1}{2}$

22. On her maiden voyage the *S.S. United States* made the trip from New York to England in 3 days, 10 hours and 40 minutes, beating the record set by the *R.M.S. Queen Mary* in 1938 by 10 hours and 2 minutes. How long did it take the *Queen Mary* to make the trip?

22-A 3 days 20 hrs. 42 mins.
22-B 3 days 15 hrs. 38 mins.
22-C 3 days 12 hrs. 2 mins.
22-D 3 days 8 hrs. 12 mins.

23. A girl purchased a blouse for $10.98. She returned the blouse the next day and selected a better one costing $12.50. She gave the clerk a five-dollar bill to pay for the difference in price. How much change should she receive?

23-A $3.58
23-B $3.48
23-C $2.52
23-D $1.52

24. Fred had a coupon worth $2.00 on the purchase of one record. Each record cost $5.98, and Fred bought two records. How much did Fred have to pay?

24-A $3.98

24-B $7.96
24-C $9.96
24-D $10.98

25. An inch on a map represents 200 miles. On the same map a distance of 375 miles is represented by

25-A $1\frac{1}{2}$ inches
25-B $1\frac{7}{8}$ inches
25-C $2\frac{1}{4}$ inches
25-D $2\frac{3}{4}$ inches

26. The library charges 5¢ for the first day and 2¢ for each additional day that a book is overdue. If a borrower paid 65¢ in late charges, for how many days was the book overdue?

26-A 15
26-B 20
26-C 30
26-D 31

27. What is the shortest board a man must buy in order to cut three sections from it each 4 feet, 8 inches long?

27-A 12 ft.
27-B 14 ft.
27-C 16 ft.
27-D 18 ft.

28. Walnuts are selling at $2.19 for a 5-pound bag. The cost for 10 pounds is

28-A $2.19 × 10
28-B $2.19 × 2
28-C $2.19 × 50
28-D $2.19 × 5 ÷ 10

29. If it takes 30 minutes to type 6 pages, how many hours will it take to type 126 pages at the same rate?

29-A 6.3
29-B 10.5
29-C 15
29-D 25

30. A decorator went to a department store and ordered curtains for 5 windows. One pair of curtains cost $14.28, 2 pairs cost $33.26 apiece, and the remaining 2 pairs cost $65.38 apiece. How much sales tax did he pay if the tax rate was 6%?

30-A $6.78
30-B $12.69
30-C $12.96
30-D $13.55

END OF PART 2

IF YOU FINISH BEFORE THE TIME IS UP, CHECK TO BE CERTAIN THAT YOU HAVE MARKED ALL OF YOUR ANSWERS ON THE ANSWER SHEET. THEN CHECK OVER YOUR WORK ON THIS PART ONLY. DO NOT RETURN TO PART ONE. DO NOT GO ON UNTIL YOU ARE TOLD TO DO SO.

PART 3

WORD KNOWLEDGE

The questions in this part test how well you understand the meanings of words. Each question has an underlined word. Read all four possible answers and decide which one has a meaning closest to the meaning of the underlined word. On your answer sheet mark the letter of the answer you choose. Try these questions.

1. Mended most nearly means

    1-A repaired
    1-B torn
    1-C clean
    1-D tied

    1. Ⓐ Ⓑ Ⓒ Ⓓ

1-A REPAIRED is the correct answer. *Mended* means *fixed* or *repaired*. *Torn* (B) might be the state of an object before it is mended. The repair might be made by *tying* (D), but not necessarily. *Clean* (C) is wrong.

2. His conduct was becoming of an officer.

    2-A happening to
    2-B turning into
    2-C improving as
    2-D proper for

    2. Ⓐ Ⓑ Ⓒ Ⓓ

2-D PROPER FOR is the correct answer. The underlined word *of* is given to you in a sentence because *becoming* may have more than one meaning. If you try to substitute each answer choice in the sentence, you will find that only (D) makes sense.

3. Entirely most nearly means

    3-A almost
    3-B largely
    3-C publicly
    3-D completely

    3. Ⓐ Ⓑ Ⓒ Ⓓ

3-D COMPLETELY is the correct answer. *Almost* (A) and *largely* (B) are incorrect because they both mean *less than entirely*. *Publicly* (C) is totally unrelated in meaning.

4. Tenant most nearly means

    4-A occupant
    4-B landlord
    4-C owner
    4-D farmer

    4. Ⓐ Ⓑ Ⓒ Ⓓ

4-A OCCUPANT is the correct answer. The most common sense of the word *tenant* is *renter*. As such, the *tenant* is never the *landlord* (B). The *owner* (C) may well be an *occupant* (A), but unless he *occupies* on a very temporary basis he is not considered a *tenant*. A *tenant farmer* (D) lives on and cultivates the land of another.

5. Adopt most nearly means

    5-A baby
    5-B change
    5-C legal
    5-D accept

    5. Ⓐ Ⓑ Ⓒ Ⓓ

5-D ACCEPT is the correct answer. The actual *adoption* is the *acceptance* as one's own. The object of *adoption* is very often a *baby* (A) and the formal process for *adoption* is a *legal* (C) one. If you answered (B) *change*, you were confusing *adopt* with *adapt*, which does mean *change*.

DO NOT TURN THE PAGE UNTIL YOU ARE TOLD TO DO SO

WORD KNOWLEDGE

TIME: 11 Minutes—35 Questions

1. Double most nearly means

   1-A almost
   1-B half
   1-C twice
   1-D more than

2. Absurd most nearly means

   2-A disgusting
   2-B foolish
   2-C reasonable
   2-D very old

3. The machine has manual controls.

   3-A self-acting
   3-B simple
   3-C hand-operated
   3-D handmade

4. The packages were kept in a secure place.

   4-A distant
   4-B safe
   4-C convenient
   4-D secret

5. Exhibit most nearly means

   5-A display
   5-B trade
   5-C sell
   5-D label

6. Grimy most nearly means

   6-A ill-fitting
   6-B poorly made
   6-C dirty
   6-D ragged

7. Captive most nearly means

   7-A savage
   7-B jailer
   7-C spy
   7-D prisoner

8. Expertly most nearly means

   8-A awkwardly
   8-B quickly
   8-C skillfully
   8-D unexpectedly

9. Competent most nearly means

   9-A busy
   9-B capable
   9-C friendly
   9-D good-natured

10. The policeman consoled the weeping child.

    10-A found
    10-B scolded
    10-C carried home
    10-D comforted

11. The cashier yearned for a vacation.

    11-A begged
    11-B longed
    11-C saved
    11-D applied

12. Huge most nearly means

    12-A ugly
    12-B tall
    12-C wide
    12-D immense

13. Villainous most nearly means

13-A untidy
13-B dignified
13-C homely
13-D wicked

14. Vigorously most nearly means

14-A sleepily
14-B thoughtfully
14-C energetically
14-D sadly

15. Vacant most nearly means

15-A quiet
15-B dark
15-C available
15-D empty

16. Juvenile most nearly means

16-A delinquent
16-B lovesick
16-C youthful
16-D humorous

17. Incredible most nearly means

17-A thrilling
17-B convincing
17-C uninteresting
17-D unbelievable

18. Power most nearly means

18-A size
18-B ambition
18-C force
18-D success

19. The principal defended the striking teachers.

19-A delayed
19-B shot at
19-C protected
19-D informed on

20. Familiar most nearly means

20-A welcome
20-B dreaded
20-C rare
20-D well-known

21. Comprehend most nearly means

21-A hear
21-B listen
21-C agree
21-D understand

22. Merchants most nearly means

22-A producers
22-B advertisers
22-C bankers
22-D storekeepers

23. Conclusion most nearly means

23-A theme
23-B suspense
23-C end
23-D beginning

24. Revolving most nearly means

24-A rocking
24-B working
24-C vibrating
24-D turning

25. Startled most nearly means

25-A surprised
25-B chased
25-C punished
25-D arrested

26. Amplified most nearly means

26-A expanded
26-B summarized
26-C analyzed
26-D shouted

27. Hazard most nearly means

27-A damage
27-B choice
27-C opportunity
27-D danger

28. Self-sufficient most nearly means

    28-A independent
    28-B conceited
    28-C stubborn
    28-D clever

29. Terminate most nearly means

    29-A continue
    29-B go by train
    29-C begin
    29-D end

30. Pedestrian most nearly means

    30-A passenger
    30-B street-crosser
    30-C walker
    30-D traffic light

31. Acquired most nearly means

    31-A sold
    31-B plowed
    31-C desired
    31-D obtained

32. Indigent people are entitled to food stamps.

    32-A poor
    32-B lazy
    32-C angry
    32-D homeless

33. The old-fashioned classroom has stationary desks.

    33-A heavy
    33-B carved
    33-C written-upon
    33-D not movable

34. Inferior most nearly means

    34-A noticeable
    34-B second-rate
    34-C lasting
    34-D excellent

35. One should eat only mature fruits.

    35-A edible
    35-B washed
    35-C ripe
    35-D sprayed

END OF PART 3

IF YOU FINISH BEFORE THE TIME IS UP, CHECK OVER YOUR WORK ON THIS PART ONLY. DO NOT RETURN TO EITHER PREVIOUS PART. DO NOT GO ON TO THE NEXT PAGE UNTIL YOU ARE TOLD TO DO SO.

PART 4

PARAGRAPH COMPREHENSION

The paragraph comprehension part of your test battery requires concentration and attention to detail. First you must read and understand the paragraph. Then you must read and understand each of the answer choices, noticing the differences of meaning or emphasis that are imparted by little words. There is one question based upon each paragraph. You must answer that question on the basis of what is stated or implied in the passage, even if you know a better answer and even if you know the information in the paragraph to be false. In some cases more than one answer might be correct, but you must choose the BEST answer and mark its letter on your answer sheet. Try these questions.

1. Some fire-resistant buildings, although wholly constructed of materials that will not burn, may be completely gutted by the spread of fire through their contents by way of hallways and other openings. They may even suffer serious structural damage by the collapse of metal beams and columns.

The paragraph best supports the statement that some fire-resistant buildings

1-A can be damaged seriously by fire
1-B have specially constructed halls and doors
1-C afford less protection to their contents than would ordinary buildings
1-D will burn readily

1. Ⓐ Ⓑ Ⓒ Ⓓ

1-A The paragraph presents the problems of fire in fire-resistant buildings. It suggests that the contents of the buildings may burn even though the structural materials themselves do not, and the ensuing fire may even cause the collapse of the buildings. The paragraph does not compare the problem of fire in fire-resistant buildings with that of fire in ordinary buildings.

2. Taxes are deducted each pay period from the amount of salaries or wages, including payments for overtime and night differential, paid to employees of the postal service in excess of the withholding exemptions allowed under the Internal Revenue Act. The amount of tax to be withheld from each payment of wages to any employee, except fourth-class postmasters, will be determined from the current official table of pay and withholding exemptions published by the Post Office Department.

The salaries of most postal employees

2-A are paid in amounts depending upon the exemptions fixed by the Department
2-B do not include overtime or night differential payments
2-C are determined by provisions of the Internal Revenue Act
2-D are subject to tax deductions

2. Ⓐ Ⓑ Ⓒ Ⓓ

2-D The paragraph states that the Post Office complies with IRS regulations in withholding taxes from salaries and wages. The IRS determines the tax, not the salaries, as suggested in choice C.

DO NOT TURN THE PAGE UNTIL YOU ARE TOLD TO DO SO

PARAGRAPH COMPREHENSION

TIME: 13 Minutes—15 Questions

1. Television reached in 20 years the goal toward which print had been working for 500; to extend its audience to include the entire population. By 1973 in the United States, nine out of ten families watched 45 million sets going an average of five hours a day.

The paragraph best supports the statement that

1-A the entire nation has TV sets
1-B nine out of ten individuals watch an average of five hours a day
1-C the TV viewing public grew much more rapidly than did the reading public
1-D there are more TV sets in the United States than in other countries

2. Specialization could not exist without the process of exchange. A farmer might specialize in raising corn. In the course of a year he would produce many more bushels of corn than he and his family could possibly consume. However, being a specialist, he can neither grow the other foods he needs, nor produce such necessities of life as clothing, shelter, newspapers, and machinery. What he does in effect is exchange his corn for those products.

As a result of specialization

2-A the process of exchange has been greatly accelerated
2-B the farm has become a business
2-C the farmer's produce must be sent to the open market for distribution
2-D food products become the specialized field of the farmer

3. Telegrams should be clear, concise, and brief. Omit all unnecessary words. The parts of speech most often used in telegrams are nouns, verbs, adjectives, and adverbs. If possible, do without pronouns, prepositions, articles, and copulative verbs. Use simple sentences, rather than complex and compound.

In writing telegrams one should always use

3-A common and simple words
3-B only nouns, verbs, adjectives, and adverbs
3-C incomplete sentences
3-D only words essential to the meaning

4. It was formerly thought that whole wheat and graham breads were far superior to white bread made from highly refined wheat flour. However, it is now believed that the general use of milk solids in white bread significantly narrows the nutritional gap between the two types of bread. About the only dietary advantages now claimed for whole wheat bread are higher content of iron and vitamin B, both easily obtainable in many other common foods.

The paragraph best supports the statement that

4-A white bread is fattening because of its milk content
4-B whole wheat bread is not much more nutritious than white bread
4-C whole wheat bread contains roughage
4-D white bread contains neither iron nor vitamin B

5. Just as municipal corporations acting in a governmental capacity are free from accident liability, so also are private corporations or associations exempt from liability when car-

rying on welfare or charitable enterprises not for profit.

The paragraph best supports the statement that

5-A municipal and charitable corporations are exempt from taxes

5-B a private hospital or clinic that treats indigent patients without making a charge would not be liable for injuries caused

5-C municipal corporations do not operate for profit

5-D an individual hurt in an automobile accident by a city chauffeur cannot sue the city if the chauffeur is incorporated

6. Many industrial processes are dangerous to the health of workers and give rise to occupational disease. The state, as the guardian of public health and welfare, has a legitimate interest in conserving the vitality of industrial workers and may, to this end, make appropriate laws, and give to boards or departments authority to make regulations to carry out the law. Such laws and rules may prohibit dangerous conditions, regulate the plant or the person, or compensate for injuries received.

The paragraph best supports the statement that

6-A workmen's compensation laws are in force in practically all states

6-B government regulation of industry is highly desirable

6-C the state is interested in lessening the occurrence of occupational disease

6-D the state compensates the worker for injuries received while carrying out the duties of his occupation

7. A survey to determine the subjects that have helped students most in their jobs shows that typewriting leads all other subjects in the business group. It also leads among the subjects college students consider most valuable and would take again if they were to return to high school.

The paragraph best supports the statement that

7-A the ability to type is an asset in business and in school

7-B students who return to night school take typing

7-C students with a knowledge of typing do superior work in college

7-D success in business is assured those who can type

8. Whenever two groups of people whose interests at the moment conflict meet to discuss a solution of that conflict, there is laid a basis for an interchange of facts and ideas which increases the total range of knowledge of both parties and tends to break down the barrier that their restricted field of information has helped to create.

Conflicts between two parties may be brought closer to a settlement through

8-A the exchange of accusations

8-B gaining a wider knowledge of facts

8-C submitting the dispute to an impartial judge

8-D limiting discussion to plans acceptable to both groups

9. The dangers of the ancient triple menace of the operating room—shock, hemorrhage, and infection—have been virtually eliminated. Transfusion of blood is employed to combat shock and hemorrhage. It is also used to build up a patient so weakened by disease that an operation would otherwise be impossible.

The paragraph best supports the statement that

9-A asepsis has removed the danger from infection

9-B operations are no longer as dangerous as they once were

9-C a blood transfusion usually precedes a serious operation

9-D operating technique has greatly improved due to the rise in standards of medical schools

10. The view is widely held that butter is more digestible and better absorbed than other fats because of its low melting point. There is little scientific authority for such a view. As margarine is made today, its melting point is close to that of butter, and tests show only the slightest degree of difference in digestibility of fats of equally low melting points.

The paragraph best supports the statement that

10-A butter is more easily digested than margarine

10-B there is not much difference in the digestibility of butter and margarine

10-C most people prefer butter to margarine

10-D it sometimes becomes necessary to use a substitute for butter

11. Even when sheep are raised as a principal business rather than a farm by-product, it is extremely difficult to produce wool of uniform quality. On a single sheep there are at least four grades. In one season, no two sheep in a flock yield exactly the same grade of wool. In addition, since quality is affected by the food the sheep eat, by the soil over which they graze, and by the weather, no two flocks in one year produce the same grade of wool.

The paragraph best supports the statement that

11-A soil is a factor in the quality of wool

11-B sheep raising is always a by-product of the meat-producing industries

11-C in one season all sheep yield exactly the same grade of wool

11-D there is a consistent change in the seasonal quality of wool

12. In the business districts of cities, collections from street letter boxes are made at stated hours, and collectors are required to observe these hours exactly. Any businessman using these boxes can rely with certainty upon the time of the next collection.

The paragraph best supports the statement that

12-A mail collections in business districts are more frequent during the day than at night

12-B mail collectors are required to observe safety regulations exactly

12-C mail collections are made often in business districts

12-D mail is collected in business districts on a regular schedule

13. Both the high school and the college should take the responsibility for preparing the student to get a job. Since the ability to write a good application letter is one of the first steps toward this goal, every teacher should be willing to do what he can to help the student learn to write such letters.

The paragraph best supports the statement that

13-A inability to write a good letter often reduces one's job prospects

13-B the major responsibility of the school is to obtain jobs for its students

13-C success is largely a matter of the kind of work the student applies for first

13-D every teacher should teach a course in the writing of application letters

14. In humid climates a thick growth of vegetation with a mattress of interlacing roots usually protects the moist soil from wind. But in dry regions vegetation is either wholly lacking, or scant growths are found huddled in detached clumps, leaving patches of unprotected ground. Since there is little or no moisture present to hold the soil particles together, they are readily lifted and scattered by the wind.

The main point of the paragraph is that

14-A vegetation is always present in humid climates

14-B lack of moisture increases cohesion

14-C moisture is an important element in soil and rock erosion

14-D wind is the chief agent in the dispersal of topsoil

15. The rates of vibration perceived by the ears as musical tones lie between fairly well-defined limits. In the ear, as in the eye, there are individual variations. However, variations are more marked in the ear, since its range of perception is greater.

The ear

15-A   is limited by the nature of its variations

15-B   is the most sensitive of the auditory organs

15-C   differs from the eye in its broader range of perception

15-D   is sensitive to a great range of musical volume

END OF PART 4

IF YOU COMPLETE YOUR WORK BEFORE TIME IS UP, CHECK OVER YOUR ANSWERS ON THIS PART ONLY. DO NOT GO BACK TO ANY PREVIOUS PART. DO NOT GO ON TO THE NEXT PART UNTIL YOU ARE TOLD TO DO SO.

PART 5

NUMERICAL OPERATIONS

The numerical operations part of your test battery consists of fifty very simple arithmetic questions which must be answered in only three minutes. Obviously, speed is a very important factor. You should not attempt to compute these answers using pencil and scratch paper. Instead, solve each problem in your head, then choose the correct answer from among the four choices and mark the letter of the correct answer on your answer sheet. If you are not sure of an answer, guess and go on to the next question. Do not skip any questions. You will most certainly not have time to go back to fill in. Since a wrong answer will not count against you, it cannot hurt to guess. Many people cannot complete all fifty questions in the three minutes allowed. Do not be upset if you cannot finish. Just answer as many questions as you can. Try these questions.

1. $3 - 1 =$

  1-A 2
  1-B 3
  1-C 4
  1-D 1

  1. Ⓐ Ⓑ Ⓒ Ⓓ

1-A $3 - 1 = 2$

2. $8 \times 2 =$

  2-A 6
  2-B 16
  2-C 12
  2-D 10

  2. Ⓐ Ⓑ Ⓒ Ⓓ

2-B $8 \times 2 = 16$

3. $6 + 6 =$

  3-A 0
  3-B 1
  3-C 12
  3-D 36

  3. Ⓐ Ⓑ Ⓒ Ⓓ

3-C $6 + 6 = 12$

4. $8 - 5 =$

  4-A 3
  4-B 13
  4-C 17
  4-D 4

  4. Ⓐ Ⓑ Ⓒ Ⓓ

4-A $8 - 5 = 3$

5. $1 + 1 =$

  5-A 0
  5-B 11
  5-C 1
  5-D 2

  5. Ⓐ Ⓑ Ⓒ Ⓓ

5-D $1 + 1 = 2$

6. $4 \times 3 =$

  6-A 9
  6-B 18
  6-C 12
  6-D 7

  6. Ⓐ Ⓑ Ⓒ Ⓓ

6-C $4 \times 3 = 12$

DO NOT TURN THE PAGE UNTIL YOU ARE TOLD TO DO SO

NUMERICAL OPERATIONS

TIME: 3 Minutes—50 Questions

1. 5 + 3 =

1-A   2
1-B   6
1-C   8
1-D   11

2. 8 − 6 =

2-A   7
2-B   2
2-C   12
2-D   14

3. 12 ÷ 2 =

3-A   10
3-B   3
3-C   4
3-D   6

4. 4 + 6 =

4-A   12
4-B   10
4-C   3
4-D   2

5. 6 × 3 =

5-A   3
5-B   9
5-C   12
5-D   18

6. 9 + 5 =

6-A   14
6-B   4
6-C   13
6-D   16

7. 10 ÷ 5 =

7-A   5
7-B   15
7-C   2
7-D   25

8. 2 × 9 =

8-A   18
8-B   36
8-C   16
8-D   15

9. 8 + 3 =

9-A   13
9-B   12
9-C   11
9-D   15

10. 1 + 6 =

10-A   5
10-B   6
10-C   7
10-D   9

11. 50 ÷ 5 =

11-A   5
11-B   10
11-C   55
11-D   11

12. 8 − 6 =

12-A   14
12-B   4
12-C   3
12-D   2

13. 6 ÷ 3 =

13-A 3
13-B 2
13-C 18
13-D 24

14. 2 × 9 =

14-A 7
14-B 17
14-C 18
14-D 19

15. 4 + 8 =

15-A 4
15-B 10
15-C 12
15-D 16

16. 7 × 9 =

16-A 45
16-B 63
16-C 72
16-D 75

17. 5 + 6 =

17-A 11
17-B 13
17-C 15
17-D 7

18. 0 + 8 =

18-A 0
18-B 1
18-C 8
18-D 18

19. 4 + 5 =

19-A 6
19-B 1
19-C 9
19-D 11

20. 64 ÷ 8 =

20-A 6
20-B 7
20-C 8
20-D 9

21. 8 + 3 =

21-A 5
21-B 11
21-C 12
21-D 13

22. 2 × 2 =

22-A 2
22-B 4
22-C 6
22-D 8

23. 6 + 1 =

23-A 16
23-B 15
23-C 7
23-D 5

24. 6 ÷ 2 =

24-A 12
24-B 8
24-C 4
24-D 3

25. 4 + 5 =

25-A 25
25-B 20
25-C 11
25-D 9

26. 7 × 8 =

26-A 56
26-B 48
26-C 42
26-D 72

27. 9 + 6 =

27-A 13
27-B 14
27-C 15
27-D 16

28. 2 + 3 =

28-A 5
28-B 7
28-C 1
28-D 6

29. 7 − 1 =

29-A 8
29-B 0
29-C 7
29-D 6

30. 8 ÷ 8 =

30-A 8
30-B 0
30-C 16
30-D 1

31. 40 ÷ 8 =

31-A 4
31-B 5
31-C 6
31-D 8

32. 7 × 6 =

32-A 24
32-B 36
32-C 42
32-D 48

33. 4 + 5 =

33-A 9
33-B 7
33-C 11
33-D 1

34. 6 × 2 =

34-A 8
34-B 4
34-C 36
34-D 12

35. 10 − 8 =

35-A 80
35-B 18
35-C 12
35-D 2

36. 7 ÷ 1 =

36-A 1
36-B 7
36-C 0
36-D 8

37. 9 + 4 =

37-A 11
37-B 13
37-C 15
37-D 17

38. 3 × 8 =

38-A 24
38-B 32
38-C 36
38-D 42

39. 1 + 7 =

39-A 6
39-B 7
39-C 8
39-D 5

40. 6 × 6 =

40-A 12
40-B 18
40-C 36
40-D 66

41. 90 ÷ 9 =

41-A 9
41-B 10
41-C 11
41-D 12

42. 2 − 2 =

42-A 1
42-B 4
42-C 2
42-D 0

43. 7 + 8 =

   43-A   9
   43-B   19
   43-C   17
   43-D   15

44. 4 − 0 =

   44-A   1
   44-B   4
   44-C   5
   44-D   8

45. 8 + 3 =

   45-A   5
   45-B   15
   45-C   13
   45-D   11

46. 3 − 2 =

   46-A   1
   46-B   2
   46-C   5
   46-D   6

47. 5 + 8 =

   47-A   12
   47-B   11
   47-C   13
   47-D   17

48. 3 ÷ 3 =

   48-A   0
   48-B   1
   48-C   3
   48-D   6

49. 9 + 1 =

   49-A   19
   49-B   9
   49-C   10
   49-D   11

50. 4 × 6 =

   50-A   28
   50-B   24
   50-C   23
   50-D   18

END OF PART 5

DO NOT GO ON UNTIL YOU ARE TOLD TO DO SO

CODING SPEED

The coding part of your exam is different from all other parts of the exam. Nothing that you have learned enters into your answering of these questions. Coding is a test of your memory, your eye-hand coordination and your working speed.

Before each set of questions you will find a "key." The key consists of ten words listed in alphabetical order. Each word has a four-digit code number assigned to it.

In the set of questions you will find the same ten words, scrambled and some-times repeated. Following each word in the test are *five* answer choices in columns labelled "A" to "E." Each answer choice is a four-digit number. The answer choices are in ascending order; that is, the lowest number is always in column A, the next higher number is in column B, and so on to the highest number in column E. You must look at the word, find the correct code number among the choices and mark on your answer sheet the letter of the column in which you found the correct code number.

On the actual examination you must work very quickly. You have only seven minutes in which to try to answer eighty-four questions. Use the sample questions that follow to develop a system that works for you—memorization, some sort of word-number association, a mathematical formula or any private method that helps you work up speed and accuracy. Many people cannot finish this part in the time allowed. Do not be upset if you cannot finish. Just do your best. Try these questions.

Key

clay 5813	fudge 1875	kiss 7871
dungeon 6214	gentle 9432	loft 4630
elf 3185	hand 5500	sock 8902
	jump 2864	

Answers

		A	B	C	D	E	
1.	gentle	2864	4630	5813	7871	9432	1. Ⓐ Ⓑ Ⓒ Ⓓ Ⓔ
2.	loft	1875	3185	4630	6214	8902	2. Ⓐ Ⓑ Ⓒ Ⓓ Ⓔ
3.	elf	1875	2864	3185	5813	8902	3. Ⓐ Ⓑ Ⓒ Ⓓ Ⓔ
4.	kiss	2864	4630	5500	7871	9432	4. Ⓐ Ⓑ Ⓒ Ⓓ Ⓔ
5.	fudge	1875	3185	5500	5813	6214	5. Ⓐ Ⓑ Ⓒ Ⓓ Ⓔ
6.	jump	2864	5813	6214	7871	8902	6. Ⓐ Ⓑ Ⓒ Ⓓ Ⓔ
7.	hand	4630	5500	5813	6214	7871	7. Ⓐ Ⓑ Ⓒ Ⓓ Ⓔ
8.	dungeon	1875	3185	4630	6214	8902	8. Ⓐ Ⓑ Ⓒ Ⓓ Ⓔ
9.	sock	2864	4630	5500	8902	9432	9. Ⓐ Ⓑ Ⓒ Ⓓ Ⓔ
10.	clay	5500	5813	6214	7871	9432	10. Ⓐ Ⓑ Ⓒ Ⓓ Ⓔ
11.	hand	1875	3185	4630	5500	5813	11. Ⓐ Ⓑ Ⓒ Ⓓ Ⓔ
12.	kiss	2864	4630	7871	8902	9432	12. Ⓐ Ⓑ Ⓒ Ⓓ Ⓔ

The correct answers are:

1-E	4-D	7-B	10-B
2-C	5-A	8-D	11-D
3-C	6-A	9-D	12-C

Key

bug 8076	grass 7601	star 2790
cow 6306	pencil 5015	uncle 9876
exit 4273	post 1119	water 4799
	rope 3838	

Answers

		A	B	C	D	E	
13.	pencil	2790	3838	4273	5015	7601	13. Ⓐ Ⓑ Ⓒ Ⓓ Ⓔ
14.	cow	4273	6306	7601	8076	9876	14. Ⓐ Ⓑ Ⓒ Ⓓ Ⓔ
15.	exit	1119	2790	4273	5015	6306	15. Ⓐ Ⓑ Ⓒ Ⓓ Ⓔ
16.	uncle	4273	4799	7601	8076	9876	16. Ⓐ Ⓑ Ⓒ Ⓓ Ⓔ
17.	rope	3838	4273	5015	7601	8076	17. Ⓐ Ⓑ Ⓒ Ⓓ Ⓔ
18.	bug	1119	2790	3838	8076	9876	18. Ⓐ Ⓑ Ⓒ Ⓓ Ⓔ
19.	grass	2790	4273	6306	7601	8076	19. Ⓐ Ⓑ Ⓒ Ⓓ Ⓔ
20.	post	1119	3838	5015	7601	9876	20. Ⓐ Ⓑ Ⓒ Ⓓ Ⓔ
21.	water	2790	4273	4799	5015	6306	21. Ⓐ Ⓑ Ⓒ Ⓓ Ⓔ
22.	cow	4273	4799	5015	6306	8076	22. Ⓐ Ⓑ Ⓒ Ⓓ Ⓔ
23.	star	2790	3838	4799	6306	7601	23. Ⓐ Ⓑ Ⓒ Ⓓ Ⓔ
24.	grass	4273	4799	7601	8076	9876	24. Ⓐ Ⓑ Ⓒ Ⓓ Ⓔ

The correct answers are:

13-D	16-E	19-D	22-D
14-B	17-A	20-A	23-A
15-C	18-D	21-C	24-C

DO NOT TURN THE PAGE UNTIL YOU ARE TOLD TO DO SO

CODING SPEED

TIME: 7 Minutes—84 Questions

Key

bird	7011	ghost	9212	rat	4643
car	6300	jury	2912	stump	8956
egg	1237	maroon	5873	window	6766
		pump	3061		

Answers

		A	B	C	D	E
1.	maroon	4643	5873	6766	8956	9212
2.	window	1237	2912	4643	6766	8956
3.	jury	2912	3061	5873	6300	7011
4.	rat	1237	3061	4643	6300	6766
5.	ghost	2912	4643	5873	8956	9212
6.	bird	3061	4643	6300	6766	7011
7.	stump	5873	6300	6766	7011	8956
8.	car	1237	3061	6300	6766	9212
9.	egg	1237	2912	3061	5873	8956
10.	pump	2912	3061	4643	6300	6766
11.	window	3061	6300	6766	7011	9212
12.	rat	3061	4643	5873	6766	8956

Key

bank	3029	eel	2270	luck	1654
candle	5605	farm	9564	mule	9984
dinner	8002	hill	6883	tuba	7240
		husk	4488		

Answers

		A	B	C	D	E
13.	candle	2270	3029	4488	5605	7240
14.	hill	1654	5605	6883	8002	9984
15.	farm	3029	4488	6883	7240	9564
16.	bank	2270	3029	5605	6883	8002
17.	dinner	4488	7240	8002	9564	9984
18.	luck	1654	3029	4488	6883	7240
19.	husk	4488	6883	7240	8002	9564
20.	mule	3029	4488	8002	9564	9984
21.	eel	2270	3029	4488	6883	8002
22.	dinner	3029	4488	6883	8002	9984
23.	tuba	5605	7240	8002	9564	9984
24.	husk	1654	2270	3029	4488	6883

Key

aunt	7959	dove	1918	ladle	3344
couch	4790	hail	1929	mark	6776
deer	8812	iron	2458	pistol	9434
		judge	5761		

Answers

		A	B	C	D	E
25.	pistol	1918	1929	4790	7959	9434
26.	iron	1929	2458	3344	6776	7959
27.	mark	3344	4790	5761	6776	7959
28.	judge	1918	1929	2458	4790	5761
29.	ladle	2458	3344	6776	7959	9434
30.	couch	4790	5761	6776	8812	9434
31.	deer	1918	2458	5761	7959	8812
32.	aunt	3344	5761	7959	8812	9434
33.	pistol	1929	3344	4790	7959	9434
34.	dove	1918	1929	2458	3344	4790
35.	mark	4790	6776	7959	8812	9434
36.	hail	1929	2458	5761	6776	7959

Key

art	1066	flower	4003	silence	6969
clue	3682	hood	7877	spoon	9060
down	5974	ice	8880	taxi	1001
		pants	2468		

Answers

		A	B	C	D	E
37.	silence	3682	4003	6969	8880	9060
38.	hood	1066	4003	5974	7877	9060
39.	pants	1001	2468	3682	4003	6969
40.	clue	3682	4003	6969	8880	9060
41.	art	1001	1066	4003	7877	8880
42.	down	2468	4003	5974	6969	7877
43.	ice	1001	1066	4003	8880	9060
44.	flower	4003	5974	6969	7877	8880
45.	spoon	2468	3682	6969	8880	9060
46.	down	1066	3682	4003	5974	6969
47.	hood	1001	2468	6969	7877	9060
48.	taxi	1001	1066	4003	8880	9060

Key

book	3498	guard	5249	pie	6765
boy	1518	hotel	9804	sea	7602
exam	2412	motel	8940	thing	5521
		navy	4404		

Answers

		A	B	C	D	E
49.	guard	1518	4404	5249	5521	6765
50.	exam	1518	2412	5521	7602	9804
51.	thing	2412	5521	5249	6765	8940
52.	motel	3498	4404	6765	8940	9804
53.	sea	5249	6765	7602	8940	9804
54.	boy	1518	2412	4404	5521	7602
55.	navy	2412	3498	4404	5249	6765
56.	book	3498	5249	5521	7602	8940
57.	hotel	1518	2412	6765	8940	9804
58.	pie	5521	6765	7602	8940	9804
59.	navy	4404	5249	5521	6765	7602
60.	book	1518	2412	3498	4404	9804

Key

air	1230	day	1010	island	9064
brush	8800	edge	6010	knee	3369
cabin	5254	fate	7946	lever	2125
		goose	4656		

Answers

		A	B	C	D	E
61.	island	1010	3369	7946	8800	9064
62.	goose	1230	2125	4656	5254	6010
63.	knee	2125	3369	5254	7946	8800
64.	fate	1010	1230	3369	4656	7946
65.	brush	2125	4656	5254	8800	9064
66.	lever	1010	1230	2125	6010	8800
67.	cabin	3369	4656	5254	7946	9064
68.	edge	1230	2125	4656	6010	8800
69.	air	1230	3369	5254	7946	9064
70.	knee	1010	1230	2125	3369	4656
71.	cabin	1230	2125	3369	4656	5254
72.	day	1010	1230	6010	8800	9064

Key

arch 2641	dress 5959	mud 7777
battle 1686	fuzz 4769	puzzle 8724
coin 9559	green 3480	stew 4162
	hair 6931	

Answers

		A	B	C	D	E
73.	puzzle	1686	4769	6931	8724	9559
74.	fuzz	2641	3480	4162	4769	5959
75.	stew	2641	4162	6931	7777	8724
76.	battle	1686	2641	4162	6931	8724
77.	mud	3480	4769	5959	7777	9559
78.	green	1686	3480	4162	6931	8724
79.	coin	2641	4162	5959	7777	9559
80.	arch	2641	4162	4769	6931	8724
81.	dress	1686	4769	5959	8724	9559
82.	hair	4162	4769	5959	6931	7777
83.	puzzle	1686	4162	6931	7777	8724
84.	dress	2641	3480	4162	4769	5959

END OF PART 6

**IF YOU FINISH BEFORE TIME IS UP, MAKE SURE YOU HAVE AN-
SWERED ALL THE QUESTIONS. DO NOT GO BACK TO ANY PREVIOUS
PART. DO NOT GO ON UNTIL YOU ARE TOLD TO DO SO.**

AUTO & SHOP INFORMATION

The auto and shop information questions test your knowledge and understanding of automobiles and of tools and shop practices. The answers to many questions come straight from your life experience. However, if this is not your area of interest, there will be questions to which you do not know the answer. Make the most sensible guess. Answer all questions. Mark the letter of your choice on your answer sheet. Try these questions.

1. The muffler on a car serves to

    1-A filter the exhaust fumes
    1-B keep the car warm
    1-C reduce exhaust sounds
    1-D protect against body damage

    1. Ⓐ Ⓑ Ⓒ Ⓓ

1-C The muffler is, in effect, a silencer. It cuts down exhaust noise. While the muffler is part of the exhaust system, it has no effect on the fumes (A).

2. Shock absorbers are part of the

    2-A engine
    2-B upholstery
    2-C suspension
    2-D exhaust system

    2. Ⓐ Ⓑ Ⓒ Ⓓ

2-C Shock absorbers are the heavy duty springs in the SUSPENSION. The rear shock absorbers are very near the exhaust system (D), but they are not part of that system. While springs in the upholstery (B) may indeed absorb shocks, they are not called *shock absorbers*.

3.

You might use the instrument below if you wanted to

    3-A pitch a tent
    3-B poke holes in a fabric
    3-C locate studs in a wall
    3-D drill holes at equal short distances along a board

    3. Ⓐ Ⓑ Ⓒ Ⓓ

3-D The *compass* above would be very useful in marking out equal short distances on a board. The compass would not, of course, be of use in the actual drilling.

4. The frequency of oiling and greasing of bearings and other moving parts of machinery depends mainly on the

    4-A size of the parts requiring lubrication
    4-B speed at which the parts move
    4-C ability of the operator
    4-D amount of use of the equipment

    4. Ⓐ Ⓑ Ⓒ Ⓓ

4-D Lubrication of machinery is scheduled according to time elapsed and amount of use. All the other reasons offered are irrelevant.

DO NOT TURN THE PAGE UNTIL YOU ARE TOLD TO DO SO

AUTO & SHOP INFORMATION

TIME: 11 Minutes—25 Questions

1. Most automobile engines run according to the

   1-A rotary cycle
   1-B intake-exhaust cycle
   1-C four-stroke cycle
   1-D two-stroke cycle

2. If the temperature gauge indicates the engine is getting overheated

   2-A allow it to cool down
   2-B pour cold water in immediately
   2-C pour hot water in immediately
   2-D pour in a cooling anti-freeze at once

3. Vapor-lock in a gasoline engine is most likely due to

   3-A an over-rich gas-air mixture
   3-B fuel forming bubbles in the gas line
   3-C a tear in the fuel pump diaphragm
   3-D the carburetor being clogged with dirt

4. A governor is used on an automobile primarily to limit its

   4-A rate of acceleration
   4-B maximum speed
   4-C fuel consumption
   4-D stopping distance

5. Water sludge in engine crankcase oil is most usually caused by

   5-A using a low viscosity oil
   5-B condensation in the crankcase
   5-C mixing different brands of motor oil
   5-D using a high viscosity oil

6. A number 10 wood screw is

   6-A thicker than a number 6
   6-B longer than a number 6
   6-C shorter than a number 6
   6-D thinner than a number 6

7. The reason that a lubricant prevents rubbing surfaces from becoming hot is that the oil

   7-A is cold and cools off the rubbing metal surfaces
   7-B is sticky, preventing the surfaces from moving over each other too rapidly
   7-C forms a smooth layer between the two surfaces, preventing their coming into contact
   7-D makes the surfaces smooth so that they move easily over each other

8. The length of a flat head screw is defined as the length

   8-A of the threaded portion
   8-B of the shank plus the threaded portion
   8-C of the complete screw
   8-D between the bottom of the head and the point

9. The saw that is never hand filed is a

   9-A rip saw
   9-B circular saw
   9-C coping saw
   9-D band saw

10. The length of a 10-penny nail is, in inches

    10-A $2\frac{1}{2}$
    10-B 3
    10-C $3\frac{1}{2}$
    10-D 4

11.

    The tool shown above is

11-A an Allen-head wrench
11-B a double scraper
11-C an offset screwdriver
11-D a nail puller

12.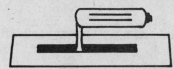

The tool pictured above is used to

12-A pry the tops off paint cans
12-B level wooden threshholds
12-C finish the surface of plastered walls
12-D pound down paving stones

13. The set in the teeth of a hand saw primarily

13-A prevents the saw from binding
13-B makes the saw cut true
13-C gives the saw a sharper edge
13-D removes the sawdust

14. A car slows down, lacks power, and a popping sound can be heard. The trouble is likely to be

14-A a faulty fuel supply
14-B a shorted sparkplug
14-C pitted breaker points
14-D faulty distributor timing

15. Manifolds are used to conduct

15-A gases out of an engine only
15-B gases into an engine only
15-C gases into or out of an engine
15-D heat into the piston

16. Reverse flushing of a clogged gasoline engine block and radiator cooling system is done properly by

16-A not removing the thermostat out of the engine block
16-B connecting the flushing gun at the bottom of the engine block
16-C using air and water
16-D using low pressure steam

17. Upon dismantling a gasoline engine, it was found that the piston rings were stuck in the grooves, not being free to rotate. This was most likely caused by

17-A operating the engine with spark setting in advanced position
17-B the thermostat maintaining too low an engine temperature
17-C dirty or contaminated lubricating oil
17-D using the wrong type of spark plugs in the engine

18. To test for leaks around the intake manifold of an idling engine, the mechanic would most likely use

18-A soap bubbles
18-B talc powder
18-C oil
18-D heavy grease

19. Wood ladders should not be painted because

19-A paint will wear off rapidly due to the conditions under which ladders are used
19-B ladders are slippery when painted
19-C it is more effective to store the ladder in a dry place
19-D paint will hide defects in the ladder

20. A screw is broken off in a tapped hole. The proper tools to use in removing the broken screw from the hole are

20-A hammer and cold chisel
20-B drill and EZY-out
20-C acetylene and oxygen torch
20-D screw driver and pliers

21. When sanding wood by hand, best results are usually obtained in finishing the surface when the sanding block is worked

21-A across the grain
21-B in a diagonal to the grain
21-C in a circular motion
21-D with the grain

22. The term "whipping" when applied to rope means

22-A binding the ends with cord to prevent unraveling

22-B coiling the rope in as tight a ball as possible
22-C lubricating the strands with tallow
22-D wetting the rope with water to cure it

23. The wrench that is used principally for pipe work is

23-A

23-B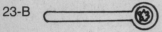

23-C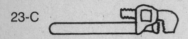

23-D

24. If an expander is used under an oil ring it must be

24-A of the diagonal joint type
24-B a rigid type

24-C of the step joint type
24-D of the vented type

25. The tool used to measure the depth of a hole is

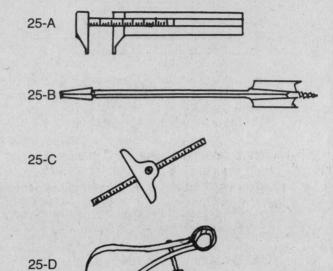

25-A

25-B

25-C

25-D

END OF PART 7

IF YOU FINISH BEFORE TIME IS UP, CHECK YOUR WORK ON THIS PART ONLY. DO NOT RETURN TO ANY PREVIOUS PART. DO NOT GO ON UNTIL YOU ARE TOLD TO DO SO.

PART 8

MATHEMATICS KNOWLEDGE

To solve the problems in this part, you must draw upon your knowledge of high school mathematics. The problems require you to use simple algebra and geometry along with arithmetic skills and reasoning power. Some questions can be answered in your head. Others will require the use of scratch paper. If you use scratch paper for your calculations, be sure to mark the letter of the correct answer on your answer sheet. Try these questions.

1. Two rectangular boards each measuring 5 feet by 3 feet are placed together to make one large board. How much shorter will the perimeter be if the two long sides are placed together than if the two short sides are placed together?

1-A 2 feet
1-B 4 feet
1-C 6 feet
1-D 8 feet

1. Ⓐ Ⓑ Ⓒ Ⓓ

1-B Perimeter $= 2\,l + 2\,w$
If the two long sides are together the perimeter will be
$5 + 3 + 3 + 5 + 3 + 3 = 22$

If the two short sides are together, the perimeter will be
$3 + 5 + 5 + 3 + 5 + 5 = 26$

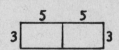

$26 - 22 = 4$ feet shorter

2. $100 - x = 5^2$ What is the value of x?

2-A 75
2-B 25
2-C 5
2-D 50

2. Ⓐ Ⓑ Ⓒ Ⓓ

2-A To square a number multiply it by itself.
$$100 - x = 5^2$$
$$100 - x = 5 \times 5$$
$$100 - x = 25$$
$$100 - 25 = x$$
$$x = 75$$

3. If an engine pumps G gallons of water per minute, then the number of gallons pumped in half an hour may be found by

3-A taking one-half of G
3-B dividing 60 by G
3-C multiplying G by 30
3-D dividing 30 by G

3. Ⓐ Ⓑ Ⓒ Ⓓ

3-C One half hour $= 30$ minutes
Amount $=$ rate (G) $\times$ time (30 minutes)

4. $+1 -1 +1 -1 +1 \ldots$ and so on where the last number is $+1$, has a sum of

4-A 0
4-B -1
4-C $+1$
4-D 2

4. Ⓐ Ⓑ Ⓒ Ⓓ

4-C Each minus 1 cancels out the plus 1 before it. Since the final term is $+1$, which is not cancelled out by a -1, the sum is $+1$.

DO NOT TURN THE PAGE UNTIL YOU ARE TOLD TO DO SO

MATHEMATICS KNOWLEDGE

TIME: 24 Minutes—25 Questions

1. If 30 is divided by .06, the result is

   1-A   5
   1-B   50
   1-C   500
   1-D   5000

2. When 2x − 1 is multiplied by 10 the result is 70. What is the value of x?

   2-A   2
   2-B   12
   2-C   3
   2-D   4

3. In a class of 24 students there are 14 boys. What fractional part of the class is girls?

   3-A $\frac{4}{12}$
   3-B $\frac{6}{12}$
   3-C $\frac{7}{12}$
   3-D   2.5/6

4. In the formula I = p + prt, what does I equal when p = 500, r = 20%, t = 2?

   4-A   10,000
   4-B   700
   4-C   8,000
   4-D   12,000

5. A car owner finds he needs 12 gallons of gas for each 120 miles he drives. If he has his carburetor adjusted, he will need only 80% as much gas. How many miles will 12 gallons of gas then last him?

   5-A   90
   5-B   150
   5-C   96
   5-D   160

6. What is the maximum number of books each $\frac{1}{4}$ inch thick that can be placed standing on a shelf 4 feet long?

   6-A   16
   6-B   192
   6-C   48
   6-D   96

7. In a bag there are red, green, black, and white marbles. If there are 6 red, 8 green, 4 black, and 12 white, and one marble is to be selected at random, what is the probability it will be white?

   7-A $\frac{1}{5}$
   7-B $\frac{2}{5}$
   7-C $\frac{4}{15}$
   7-D $\frac{2}{15}$

8.

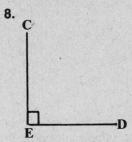

In the diagram above, CE ⊥ ED. If CE = 7 and ED = 6, what is the shortest distance from C to D?

   8-A   6
   8-B $4\sqrt{12}$
   8-C   7
   8-D $\sqrt{85}$

9. 60 is what percent of $\frac{1}{2}$?

   9-A   25
   9-B   12,000

9-C 1,000
9-D 24,000

10. Find 5½% of $2,800

10-A $15.40
10-B $16.40
10-C $154
10-D $160

11. A line of print in a magazine article contains an average of 6 words. There are 5 lines to the inch. If 8 inches are available for an article which contains 270 words, how must the article be changed?

11-A Add 30 words
11-B Delete 30 words
11-C Delete 40 words
11-D Add 60 words

12.

Triangle R is 3 times triangle S.
Triangle S is 3 times triangle T.
If triangle S = 1, what is the sum of the three triangles?

12-A $2\frac{1}{3}$
12-B $3\frac{1}{3}$
12-C $4\frac{1}{3}$
12-D 6

13. If $\frac{3}{4}$ of a class is absent and $\frac{2}{3}$ of those present leave the room, what fraction of the original class remains in the room?

13-A $\frac{1}{24}$
13-B $\frac{1}{4}$
13-C $\frac{1}{12}$
13-D $\frac{1}{8}$

14. If $2 - x = x - 2$, then $x =$

14-A -2
14-B 2
14-C 0
14-D $\frac{1}{2}$

15. If $D = R \times T$, then $R =$

15-A $D \times T$
15-B $T \div R$
15-C $T - D$
15-D $D \div T$

16. If $.04y = 1$, then $y =$

16-A .025
16-B 25
16-C .25
16-D 250

17. If all P are S and no S are Q, it necessarily follows that

17-A all Q are S
17-B all Q are P
17-C no P are Q
17-D no S are P

18. A is older than B. With the passage of time

18-A the ratio of the ages of A and B remains unchanged
18-B the ratio of the ages of A and B increases
18-C the ratio of the ages of A and B decreases
18-D the difference in their ages varies

19. From a temperature of 15°, a drop of 21° would result in a temperature of

19-A $-36°$
19-B $36°$
19-C $-6°$
19-D $-30°$

20. If a piece of wood measuring 4 feet 2 inches is divided into three equal parts, each part is

20-A 1 foot $4\frac{2}{3}$ inches
20-B 1 foot $2\frac{1}{3}$ inches
20-C 1 foot 4 inches
20-D 1 foot $\frac{7}{18}$ inch

21. The sum of -24 and -3 is

21-A 8
21-B 21
21-C -8
21-D -27

22. 1.1 × .00001 =

22-A .0022
22-B .00022
22-C .000022
22-D .0000022

23. The number of digits in the square root of 64,048,009 is

23-A 4
23-B 5
23-C 6
23-D 7

24. A cog wheel having 8 cogs plays into another cog wheel having 24 cogs. When the small

wheel has made 42 revolutions, how many has the larger wheel made?

24-A 14
24-B 16
24-C 20
24-D 10

25. If T tons of snow fall in 1 second, how many tons fall in M minutes?

25-A 60 MT
25-B MT + 60
25-C MT
25-D $\frac{60 M}{T}$

END OF PART 8

IF YOU COMPLETE YOUR WORK BEFORE TIME IS UP, CHECK TO BE SURE THAT YOU HAVE MARKED ALL THE ANSWERS ON YOUR ANSWER SHEET. THEN CHECK OVER YOUR WORK ON THIS PART ONLY. DO NOT GO BACK TO ANY PREVIOUS PART. DO NOT GO ON TO THE NEXT PAGE UNTIL YOU ARE TOLD TO DO SO.

PART 9

MECHANICAL COMPREHENSION

Part 9 consists of questions about your understanding of general mechanical and physical principles. Your understanding of these principles will come from your own observations, from experience in working with mechanical devices and from your reading and school courses. Answer all the questions as best you can, marking the letter of your choice on your answer sheet. Try these questions.

1.

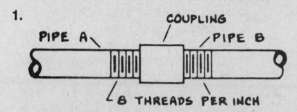

If both pipes A and B are free to move back and forth but are held so they cannot turn, and the coupling is turned 4 revolutions with a wrench, the overall length of the pipes and coupling will:

1-A   decrease $\frac{1}{2}''$
1-B   remain the same
1-C   increase or decrease 1″ depending upon the direction of turning
1-D   increase $\frac{1}{2}''$

1. Ⓐ Ⓑ Ⓒ Ⓓ

1-B If the coupling is turned, but the pipes are held firm so that they cannot turn, then the coupling will move along the length of one or the other pipes, but the overall length of the three pieces will remain the same.

2.

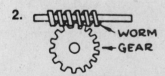

The figure here shows a worm and a gear. If the worm rotates slowly on its shaft, the gear will

2-A   not turn
2-B   turn very slowly

2-C   turn rapidly
2-D   oscillate

2. Ⓐ Ⓑ Ⓒ Ⓓ

2-B Since the teeth of the gear are meshed with the worm, the movement of one demands the movement of the other. If the worm were to rotate very rapidly, the gear would spin rapidly. Since the worm is rotating slowly, the gear will turn slowly.

3.

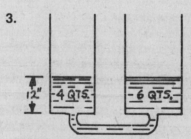

To bring the level of the water in the tanks to a height of $2\frac{1}{2}$ feet, the quantity of water to be added is

3-A   10 qts
3-B   20 qts.
3-C   15 qts.
3-D   25 qts.

3. Ⓐ Ⓑ Ⓒ Ⓓ

3-C Ten quarts of water have brought the water level to one foot. An additional fifteen quarts would raise the water level by one and one-half feet to a total height of two and one-half feet.

DO NOT TURN THE PAGE UNTIL YOU ARE TOLD TO DO SO

MECHANICAL COMPREHENSION

TIME: 19 Minutes—25 Questions

1.

The figure above represents a pulley, with practically no friction, from which two ten-pound weights are suspended as indicated. If a downward force is applied to weight 1, it is most likely that weight 1 will

1-A come to rest at the present level of weight 2

1-B move downward until it is level with weight 2

1-C move downward until it reaches the floor

1-D pass weight 2 in its downward motion and then return to its present position

2.

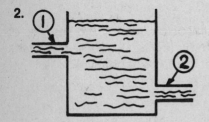

The figure above represents a water tank containing water. The number 1 indicates an intake pipe and 2 indicates a discharge pipe. Of the following, the statement which is *least* accurate is that the

2-A tank will eventually overflow if water flows through the intake pipe at a faster rate than it flows out through the discharge pipe

2-B tank will empty completely if the intake pipe is closed and the discharge pipe is allowed to remain open

2-C water in the tank will remain at a constant level if the rate of intake is equal to the rate of discharge

2-D water in the tank will rise if the intake pipe is operating when the discharge pipe is closed

3.

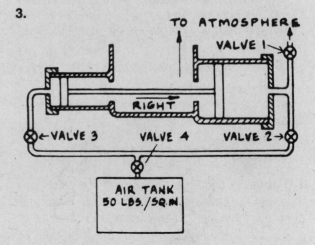

If all valves are closed at the start, in order to have air pressure from the tank move the pistons to the right, the valves to be opened are

3-A 2 and 4

3-B 2, 3, and 4

3-C 1 and 2

3-D 1, 3 and 4

4. The purpose of an air valve in a heating system is to

4-A prevent pressure from building up in a room due to the heated air

4-B   relieve the air from steam radiators
4-C   allow excessive steam pressure in the boiler to escape to the atmosphere
4-D   control the temperature in the room

5. Sweating usually occurs on pipes that

5-A   contain cold water
5-B   contain hot water
5-C   are chrome plated
5-D   require insulation

6.

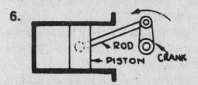

The figure above shows a crank and piston. The piston moves from mid-position to the extreme right if the crank

6-A   makes $\frac{1}{2}$ turn
6-B   makes a $\frac{3}{4}$ turn
6-C   makes one turn
6-D   makes $1\frac{1}{2}$ turns

7.

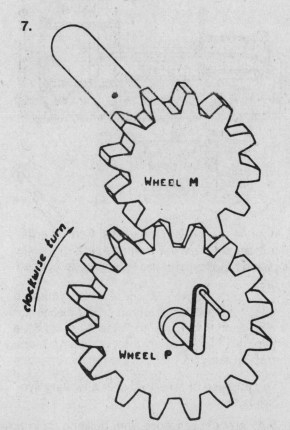

Study the gear wheels in the figure below, then determine which of the following statements is true.

7-A   If you turn wheel M clockwise by means of the handle, wheel P will also turn clockwise.
7-B   It will take the same time for a tooth of wheel P to make a full turn as it will for a tooth of wheel M.
7-C   It will take less time for a tooth of wheel P to make a full turn than it will take a tooth of wheel M.
7-D   It will take more time for a tooth of wheel P to make a full turn than it will for a tooth of wheel M.

8. Assume that the color of the flame from a gas stove is bright yellow. To correct this, you should

8-A   close the air flap
8-B   increase the size of the gas opening
8-C   increase the gas pressure
8-D   open the air flap

9. The try-cocks of steam boilers are used to

9-A   act as safety valves
9-B   empty the boiler of water
9-C   test steam pressure in the boiler
9-D   find the height of water in the boiler

10.

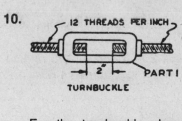

For the turnbuckle shown, the number of complete turns of Part 1 required to make the ends of the threaded rods meet is

10-A   6
10-B   18
10-C   12
10-D   24

11.

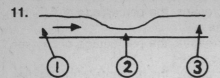

The figure above represents a pipe through which water is flowing in the direction of the arrow. There is a constriction in the pipe at the point indicated by the number 2. Water is being pumped into the pipe at a constant rate of 350 gallons per minute. Of the following, the most accurate statement is that

11-A the velocity of the water at point 2 is the same as the velocity of the water at point 3

11-B a greater volume of water is flowing past point 1 in a minute than is flowing past point 2

11-C the velocity of the water at point 1 is greater than the velocity at point 2

11-D the volume of water flowing past point 2 in a minute is the same as the volume of water flowing past point 1 in a minute

12.

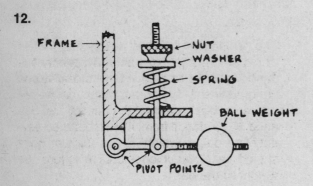

If the ball and spring mechanism are balanced in the position shown, the ball will move upward if

12-A the nut is loosened

12-B ball is moved away from the frame

12-C the nut is loosened and the ball moved away from the frame

12-D the nut is tightened

13.

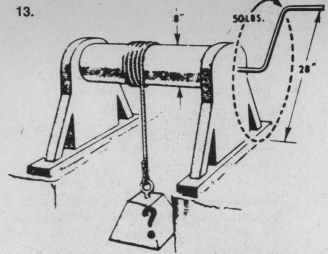

In the diagram above, the axle eight inches in diameter has attached a handle 28 inches in diameter. If a force of 50 lb. is applied to the handle, the axle will lift a weight of

13-A 224 lb.

13-B 175 lb.

13-C 200 lb.

13-D   88 lb.

14.

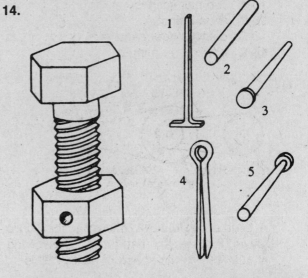

The figure above shows a bolt and nut and five numbered pieces. If all of the pieces are long enough to go through the bolt, and if the circular hole extends through the bolt and through the other side of the nut, which piece must you use to fix the nut in a stationary position?

14-A 1
14-B 3
14-C 2
14-D 4

15.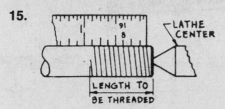

A very light cut (trace) is being measured as a check before cutting the thread on the lathe. The number of threads per inch shown is:

15-A 12
15-B 14
15-C 13
15-D 15

16. The standing end of a rope used to hoist a boatswain's chair should be tied to the eye of the ropes holding the chair by means of (a)

16-A two half hitches
16-B square knot
16-C double sheet bend
16-D bowline on a bight

17.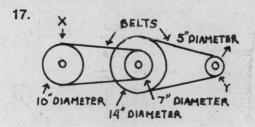

A double belt drive is shown in the figure above. If the pulley marked "X" is revolving at 100 R.P.M., the speed of pulley "Y" is

17-A 800 R.P.M.
17-B 200 R.P.M.
17-C 400 R.P.M.
17-D 25 R.P.M.

18. Analysis of the flue gases shows that as the percentage of excess air

18-A increases, the percentage of CO_2 increases
18-B increases, the percentage of oxygen decreases
18-C increases, the percentage of CO_2 decreases
18-D decreases, the percentage of oxygen decreases

19. If the flush tank of a water-closet fixture overflows, the fault is likely to be

19-A failure of the ball to seat properly
19-B excessive water pressure
19-C defective trap in the toilet bowl
19-D water-logged float

20.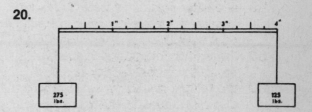

The bar above, which is exactly four inches in length, has a two hundred seventy-five pound weight hung on one end and a one hundred twenty-five pound weight on the opposite end. In order that the bar will just balance, the distance from the two hundred seventy-five pound weight to the fulcrum point should be (In your computation ignore the weight of the bar.)

20-A $\frac{1}{2}$ inch
20-B 1 inch
20-C $\frac{3}{4}$ inch
20-D $1\frac{1}{4}$ inches

21. If the float of a flush tank leaks and fills with water, the most probable result will be

21-A no water in the tank
21-B ball cock will remain open
21-C water will flow over tank rim onto floor
21-D flush ball will not seat properly

22.

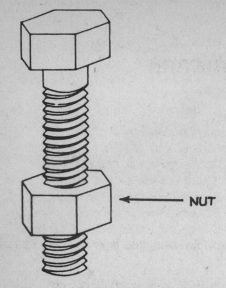

← NUT

Which of the following statements is true?

22-A If the nut is held stationary and the head turned clockwise, the bolt will move up.

22-B If the head of the bolt is held stationary and the nut is turned clockwise, the nut will move down.

22-C If the head of the bolt is held stationary and the nut is turned clockwise, the nut will move up.

22-D If the nut is held stationary and the bolt is turned counterclockwise, the nut will move up.

23.

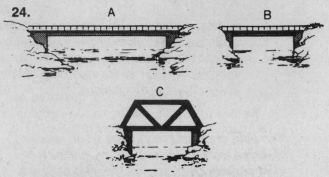

Which spoon is hottest?

23-A wood
23-B silver
23-C steel
23-D silver and steel are equally hot

24.

A   B

C

Which bridge is the strongest?

24-A A
24-B B
24-C C
24-D All are equally strong

25.

If the adult backs to the end of the seesaw, the child will

25-A remain stationary
25-B fly into the air
25-C hit the ground hard
25-D slide to its end of the seesaw

END OF PART 9

IF YOU FINISH BEFORE TIME IS UP, CHECK OVER YOUR WORK ON THIS PART ONLY. DO NOT RETURN TO ANY PREVIOUS PART. DO NOT GO ON UNTIL YOU ARE TOLD TO DO SO.

PART 10

ELECTRONICS INFORMATION

The questions in this part test your knowledge and understanding of electricity, radio and electronics. To answer some of the questions all you need is common sense. Other questions can be answered on the basis of experience, courses and reading. Answer all the questions. Mark the letter of your answer on the answer sheet. Try these questions.

1. The plug of a portable tool should be removed from the convenience outlet by grasping the plug and not by pulling on the cord because

   1-A the plug is easier to grip than the cord
   1-B pulling on the cord may allow the plug to fall on the floor and break
   1-C pulling on the cord may break the wires off the plug terminals
   1-D the plug is generally better insulated than the cord

   1. Ⓐ Ⓑ Ⓒ Ⓓ

1-C Yanking at an electric cord can cause hidden damage inside the plug. The force can cause terminals to loosen or bits of wire to break off and fray. Frayed wires can in turn come into contact with the opposite pole, causing fire or short circuit in the plug at some later date.

2. A copper wire with twice the diameter of another copper wire has a current carrying capacity

   2-A four times as great
   2-B twice as great
   2-C half as great
   2-D three times as great

   2. Ⓐ Ⓑ Ⓒ Ⓓ

2-A A copper wire with twice the diameter of another copper wire is four times as heavy and therefore can carry four times as much current. You can prove this to yourself by substituting some simple figures in the formula for the area of a circle, $A = \pi r^2$.

If the diameter of a wire is 6cm., then its radius is 3cm.

$\pi \times 3^2 = 3.14 \times 9 = 28.26$ sq. cm.

If the diameter of wire is 12cm, then its radius is 6cm.

$\pi \times 6^2 = 3.14 \times 36 = 113.04$ sq. cm., which is four times 28.26 sq. cm.

3. When removing the insulation from a wire before making a splice, care should be taken to avoid nicking the wire mainly because the

   3-A current carrying capacity will be reduced
   3-B resistance will be increased
   3-C wire tinning will be injured
   3-D wire is more likely to break

   3. Ⓐ Ⓑ Ⓒ Ⓓ

3-D A nick in wire can be dangerous because it weakens the wire at that point and can lead to breakage. If the wire is nicked during stripping, you should cut off the weakened portion and begin again. Later breakage from an unnoticed weakness can lead to a short circuit.

4. A megawatt is

   4-A ten watts
   4-B one hundred watts
   4-C one thousand watts
   4-D one million watts

   4. Ⓐ Ⓑ Ⓒ Ⓓ

4-D *Mega,* from the Greek, means a million or multiplied by a million.

DO NOT TURN THE PAGE UNTIL YOU ARE TOLD TO DO SO

ELECTRONICS INFORMATION

TIME: 9 Minutes—20 Questions

1. The core of an electro-magnet is usually

   1-A aluminum
   1-B lead
   1-C brass
   1-D iron

2. A direct-current supply may be obtained from an alternating-current source by means of

   2-A a frequency changer set
   2-B an inductance-capacitance filter
   2-C a tungar bulb rectifier
   2-D none of the devices mentioned above

3. A "mil" measures

   3-A an eighth of an inch
   3-B a millionth of an inch
   3-C a thousandth of an inch
   3-D a ten-thousandth of an inch

4. The device used to change a.c. to d.c. is a

   4-A frequency changer
   4-B regulator
   4-C transformer
   4-D rectifier

5. A load is missing from a D.C. shunt wound motor. If you happen to open the field circuit

   5-A the speed of the motor will slow down greatly
   5-B the speed of the motor will be much greater
   5-C the speed will be the same
   5-D the motor will cease to operate

6. The electrical contacts in the tuner of a television set are usually plated with silver. Silver is used to

   6-A avoid tarnish
   6-B improve conductivity
   6-C improve appearance
   6-D avoid arcing

7. Electrical contacts are opened or closed when the electrical current energizes the coils of a device called a

   7-A reactor
   7-B transtat
   7-C relay
   7-D thermostat

8. If a live conductor is contacted accidentally, the severity of the electrical shock is determined primarily by

   8-A the size of the conductor
   8-B the current in the conductor
   8-C whether the current is a.c. or d.c.
   8-D the contact resistance

9. Metal cabinets used for lighting circuits are grounded to

   9-A eliminate electrolysis
   9-B assure that the fuse in a defective circuit will blow
   9-C reduce shock hazard
   9-D simplify wiring

10. When connecting a lamp bank or portable tool to a live 600-volt d.c. circuit, the best procedure is to make the negative or ground connection first and then the positive connection. The reason for this procedure is that

    10-A electricity flows from positive to negative
    10-B there is less danger of accidental shock

10-C the reverse procedure may blow the fuse

10-D less arcing will occur when the connection is made

11. A material *not* used in the make-up of lighting wires or cables is

11-A rubber

11-B paper

11-C lead

11-D cotton

12. A polarized plug generally has

12-A two parallel prongs of the same size

12-B prongs at an angle with one another

12-C magnetized prongs

12-D prongs marked plus and minus

13. In comparing Nos. 00, 8, 12 and 6 A.W.G. wires, the smallest of the group is

13-A No. 00

13-B No. 8

13-C No. 12

13-D No. 6

14. Direct current arcs are "hotter" and harder to extinguish than alternating current arcs, so that electrical appliances which include a thermostat are frequently marked for use on "a.c. only." One appliance which might be so marked *because it includes a thermostat* is a

14-A soldering iron

14-B floor waxer

14-C vacuum cleaner

14-D household iron

15. Neutral wire can be quickly recognized by the

15-A greenish color

15-B bluish color

15-C natural or whitish color

15-D black color

16.

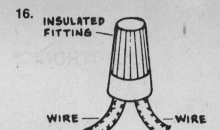

Wires are often spliced by the use of a fitting like the one shown above. The use of this fitting does away with the need for

16-A skinning

16-B cleaning

16-C twisting

16-D soldering

17.

The device shown above is a

17-A C-clamp

17-B test clip

17-C battery connector

17-D ground clamp

18. A good magnetic material is

18-A copper

18-B iron

18-C tin

18-D brass

19.

The sketch shows a head-on view of a three-pronged plug used with portable electrical power tools. Considering the danger of shock when using such tools, it is evident that the function of the U-shaped prong is to

19-A   insure that the other two prongs enter the outlet with the proper polarity
19-B   provide a half-voltage connection when doing light work
19-C   prevent accidental pulling of the plug from the outlet
19-D   connect the metallic shell of the tool motor to ground

20. The instrument by which electric power may be measured is a

20-A   rectifier
20-B   scanner drum
20-C   ammeter
20-D   wattmeter

END OF EXAMINATION

IF YOU FINISH BEFORE THE TIME IS UP, CHECK OVER YOUR WORK ON THIS PART ONLY. DO NOT GO BACK TO ANY PREVIOUS PART.

CORRECT ANSWERS—SECOND MODEL EXAM

PART 1—GENERAL SCIENCE

1. C	5. A	8. C	11. C	14. C	17. D	20. B	23. C
2. C	6. C	9. D	12. B	15. B	18. B	21. D	24. D
3. C	7. C	10. C	13. D	16. D	19. B	22. B	25. D
4. B							

PART 2—ARITHMETIC REASONING

1. D	5. C	9. B	13. B	17. C	21. B	25. B	28. B
2. B	6. A	10. C	14. D	18. D	22. A	26. D	29. B
3. C	7. C	11. A	15. A	19. A	23. B	27. B	30. B
4. D	8. B	12. A	16. B	20. A	24. C		

PART 3—WORD KNOWLEDGE

1. C	6. C	11. B	16. C	20. D	24. D	28. A	32. A
2. B	7. D	12. D	17. D	21. D	25. A	29. D	33. D
3. C	8. C	13. D	18. C	22. D	26. A	30. C	34. B
4. B	9. B	14. C	19. C	23. C	27. D	31. D	35. C
5. A	10. D	15. D					

PART 4—PARAGRAPH COMPREHENSION

1. C	3. D	5. B	7. A	9. B	11. A	13. A	15. C
2. A	4. B	6. C	8. B	10. C	12. D	14. D	

PART 5—NUMERICAL OPERATIONS

1. C	8. A	15. C	21. B	27. C	33. A	39. C	45. D
2. B	9. C	16. B	22. B	28. A	34. D	40. C	46. A
3. D	10. C	17. A	23. C	29. D	35. D	41. B	47. C
4. B	11. B	18. C	24. D	30. D	36. B	42. D	48. B
5. D	12. D	19. C	25. D	31. B	37. B	43. D	49. C
6. A	13. B	20. C	26. A	32. C	38. A	44. B	50. B
7. C	14. C						

PART 6—CODING SPEED

1. B	12. B	23. B	34. A	45. E	55. C	65. D	75. B
2. D	13. D	24. D	35. B	46. D	56. A	66. C	76. A
3. A	14. C	25. E	36. A	47. D	57. E	67. C	77. D
4. C	15. E	26. B	37. C	48. A	58. B	68. D	78. B
5. E	16. B	27. D	38. D	49. C	59. A	69. A	79. E
6. E	17. C	28. E	39. B	50. B	60. C	70. D	80. A
7. E	18. A	29. B	40. A	51. B	61. E	71. E	81. C
8. C	19. A	30. A	41. B	52. D	62. C	72. A	82. D
9. A	20. E	31. E	42. C	53. C	63. B	73. D	83. E
10. B	21. A	32. C	43. D	54. A	64. E	74. D	84. E
11. C	22. D	33. E	44. A				

PART 7—AUTO & SHOP INFORMATION

1. C	5. B	8. C	11. C	14. A	17. C	20. B	23. C
2. A	6. A	9. C	12. C	15. C	18. C	21. D	24. D
3. B	7. C	10. B	13. A	16. C	19. D	22. A	25. C
4. B							

PART 8—MATHEMATICS KNOWLEDGE

1. C	5. B	8. D	11. B	14. B	17. C	20. A	23. A
2. D	6. B	9. B	12. C	15. D	18. C	21. D	24. A
3. D	7. B	10. C	13. C	16. B	19. C	22. C	25. A
4. B							

PART 9—MECHANICAL COMPREHENSION

1. C	5. A	8. D	11. D	14. D	17. C	20. D	23. B
2. B	6. B	9. D	12. D	15. C	18. C	21. B	24. C
3. D	7. D	10. C	13. B	16. C	19. D	22. B	25. B
4. B							

PART 10—ELECTRONICS INFORMATION

1. D	4. D	7. C	10. B	13. C	15. C	17. D	19. D
2. C	5. B	8. D	11. B	14. D	16. D	18. B	20. D
3. C	6. B	9. C	12. B				

SCORE SHEET—SECOND MODEL EXAM

PART	NUMBER CORRECT		NUMBER OF QUESTIONS		
GENERAL SCIENCE	_18_	÷ 25 =	_1_	× 100 = _900_ %	
ARITHMETIC REASONING	_____	÷ 30 =	_____	× 100 = _____%	
WORD KNOWLEDGE	_____	÷ 35 =	_____	× 100 = _____%	
PARAGRAPH COMPREHENSION	_____	÷ 15 =	_____	× 100 = _____%	
NUMERICAL OPERATIONS	_____	÷ 50 =	_____	× 100 = _____%	
CODING SPEED	_____	÷ 84 =	_____	× 100 = _____%	
AUTO & SHOP INFORMATION	_____	÷ 25 =	_____	× 100 = _____%	
MATHEMATICS KNOWLEDGE	_____	÷ 25 =	_____	× 100 = _____%	
MECHANICAL COMPREHENSION	_____	÷ 25 =	_____	× 100 = _____%	
ELECTRONICS INFORMATION	_____	÷ 20 =	_____	× 100 = _____%	
TOTAL	_____	÷ 334 =	_____	× 100 = _____%	

PROGRESS CHART

	Exam I	Exam II
GENERAL SCIENCE	%	%
ARITHMETIC REASONING	%	%
WORD KNOWLEDGE	%	%
PARAGRAPH COMPREHENSION	%	%
NUMERICAL OPERATIONS	%	%
CODING SPEED	%	%
AUTO & SHOP INFORMATION	%	%
MATHEMATICS KNOWLEDGE	%	%
MECHANICAL COMPREHENSION	%	%
ELECTRONICS INFORMATION	%	%
TOTAL	%	%

THIRD MODEL EXAM

ANSWER SHEET—THIRD MODEL EXAM

PART 1—GENERAL SCIENCE

1 Ⓐ Ⓑ Ⓒ Ⓓ   6 Ⓐ Ⓑ Ⓒ Ⓓ   11 Ⓐ Ⓑ Ⓒ Ⓓ   16 Ⓐ Ⓑ Ⓒ Ⓓ   21 Ⓐ Ⓑ Ⓒ Ⓓ

2 Ⓐ Ⓑ Ⓒ Ⓓ   7 Ⓐ Ⓑ Ⓒ Ⓓ   12 Ⓐ Ⓑ Ⓒ Ⓓ   17 Ⓐ Ⓑ Ⓒ Ⓓ   22 Ⓐ Ⓑ Ⓒ Ⓓ

3 Ⓐ Ⓑ Ⓒ Ⓓ   8 Ⓐ Ⓑ Ⓒ Ⓓ   13 Ⓐ Ⓑ Ⓒ Ⓓ   18 Ⓐ Ⓑ Ⓒ Ⓓ   23 Ⓐ Ⓑ Ⓒ Ⓓ

4 Ⓐ Ⓑ Ⓒ Ⓓ   9 Ⓐ Ⓑ Ⓒ Ⓓ   14 Ⓐ Ⓑ Ⓒ Ⓓ   19 Ⓐ Ⓑ Ⓒ Ⓓ   24 Ⓐ Ⓑ Ⓒ Ⓓ

5 Ⓐ Ⓑ Ⓒ Ⓓ   10 Ⓐ Ⓑ Ⓒ Ⓓ   15 Ⓐ Ⓑ Ⓒ Ⓓ   20 Ⓐ Ⓑ Ⓒ Ⓓ   25 Ⓐ Ⓑ Ⓒ Ⓓ

PART 2—ARITHMETIC REASONING

1 Ⓐ Ⓑ Ⓒ Ⓓ   7 Ⓐ Ⓑ Ⓒ Ⓓ   13 Ⓐ Ⓑ Ⓒ Ⓓ   19 Ⓐ Ⓑ Ⓒ Ⓓ   25 Ⓐ Ⓑ Ⓒ Ⓓ

2 Ⓐ Ⓑ Ⓒ Ⓓ   8 Ⓐ Ⓑ Ⓒ Ⓓ   14 Ⓐ Ⓑ Ⓒ Ⓓ   20 Ⓐ Ⓑ Ⓒ Ⓓ   26 Ⓐ Ⓑ Ⓒ Ⓓ

3 Ⓐ Ⓑ Ⓒ Ⓓ   9 Ⓐ Ⓑ Ⓒ Ⓓ   15 Ⓐ Ⓑ Ⓒ Ⓓ   21 Ⓐ Ⓑ Ⓒ Ⓓ   27 Ⓐ Ⓑ Ⓒ Ⓓ

4 Ⓐ Ⓑ Ⓒ Ⓓ   10 Ⓐ Ⓑ Ⓒ Ⓓ   16 Ⓐ Ⓑ Ⓒ Ⓓ   22 Ⓐ Ⓑ Ⓒ Ⓓ   28 Ⓐ Ⓑ Ⓒ Ⓓ

5 Ⓐ Ⓑ Ⓒ Ⓓ   11 Ⓐ Ⓑ Ⓒ Ⓓ   17 Ⓐ Ⓑ Ⓒ Ⓓ   23 Ⓐ Ⓑ Ⓒ Ⓓ   29 Ⓐ Ⓑ Ⓒ Ⓓ

6 Ⓐ Ⓑ Ⓒ Ⓓ   12 Ⓐ Ⓑ Ⓒ Ⓓ   18 Ⓐ Ⓑ Ⓒ Ⓓ   24 Ⓐ Ⓑ Ⓒ Ⓓ   30 Ⓐ Ⓑ Ⓒ Ⓓ

PART 3—WORD KNOWLEDGE

1 Ⓐ Ⓑ Ⓒ Ⓓ   8 Ⓐ Ⓑ Ⓒ Ⓓ   15 Ⓐ Ⓑ Ⓒ Ⓓ   22 Ⓐ Ⓑ Ⓒ Ⓓ   29 Ⓐ Ⓑ Ⓒ Ⓓ

2 Ⓐ Ⓑ Ⓒ Ⓓ   9 Ⓐ Ⓑ Ⓒ Ⓓ   16 Ⓐ Ⓑ Ⓒ Ⓓ   23 Ⓐ Ⓑ Ⓒ Ⓓ   30 Ⓐ Ⓑ Ⓒ Ⓓ

3 Ⓐ Ⓑ Ⓒ Ⓓ   10 Ⓐ Ⓑ Ⓒ Ⓓ   17 Ⓐ Ⓑ Ⓒ Ⓓ   24 Ⓐ Ⓑ Ⓒ Ⓓ   31 Ⓐ Ⓑ Ⓒ Ⓓ

4 Ⓐ Ⓑ Ⓒ Ⓓ   11 Ⓐ Ⓑ Ⓒ Ⓓ   18 Ⓐ Ⓑ Ⓒ Ⓓ   25 Ⓐ Ⓑ Ⓒ Ⓓ   32 Ⓐ Ⓑ Ⓒ Ⓓ

5 Ⓐ Ⓑ Ⓒ Ⓓ   12 Ⓐ Ⓑ Ⓒ Ⓓ   19 Ⓐ Ⓑ Ⓒ Ⓓ   26 Ⓐ Ⓑ Ⓒ Ⓓ   33 Ⓐ Ⓑ Ⓒ Ⓓ

6 Ⓐ Ⓑ Ⓒ Ⓓ   13 Ⓐ Ⓑ Ⓒ Ⓓ   20 Ⓐ Ⓑ Ⓒ Ⓓ   27 Ⓐ Ⓑ Ⓒ Ⓓ   34 Ⓐ Ⓑ Ⓒ Ⓓ

7 Ⓐ Ⓑ Ⓒ Ⓓ   14 Ⓐ Ⓑ Ⓒ Ⓓ   21 Ⓐ Ⓑ Ⓒ Ⓓ   28 Ⓐ Ⓑ Ⓒ Ⓓ   35 Ⓐ Ⓑ Ⓒ Ⓓ

PART 4—PARAGRAPH COMPREHENSION

1 Ⓐ Ⓑ Ⓒ Ⓓ   5 Ⓐ Ⓑ Ⓒ Ⓓ   9 Ⓐ Ⓑ Ⓒ Ⓓ   13 Ⓐ Ⓑ Ⓒ Ⓓ

2 Ⓐ Ⓑ Ⓒ Ⓓ   6 Ⓐ Ⓑ Ⓒ Ⓓ   10 Ⓐ Ⓑ Ⓒ Ⓓ   14 Ⓐ Ⓑ Ⓒ Ⓓ

3 Ⓐ Ⓑ Ⓒ Ⓓ   7 Ⓐ Ⓑ Ⓒ Ⓓ   11 Ⓐ Ⓑ Ⓒ Ⓓ   15 Ⓐ Ⓑ Ⓒ Ⓓ

4 Ⓐ Ⓑ Ⓒ Ⓓ   8 Ⓐ Ⓑ Ⓒ Ⓓ   12 Ⓐ Ⓑ Ⓒ Ⓓ

PART 5—NUMERICAL OPERATIONS

1 Ⓐ Ⓑ Ⓒ Ⓓ	11 Ⓐ Ⓑ Ⓒ Ⓓ	21 Ⓐ Ⓑ Ⓒ Ⓓ	31 Ⓐ Ⓑ Ⓒ Ⓓ	41 Ⓐ Ⓑ Ⓒ Ⓓ
2 Ⓐ Ⓑ Ⓒ Ⓓ	12 Ⓐ Ⓑ Ⓒ Ⓓ	22 Ⓐ Ⓑ Ⓒ Ⓓ	32 Ⓐ Ⓑ Ⓒ Ⓓ	42 Ⓐ Ⓑ Ⓒ Ⓓ
3 Ⓐ Ⓑ Ⓒ Ⓓ	13 Ⓐ Ⓑ Ⓒ Ⓓ	23 Ⓐ Ⓑ Ⓒ Ⓓ	33 Ⓐ Ⓑ Ⓒ Ⓓ	43 Ⓐ Ⓑ Ⓒ Ⓓ
4 Ⓐ Ⓑ Ⓒ Ⓓ	14 Ⓐ Ⓑ Ⓒ Ⓓ	24 Ⓐ Ⓑ Ⓒ Ⓓ	34 Ⓐ Ⓑ Ⓒ Ⓓ	44 Ⓐ Ⓑ Ⓒ Ⓓ
5 Ⓐ Ⓑ Ⓒ Ⓓ	15 Ⓐ Ⓑ Ⓒ Ⓓ	25 Ⓐ Ⓑ Ⓒ Ⓓ	35 Ⓐ Ⓑ Ⓒ Ⓓ	45 Ⓐ Ⓑ Ⓒ Ⓓ
6 Ⓐ Ⓑ Ⓒ Ⓓ	16 Ⓐ Ⓑ Ⓒ Ⓓ	26 Ⓐ Ⓑ Ⓒ Ⓓ	36 Ⓐ Ⓑ Ⓒ Ⓓ	46 Ⓐ Ⓑ Ⓒ Ⓓ
7 Ⓐ Ⓑ Ⓒ Ⓓ	17 Ⓐ Ⓑ Ⓒ Ⓓ	27 Ⓐ Ⓑ Ⓒ Ⓓ	37 Ⓐ Ⓑ Ⓒ Ⓓ	47 Ⓐ Ⓑ Ⓒ Ⓓ
8 Ⓐ Ⓑ Ⓒ Ⓓ	18 Ⓐ Ⓑ Ⓒ Ⓓ	28 Ⓐ Ⓑ Ⓒ Ⓓ	38 Ⓐ Ⓑ Ⓒ Ⓓ	48 Ⓐ Ⓑ Ⓒ Ⓓ
9 Ⓐ Ⓑ Ⓒ Ⓓ	19 Ⓐ Ⓑ Ⓒ Ⓓ	29 Ⓐ Ⓑ Ⓒ Ⓓ	39 Ⓐ Ⓑ Ⓒ Ⓓ	49 Ⓐ Ⓑ Ⓒ Ⓓ
10 Ⓐ Ⓑ Ⓒ Ⓓ	20 Ⓐ Ⓑ Ⓒ Ⓓ	30 Ⓐ Ⓑ Ⓒ Ⓓ	40 Ⓐ Ⓑ Ⓒ Ⓓ	50 Ⓐ Ⓑ Ⓒ Ⓓ

PART 6—CODING SPEED

1 Ⓐ Ⓑ Ⓒ Ⓓ Ⓔ	15 Ⓐ Ⓑ Ⓒ Ⓓ Ⓔ	29 Ⓐ Ⓑ Ⓒ Ⓓ Ⓔ	43 Ⓐ Ⓑ Ⓒ Ⓓ Ⓔ	57 Ⓐ Ⓑ Ⓒ Ⓓ Ⓔ	71 Ⓐ Ⓑ Ⓒ Ⓓ Ⓔ
2 Ⓐ Ⓑ Ⓒ Ⓓ Ⓔ	16 Ⓐ Ⓑ Ⓒ Ⓓ Ⓔ	30 Ⓐ Ⓑ Ⓒ Ⓓ Ⓔ	44 Ⓐ Ⓑ Ⓒ Ⓓ Ⓔ	58 Ⓐ Ⓑ Ⓒ Ⓓ Ⓔ	72 Ⓐ Ⓑ Ⓒ Ⓓ Ⓔ
3 Ⓐ Ⓑ Ⓒ Ⓓ Ⓔ	17 Ⓐ Ⓑ Ⓒ Ⓓ Ⓔ	31 Ⓐ Ⓑ Ⓒ Ⓓ Ⓔ	45 Ⓐ Ⓑ Ⓒ Ⓓ Ⓔ	59 Ⓐ Ⓑ Ⓒ Ⓓ Ⓔ	73 Ⓐ Ⓑ Ⓒ Ⓓ Ⓔ
4 Ⓐ Ⓑ Ⓒ Ⓓ Ⓔ	18 Ⓐ Ⓑ Ⓒ Ⓓ Ⓔ	32 Ⓐ Ⓑ Ⓒ Ⓓ Ⓔ	46 Ⓐ Ⓑ Ⓒ Ⓓ Ⓔ	60 Ⓐ Ⓑ Ⓒ Ⓓ Ⓔ	74 Ⓐ Ⓑ Ⓒ Ⓓ Ⓔ
5 Ⓐ Ⓑ Ⓒ Ⓓ Ⓔ	19 Ⓐ Ⓑ Ⓒ Ⓓ Ⓔ	33 Ⓐ Ⓑ Ⓒ Ⓓ Ⓔ	47 Ⓐ Ⓑ Ⓒ Ⓓ Ⓔ	61 Ⓐ Ⓑ Ⓒ Ⓓ Ⓔ	75 Ⓐ Ⓑ Ⓒ Ⓓ Ⓔ
6 Ⓐ Ⓑ Ⓒ Ⓓ Ⓔ	20 Ⓐ Ⓑ Ⓒ Ⓓ Ⓔ	34 Ⓐ Ⓑ Ⓒ Ⓓ Ⓔ	48 Ⓐ Ⓑ Ⓒ Ⓓ Ⓔ	62 Ⓐ Ⓑ Ⓒ Ⓓ Ⓔ	76 Ⓐ Ⓑ Ⓒ Ⓓ Ⓔ
7 Ⓐ Ⓑ Ⓒ Ⓓ Ⓕ	21 Ⓐ Ⓑ Ⓒ Ⓓ Ⓔ	35 Ⓐ Ⓑ Ⓒ Ⓓ Ⓔ	49 Ⓐ Ⓑ Ⓒ Ⓓ Ⓔ	63 Ⓐ Ⓑ Ⓒ Ⓓ Ⓔ	77 Ⓐ Ⓑ Ⓒ Ⓓ Ⓔ
8 Ⓐ Ⓑ Ⓒ Ⓓ Ⓔ	22 Ⓐ Ⓑ Ⓒ Ⓓ Ⓔ	36 Ⓐ Ⓑ Ⓒ Ⓓ Ⓔ	50 Ⓐ Ⓑ Ⓒ Ⓓ Ⓔ	64 Ⓐ Ⓑ Ⓒ Ⓓ Ⓔ	78 Ⓐ Ⓑ Ⓒ Ⓓ Ⓔ
9 Ⓐ Ⓑ Ⓒ Ⓓ Ⓔ	23 Ⓐ Ⓑ Ⓒ Ⓓ Ⓔ	37 Ⓐ Ⓑ Ⓒ Ⓓ Ⓔ	51 Ⓐ Ⓑ Ⓒ Ⓓ Ⓔ	65 Ⓐ Ⓑ Ⓒ Ⓓ Ⓔ	79 Ⓐ Ⓑ Ⓒ Ⓓ Ⓔ
10 Ⓐ Ⓑ Ⓒ Ⓓ Ⓔ	24 Ⓐ Ⓑ Ⓒ Ⓓ Ⓔ	38 Ⓐ Ⓑ Ⓒ Ⓓ Ⓔ	52 Ⓐ Ⓑ Ⓒ Ⓓ Ⓔ	66 Ⓐ Ⓑ Ⓒ Ⓓ Ⓔ	80 Ⓐ Ⓑ Ⓒ Ⓓ Ⓔ
11 Ⓐ Ⓑ Ⓒ Ⓓ Ⓔ	25 Ⓐ Ⓑ Ⓒ Ⓓ Ⓔ	39 Ⓐ Ⓑ Ⓒ Ⓓ Ⓔ	53 Ⓐ Ⓑ Ⓒ Ⓓ Ⓔ	67 Ⓐ Ⓑ Ⓒ Ⓓ Ⓔ	81 Ⓐ Ⓑ Ⓒ Ⓓ Ⓔ
12 Ⓐ Ⓑ Ⓒ Ⓓ Ⓔ	26 Ⓐ Ⓑ Ⓒ Ⓓ Ⓔ	40 Ⓐ Ⓑ Ⓒ Ⓓ Ⓔ	54 Ⓐ Ⓑ Ⓒ Ⓓ Ⓔ	68 Ⓐ Ⓑ Ⓒ Ⓓ Ⓔ	82 Ⓐ Ⓑ Ⓒ Ⓓ Ⓔ
13 Ⓐ Ⓑ Ⓒ Ⓓ Ⓔ	27 Ⓐ Ⓑ Ⓒ Ⓓ Ⓔ	41 Ⓐ Ⓑ Ⓒ Ⓓ Ⓔ	55 Ⓐ Ⓑ Ⓒ Ⓓ Ⓔ	69 Ⓐ Ⓑ Ⓒ Ⓓ Ⓔ	83 Ⓐ Ⓑ Ⓒ Ⓓ Ⓔ
14 Ⓐ Ⓑ Ⓒ Ⓓ Ⓔ	28 Ⓐ Ⓑ Ⓒ Ⓓ Ⓔ	42 Ⓐ Ⓑ Ⓒ Ⓓ Ⓔ	56 Ⓐ Ⓑ Ⓒ Ⓓ Ⓔ	70 Ⓐ Ⓑ Ⓒ Ⓓ Ⓔ	84 Ⓐ Ⓑ Ⓒ Ⓓ Ⓔ

PART 7—AUTO & SHOP INFORMATION

1 Ⓐ Ⓑ Ⓒ Ⓓ	6 Ⓐ Ⓑ Ⓒ Ⓓ	11 Ⓐ Ⓑ Ⓒ Ⓓ	16 Ⓐ Ⓑ Ⓒ Ⓓ	21 Ⓐ Ⓑ Ⓒ Ⓓ
2 Ⓐ Ⓑ Ⓒ Ⓓ	7 Ⓐ Ⓑ Ⓒ Ⓓ	12 Ⓐ Ⓑ Ⓒ Ⓓ	17 Ⓐ Ⓑ Ⓒ Ⓓ	22 Ⓐ Ⓑ Ⓒ Ⓓ
3 Ⓐ Ⓑ Ⓒ Ⓓ	8 Ⓐ Ⓑ Ⓒ Ⓓ	13 Ⓐ Ⓑ Ⓒ Ⓓ	18 Ⓐ Ⓑ Ⓒ Ⓓ	23 Ⓐ Ⓑ Ⓒ Ⓓ
4 Ⓐ Ⓑ Ⓒ Ⓓ	9 Ⓐ Ⓑ Ⓒ Ⓓ	14 Ⓐ Ⓑ Ⓒ Ⓓ	19 Ⓐ Ⓑ Ⓒ Ⓓ	24 Ⓐ Ⓑ Ⓒ Ⓓ
5 Ⓐ Ⓑ Ⓒ Ⓓ	10 Ⓐ Ⓑ Ⓒ Ⓓ	15 Ⓐ Ⓑ Ⓒ Ⓓ	20 Ⓐ Ⓑ Ⓒ Ⓓ	25 Ⓐ Ⓑ Ⓒ Ⓓ

PART 8—MATHEMATICS KNOWLEDGE

1 Ⓐ Ⓑ Ⓒ Ⓓ	6 Ⓐ Ⓑ Ⓒ Ⓓ	11 Ⓐ Ⓑ Ⓒ Ⓓ	16 Ⓐ Ⓑ Ⓒ Ⓓ	21 Ⓐ Ⓑ Ⓒ Ⓓ
2 Ⓐ Ⓑ Ⓒ Ⓓ	7 Ⓐ Ⓑ Ⓒ Ⓓ	12 Ⓐ Ⓑ Ⓒ Ⓓ	17 Ⓐ Ⓑ Ⓒ Ⓓ	22 Ⓐ Ⓑ Ⓒ Ⓓ
3 Ⓐ Ⓑ Ⓒ Ⓓ	8 Ⓐ Ⓑ Ⓒ Ⓓ	13 Ⓐ Ⓑ Ⓒ Ⓓ	18 Ⓐ Ⓑ Ⓒ Ⓓ	23 Ⓐ Ⓑ Ⓒ Ⓓ
4 Ⓐ Ⓑ Ⓒ Ⓓ	9 Ⓐ Ⓑ Ⓒ Ⓓ	14 Ⓐ Ⓑ Ⓒ Ⓓ	19 Ⓐ Ⓑ Ⓒ Ⓓ	24 Ⓐ Ⓑ Ⓒ Ⓓ
5 Ⓐ Ⓑ Ⓒ Ⓓ	10 Ⓐ Ⓑ Ⓒ Ⓓ	15 Ⓐ Ⓑ Ⓒ Ⓓ	20 Ⓐ Ⓑ Ⓒ Ⓓ	25 Ⓐ Ⓑ Ⓒ Ⓓ

PART 9—MECHANICAL COMPREHENSION

1 Ⓐ Ⓑ Ⓒ Ⓓ	6 Ⓐ Ⓑ Ⓒ Ⓓ	11 Ⓐ Ⓑ Ⓒ Ⓓ	16 Ⓐ Ⓑ Ⓒ Ⓓ	21 Ⓐ Ⓑ Ⓒ Ⓓ
2 Ⓐ Ⓑ Ⓒ Ⓓ	7 Ⓐ Ⓑ Ⓒ Ⓓ	12 Ⓐ Ⓑ Ⓒ Ⓓ	17 Ⓐ Ⓑ Ⓒ Ⓓ	22 Ⓐ Ⓑ Ⓒ Ⓓ
3 Ⓐ Ⓑ Ⓒ Ⓓ	8 Ⓐ Ⓑ Ⓒ Ⓓ	13 Ⓐ Ⓑ Ⓒ Ⓓ	18 Ⓐ Ⓑ Ⓒ Ⓓ	23 Ⓐ Ⓑ Ⓒ Ⓓ
4 Ⓐ Ⓑ Ⓒ Ⓓ	9 Ⓐ Ⓑ Ⓒ Ⓓ	14 Ⓐ Ⓑ Ⓒ Ⓓ	19 Ⓐ Ⓑ Ⓒ Ⓓ	24 Ⓐ Ⓑ Ⓒ Ⓓ
5 Ⓐ Ⓑ Ⓒ Ⓓ	10 Ⓐ Ⓑ Ⓒ Ⓓ	15 Ⓐ Ⓑ Ⓒ Ⓓ	20 Ⓐ Ⓑ Ⓒ Ⓓ	25 Ⓐ Ⓑ Ⓒ Ⓓ

PART 10—ELECTRONICS INFORMATION

1 Ⓐ Ⓑ Ⓒ Ⓓ	6 Ⓐ Ⓑ Ⓒ Ⓓ	11 Ⓐ Ⓑ Ⓒ Ⓓ	16 Ⓐ Ⓑ Ⓒ Ⓓ
2 Ⓐ Ⓑ Ⓒ Ⓓ	7 Ⓐ Ⓑ Ⓒ Ⓓ	12 Ⓐ Ⓑ Ⓒ Ⓓ	17 Ⓐ Ⓑ Ⓒ Ⓓ
3 Ⓐ Ⓑ Ⓒ Ⓓ	8 Ⓐ Ⓑ Ⓒ Ⓓ	13 Ⓐ Ⓑ Ⓒ Ⓓ	18 Ⓐ Ⓑ Ⓒ Ⓓ
4 Ⓐ Ⓑ Ⓒ Ⓓ	9 Ⓐ Ⓑ Ⓒ Ⓓ	14 Ⓐ Ⓑ Ⓒ Ⓓ	19 Ⓐ Ⓑ Ⓒ Ⓓ
5 Ⓐ Ⓑ Ⓒ Ⓓ	10 Ⓐ Ⓑ Ⓒ Ⓓ	15 Ⓐ Ⓑ Ⓒ Ⓓ	20 Ⓐ Ⓑ Ⓒ Ⓓ

GENERAL SCIENCE

The general science part of your examination asks questions based upon the science you learned in high school. For each question there are four possible answers. Only one answer is correct. Choose the answer which you think is correct and mark the corresponding space on your answer sheet. Try these questions.

1. The functions of plant roots may normally include all of the following *except*

1-A photosynthesis
1-B absorption
1-C food storage
1-D support

1. Ⓐ Ⓑ Ⓒ Ⓓ

1-A PHOTOSYNTHESIS is the correct answer. Photosynthesis is the process by which the leaves of a plant manufacture food for that plant. Since light is required for photosynthesis, the roots of the plant are not involved with the process. The roots do help store the food (C), absorb water (B) and support the plant (D).

2. Of the following, the physical property *least* frequently used in determining the nature of an unknown chemical is

2-A taste
2-B odor
2-C solubility
2-D state

2. Ⓐ Ⓑ Ⓒ Ⓓ

2-A TASTE is the correct answer. An unknown substance might well be poisonous, hence it is dangerous to routinely use a taste test. Odor (B), solubility (C) and state (solid, liquid, gaseous) (D) are all less hazardous measures for use in the chemical laboratory.

3. The "wind chill factor" as reported by weather forecasters affects

3-A the speed of the wind
3-B the freezing point of water
3-C the amount of snow likely
3-D how cold you feel

3. Ⓐ Ⓑ Ⓒ Ⓓ

3-D HOW COLD YOU FEEL is the correct answer. The wind chill factor is based on a mathematical formula which describes the effect upon the senses of the combined temperature and wind speed. The wind chill factor is affected by the speed of the wind (A), not vice-versa. Water freezes at 32° F or 0° C (B). The amount of snowfall (C) is not dependent on the wind chill factor.

4. Cholesterol is

4-A a basic part of bone structure
4-B a carbohydrate
4-C a substance found in blood
4-D the cause of colitis

4. Ⓐ Ⓑ Ⓒ Ⓓ

4-C A SUBSTANCE FOUND IN BLOOD is the correct answer. Cholesterol is an alcohol formed in the body. While cholesterol is important to the proper function of nerves, excess amounts in the blood may cause the clogging of arteries and lead to heart attacks. In some individuals dietary fat contributes to the buildup of cholesterol in the blood. The substance basic to bones (A) is calcium. Cholesterol is not a carbohydrate (B), nor is it known to be a cause of colitis (D), inflamation of the large intestine.

DO NOT TURN THE PAGE UNTIL YOU ARE TOLD TO DO SO

GENERAL SCIENCE

TIME: 11 Minutes—25 Questions

1. The only pouched mammal native to the United States is the

   1-A kangaroo
   1-B armadillo
   1-C opossum
   1-D raccoon

2. The transparent, slightly bulging tissue that covers the front sixth of the eyeball and is frequently referred to as the "window of the eyes" is the:

   2-A iris
   2-B sciera
   2-C cornea
   2-D retina

3. Of the following, a condition *not* associated with heavy cigarette smoking is

   3-A shorter life span
   3-B slowing of the heartbeat
   3-C cancer of the lung
   3-D heart disease

4. The Wassermann test may indicate the presence of

   4-A syphilis
   4-B tuberculosis
   4-C measles
   4-D polio

5. A person with high blood-pressure should

   5-A take frequent naps
   5-B avoid salt
   5-C eat only iodized salt
   5-D exercise vigorously

6. During what season is hail most likely to occur during thunderstorms?

   6-A fall
   6-B spring
   6-C winter
   6-D summer

7. The process which is responsible for the continuous removal of carbon dioxide from the atmosphere is

   7-A respiration
   7-B oxidation
   7-C metabolism
   7-D photosynthesis

8. An important ore of uranium is called

   8-A hematite
   8-B chalcopyrite
   8-C bauxite
   8-D pitchblende

9. The time that it takes for the earth to complete a 60 degree rotation is

   9-A 1 hour
   9-B 6 hours
   9-C 4 hours
   9-D 24 hours

10. Saliva contains an enzyme which acts on

    10-A carbohydrates
    10-B proteins
    10-C minerals
    10-D vitamins

11. The time it takes for light from the sun to reach the earth is approximately

    11-A four years
    11-B eight minutes
    11-C four months
    11-D sixteen years

12. Of the following, the statement that best describes a "high" on a weather map is

12-A   the air extends farther up than normal
12-B   the air pressure is greater than normal
12-C   the air temperature is higher than normal
12-D   the air moves faster than normal

13. To reduce soil acidity a farmer should use

13-A   lime
13-B   phosphate
13-C   manure
13-D   peat moss

14. The statement that carrots help one to see in the dark is

14-A   ridiculous
14-B   reasonable because orange is a reflective color
14-C   reasonable because carrots are high in Vitamin A
14-D   reasonable because rabbits see very well at night

15. The primary reason why fungi are often found growing in abundance deep in the forest is that there

15-A   it is cooler
15-B   it is warmer
15-C   they have little exposure to sunlight for photosynthesis
15-D   they have a plentiful supply of organic matter

16. Of the following, the food which contains the largest amount of Vitamin C is

16-A   carrots
16-B   sweet potatoes
16-C   lima beans
16-D   tomatoes

17. Limes were eaten by British sailors in order to

17-A   justify their nickname, "Limeys"
17-B   pucker their mouths to resist the wind
17-C   satisfy their craving for something acid
17-D   prevent scurvy

18. A 1000-ton ship must displace a weight of water equal to

18-A   500 tons
18-B   1500 tons
18-C   1000 tons
18-D   2000 tons

19. A person is more buoyant when swimming in salt water than in fresh water because

19-A   he keeps his head out of salt water
19-B   salt coats his body with a floating membrane
19-C   salt water has greater tensile strength
19-D   salt water weighs more than an equal volume of fresh water

20. All of the following are Amphibia *except* the

20-A   salamander
20-B   frog
20-C   lizard
20-D   toad

21. The normal height of a mercury barometer at sea level is

21-A   15 inches
21-B   32 feet
21-C   30 inches
21-D   34 feet

22. A tumor is

22-A   cancer
22-B   a growth
22-C   a sore spot
22-D   a kind of mushroom

23. A circuit breaker is used in many homes instead of a

23-A   switch
23-B   fire extinguisher
23-C   fuse
23-D   meter box

24. Of the following substances, the one which is non-magnetic is

24-A   iron
24-B   aluminum

24-C nickel
24-D cobalt

25. Of the following animals, the one which is most closely related to the extinct dinosaur is the

25-A sloth
25-B lizard
25-C elephant
25-D whale

STOP

IF YOU FINISH THIS PART BEFORE THE TIME IS UP, CHECK OVER YOUR WORK ON THIS PART ONLY. DO NOT GO ON UNTIL YOU ARE TOLD TO DO SO.

PART 2

ARITHMETIC REASONING

The arithmetic reasoning questions require careful thinking as well as arithmetic calculation. Some problems require more than one step for their solutions. You must decide exactly what the question asks; then you must determine the best method for finding the answer; finally, you must work out the problem on your scratch paper. Be sure to mark the letter of the correct answer on your answer sheet. Try these questions.

1. Six girls sold the following number of boxes of cookies: 42, 35, 28, 30, 24, 27. What was the average number of boxes sold by each girl?

1-A 26
1-B 29
1-C 30
1-D 31

1. Ⓐ Ⓑ Ⓒ Ⓓ

1-D To find the average, add all the numbers and divide the sum by the number of terms. 42 + 35 + 28 + 30 + 24 + 27 = 186 ÷ 6 = 31

2. The cost of sending a telegram is 52 cents for the first ten words and $2\frac{1}{2}$ cents for each additional word. The cost of sending a 14-word telegram is

2-A 62 cents
2-B 63 cents
2-C 69 cents
2-D 87 cents

2. Ⓐ Ⓑ Ⓒ Ⓓ

2-A 14 words = 10 words + 4 words
10 words cost 52 cents
4 words @ 2.5 cents = 4 × 2.5 = 10 cents
52 cents + 10 cents = 62 cents

3. Perform the indicated operations and express your answer in inches: 12 feet, minus 7 inches, plus 2 feet 1 inch, minus 7 feet, minus 1 yard, plus 2 yards 1 foot 3 inches.

3-A 130 inches
3-B 128 inches

3-C 129 inches
3-D 131 inches

3. Ⓐ Ⓑ Ⓒ Ⓓ

3-C First convert all the yards and feet into inches so that all addition and subtraction can be done using the same units.

$$
\begin{array}{rl}
12 \text{ feet} = & 144 \text{ inches} \\
-7 \text{ inches} = - & 7 \text{ inches} \\
+2 \text{ feet, 1 inch} = + & 25 \text{ inches} \\
-7 \text{ feet} = - & 84 \text{ inches} \\
-1 \text{ yard} = - & 36 \text{ inches} \\
+2 \text{ yards, 1 foot, 3 inches} = + & \underline{87 \text{ inches}} \\
& 129 \text{ inches}
\end{array}
$$

4. Two years ago a company purchased 500 dozen pencils at 40 cents per dozen. This year only 75 percent as many pencils were purchased as were purchased two years ago, but the price was 20 percent higher than the old price. What was the total cost of pencils purchased by the company this year?

4-A $180
4-B $187.50
4-C $240
4-D $257.40

4. Ⓐ Ⓑ Ⓒ Ⓓ

4-A 500 dozen @ $.40 per dozen = purchase of two years ago
75% of 500 dozen = 375 dozen pencils purchased this year
20% of $.40 = $.08 increase in cost per dozen
375 × $.48 = $180 spent on pencils this year

DO NOT TURN THE PAGE UNTIL YOU ARE TOLD TO DO SO

ARITHMETIC REASONING

TIME: 36 Minutes—30 Questions

1. A man owned 75 shares of stock worth $50 each. The corporation declared a dividend of 8%, payable in stock. How many shares did he then own?

   1-A 81 shares
   1-B 90 shares
   1-C 80 shares
   1-D 85 shares

2. If a load of snow contains 3 tons, it will weigh how many lbs.?

   2-A 3,000 lbs.
   2-B 1,500 lbs.
   2-C 12,000 lbs.
   2-D 6,000 lbs.

3. If a woman bought some pillow cases for a total cost of $8.46, and the average per unit cost was $2.82, how many pillow cases did she buy?

   3-A 4
   3-B 2
   3-C 3
   3-D 5

4. A clerk divided his 35 hour work week as follows: $\frac{1}{5}$ of his time in sorting mail; $\frac{1}{2}$ of his time in filing letters; and $\frac{1}{7}$ of his time in reception work. The rest of his time was devoted to messenger work. The percentage of time spent on messenger work by the clerk during the week was most nearly

   4-A 6%
   4-B 14%
   4-C 10%
   4-D 16%

5. A boy deposited in his savings account the money he had saved during the summer. Find the amount of his deposit if he had 10 one-dollar bills, 9 half dollars, 8 quarters, 16 dimes, and 25 nickels.

   5-A $16.20
   5-B $17.42
   5-C $18.60
   5-D $19.35

6. One-sixth of an audience consisted of boys and $\frac{1}{3}$ of it consisted of girls. What percent of the audience consisted of children?

   6-A $66\frac{2}{3}$
   6-B 50
   6-C $37\frac{1}{2}$
   6-D 40

7. Six gross of special drawing pencils were purchased for use in a City department. If the pencils were used at the rate of 24 a week, the maximum number of weeks that the six gross of pencils would last is

   7-A 6 weeks
   7-B 24 weeks
   7-C 12 weeks
   7-D 36 weeks

8. On a scale drawing, a line $\frac{1}{4}$ inch long represents a length of 1 foot. On the same drawing, what length represents 4 feet?

   8-A 1 inch
   8-B 2 inches
   8-C 3 inches
   8-D 4 inches

9. It costs 31 cents a square foot to lay linoleum. To lay 20 square yards of linoleum it will cost

9-A $16.20
9-B $18.60
9-C $55.80
9-D $62.00

10. A teenager had to walk 2 miles to school. If he walked at an average of 3 miles per hour, how many minutes did it take him to walk to school?

10-A 40
10-B 20
10-C 50
10-D 45

11. If 3 apples cost 24¢, how many dozen apples can be bought for $1.92?

11-A $1\frac{1}{2}$
11-B 1
11-C 2
11-D $5\frac{1}{3}$

12. What is the simple interest on $600 at 4% for 2 years?

12-A $36
12-B $52
12-C $48
12-D $56

13. A man deposited a check for $1000 to open an account. Shortly after that, he withdrew $941.20. How much did he have left in his account?

13-A $56.72
13-B $58.80
13-C $59.09
13-D $60.60

14. A man's weekly salary is increased from $350 to $380. The percent of increase is, most nearly,

14-A 6 percent
14-B $8\frac{1}{2}$ percent
14-C 10 percent
14-D $12\frac{1}{2}$ percent

15. A team played 24 games of which it won 18. What percent of the games played did it win?

15-A 50%
15-B 80%
15-C 75%
15-D 85%

16. The temperature yesterday at noon was 68.5 degrees. Today at noon it was 59.9 degrees. What was the difference in temperature?

16-A 8.4 degrees
16-B 8.5 degrees
16-C 8.6 degrees
16-D 8.7 degrees

17. If a salary of $20,000 is subject to a 20 percent deduction, the net salary is

17-A $14,000
17-B $15,500
17-C $16,000
17-D $18,000

18. A man earns $20.56 on Monday; $32.90 on Tuesday; $20.78 on Wednesday. He spends half of all that he earns during the three days. How much has he left?

18-A $29.19
18-B $31.23
18-C $34.27
18-D $37.12

19. A woman bought a house dress for $17.95, a purse for $10.95, and a warm hat for $7.95. What is the total amount she had to pay for these items?

19-A $35.75
19-B $36.85
19-C $26.85
19-D $34.85

20. If an annual salary of $21,600 is increased by a bonus of $720 and by a service increment of $1200, the total pay rate is

20-A $22,320
20-B $22,800
20-C $23,320
20-D $23,520

21. A boy saved up $4.56 the first month, $3.82

the second month, and $5.06 the third month. How much did he save altogether?

21-A $12.56
21-B $13.28
21-C $13.44
21-D $14.02

22. A woman bowled 3 games. Her scores were 136, 133, and 139. She had an average of 134 for her previous 3 games. What is her average now?

22-A 135
22-B 138
22-C 136
22-D 134

23. A recipe for a cake calls for $2\frac{1}{2}$ cups of milk and 3 cups of flour. With this recipe, a cake was baked using 14 cups of flour. How many cups of milk were required?

23-A $10\frac{1}{3}$
23-B $10\frac{3}{4}$
23-C 11
23-D $11\frac{2}{3}$

24. The daily almanac report for one day during the summer stated that the sun rose at 6:14 a.m. and set at 6:06 p.m. Find the number of hours and minutes in the time between the rising and setting of the sun on that day.

24-A 11 hr. 52 min.
24-B 11 hr. 2 min.
24-C 12 hr. 8 min.
24-D 12 hr. 48 min.

25. An officer traveled 1200 miles in 20 hours. How many miles per hour did she average?

25-A 45
25-B 60
25-C 50
25-D 65

26. The number of half-pound packages of tea that can be made up from a box which holds $10\frac{1}{4}$ pounds of tea is

26-A 5
26-B $10\frac{1}{2}$
26-C 20
26-D $20\frac{1}{2}$

27. How many slices of bread, each weighing 2 ounces, are needed to balance 2 pounds of apples?

27-A 8
27-B 12
27-C 16
27-D 24

28. A girl had to buy a sweater, a blouse, and a scarf. The sweater cost $21.00, the blouse $14.98, and the scarf $4.97. What was the total cost of her purchases?

28-A $35.50
28-B $40.85
28-C $30.85
28-D $40.95

29. Five girls each ate 3 cookies from a box containing 2 dozen. What part of a dozen was left?

29-A $\frac{1}{8}$
29-B $\frac{1}{4}$
29-C $\frac{3}{4}$
29-D $\frac{7}{8}$

30. A night watchman must check a certain storage area every 45 minutes. If he first checks the area as he begins a 9-hour tour of duty, how many times will he have checked this storage area?

30-A 10
30-B 11
30-C 12
30-D 13

END OF PART 2

IF YOU FINISH BEFORE THE TIME IS UP, CHECK TO BE CERTAIN THAT YOU HAVE MARKED ALL OF YOUR ANSWERS ON THE ANSWER SHEET. THEN CHECK OVER YOUR WORK ON THIS PART ONLY. DO NOT RETURN TO PART ONE. DO NOT GO ON TO THE NEXT PART UNTIL YOU ARE TOLD TO DO SO.

PART 3

WORD KNOWLEDGE

The questions in this part test how well you understand the meanings of words. Each question has an underlined word. Read all four possible answers and decide which one has a meaning closest to the meaning of the underlined word. On your answer sheet mark the letter of the answer you choose. Try these questions.

1. Speak most nearly means

   1-A tell
   1-B talk
   1-C explain
   1-D question

1. Ⓐ Ⓑ Ⓒ Ⓓ

1-B TALK is the correct answer. When one *speaks* or *talks* one may *tell* (A), *explain* (C) or *question* (D). Since both *speak* and *talk* include all the other choices, they are most nearly alike in meaning.

2. They discovered the missing boxes in the morning.

   2-A sought
   2-B opened
   2-C found
   2-D noticed

2. Ⓐ Ⓑ Ⓒ Ⓓ

2-C FOUND is the best answer. *Noticed* (D) could be a correct answer, but, since the boxes were missing, a search is suggested and *found* is the best meaning for *discovered*. (A) *sought* and (B) *opened* are wrong.

3. The rent bill is payable on the first of the month.

   3-A late
   3-B profitable
   3-C due
   3-D paid

3. Ⓐ Ⓑ Ⓒ Ⓓ

3-C DUE is the only correct answer. A bill which is *payable* is *due;* it is not yet *late* (A) nor has it been *paid* (D). *Profitable* (B) is not the meaning of *payable*.

4. Oral most nearly means

   4-A spoken
   4-B loud
   4-C secret
   4-D by heart

4. Ⓐ Ⓑ Ⓒ Ⓓ

4-A SPOKEN is the correct answer. Something *oral* is always *spoken,* whether *loudly* (B) or in *secret* (C) or *from memory* (D).

5. The novice skier broke his ankle when he fell.

   5-A competitive
   5-B clumsy
   5-C aged
   5-D beginning

5. Ⓐ Ⓑ Ⓒ Ⓓ

5-D BEGINNING is the correct answer. A *novice* is a *beginner.* A *novice* may, of course, be *competitive* (A), *clumsy* (B) or *aged* (D), but it is his being a *beginner* that makes him a *novice*.

6. Perform most nearly means

   6-A fail
   6-B applaud
   6-C do
   6-D exchange

6. Ⓐ Ⓑ Ⓒ Ⓓ

6-C DO is the correct answer. *Perform* has a number of meanings, including *act, accomplish* and *fulfill,* but the only meaning given here is *do.* All the other choices are wrong.

DO NOT TURN THE PAGE UNTIL YOU ARE TOLD TO DO SO

WORD KNOWLEDGE

TIME: 11 Minutes—35 Questions

1. <u>Revenue</u> most nearly means

   1-A taxes
   1-B income
   1-C expenses
   1-D produce

2. <u>Purchase</u> most nearly means

   2-A charge
   2-B supply
   2-C order
   2-D buy

3. Be careful, that liquid is <u>inflammable</u>!

   3-A poisonous
   3-B valuable
   3-C explosive
   3-D likely to give off fumes

4. <u>Deportment</u> most nearly means

   4-A attendance
   4-B intelligence
   4-C neatness
   4-D behavior

5. <u>Customary</u> most nearly means

   5-A curious
   5-B necessary
   5-C difficult
   5-D common

6. We <u>assumed</u> that our candidate had been elected.

   6-A knew
   6-B wished
   6-C decided
   6-D supposed

7. <u>Approximate</u> most nearly means

   7-A mathematically correct
   7-B nearly exact
   7-C remarkable
   7-D worthless

8. <u>Vegetation</u> most nearly means

   8-A food
   8-B plant life
   8-C moisture
   8-D bird life

9. <u>Marshy</u> most nearly means

   9-A swampy
   9-B sandy
   9-C wooded
   9-D rocky

10. All air traffic was <u>suspended</u> during the emergency.

    10-A turned back
    10-B checked carefully
    10-C regulated strictly
    10-D stopped temporarily

11. The <u>preface</u> of the book was very interesting.

    11-A title page
    11-B introduction
    11-C table of contents
    11-D appendix

12. <u>Summit</u> most nearly means

    12-A face
    12-B top
    12-C base
    12-D side

13. Prevented most nearly means

    13-A allowed
    13-B suggested
    13-C hindered —
    13-D urged

14. It is my conviction that you are wrong.

    14-A guilt
    14-B imagination
    14-C firm belief —
    14-D fault

15. Imitate most nearly means

    15-A copy —
    15-B attract
    15-C study
    15-D appreciate

16. Irritating most nearly means

    16-A nervous
    16-B unsuitable
    16-C annoying —
    16-D noisy

17. Concisely most nearly means

    17-A accurately
    17-B briefly
    17-C fully
    17-D officially

18. With a full month for vacation, we made a very leisurely trip to California.

    18-A roundabout
    18-B unhurried —
    18-C unforgettable
    18-D tiresome

19. The sailors reached the shore in a landing barge.

    19-A gulf
    19-B coast —
    19-C inlet
    19-D alien

20. The aim of the enlistee was to join the Navy.

    20-A bullseye
    20-B goal
    20-C duty
    20-D promise

21. He had an acute pain in his back.

    21-A dull
    21-B slight
    21-C alarming
    21-D sharp —

22. Instructor most nearly means

    22-A expert
    22-B assistant
    22-C teacher —
    22-D foreman

23. Compel most nearly means

    23-A tempt
    23-B persuade
    23-C force —
    23-D disable

24. Don't you like the aroma of fresh-brewed coffee?

    24-A flavor
    24-B warmth
    24-C fragrance —
    24-D steam

25. Alert most nearly means

    25-A watchful —
    25-B busy
    25-C helpful
    25-D honest

26. Forthcoming events are listed on the bulletin board.

    26-A weekly
    26-B interesting
    26-C social
    26-D approaching —

27. One of the cars in the accident remained intact.

    27-A unattended
    27-B undamaged —

27-C a total loss
27-D unmoved

28. The <u>blemish</u> on the tomato appears to be caused by disease.

28-A color
28-B insect
28-C flaw
28-D design

29. In his hand the hiker carried a sturdy <u>staff</u>.

29-A pack
29-B stick
29-C loaf
29-D musical instrument

30. The face on the poster was that of a <u>notorious</u> bank robber,

30-A convicted
30-B dangerous
30-C well-known
30-D escaped

31. <u>Attorney</u> most nearly means

31-A banker
31-B lawyer

31-C foot doctor
31-D accountant

32. <u>Exhaustion</u> most nearly means

32-A fear
32-B overconfidence
32-C extreme tiredness
32-D unsteadiness

33. <u>Technique</u> most nearly means

33-A computed
33-B engineered
33-C calculation
33-D method

34. The only sound was the <u>steady</u> ticking of the clock.

34-A noisy
34-B eerie
34-C tiresome
34-D regular

35. The hikers noticed several <u>crevices</u> in the rocks.

35-A plants
35-B uneven spots
35-C cracks
35-D puddles

END OF PART 3

IF YOU FINISH BEFORE TIME IS UP, CHECK YOUR WORK ON THIS PART ONLY. DO NOT GO BACK TO EITHER PREVIOUS PART. DO NOT GO ON TO THE NEXT PART UNTIL YOU ARE TOLD TO DO SO.

PART 4

PARAGRAPH COMPREHENSION

The paragraph comprehension part of your test battery requires concentration and attention to detail. First you must read and understand the paragraph. Then you must read and understand each of the answer choices, noticing the differences of meaning or emphasis that are imparted by little words. There is one question based upon each paragraph. You must answer that question on the basis of what is stated or implied in the passage, even if you know a better answer and even if you know the information in the paragraph to be false. In some cases more than one answer might be correct, but you must choose the BEST answer and mark its letter on your answer sheet. Try these questions.

1. Life is too short for one person to do very many things well. The person who determines fairly early what he can do that he likes to do, and who goes at it hard and stays with it, is likely to do the best work and find the most peace of mind.

The reason the average man does not master many different jobs is that he

1-A desires peace of mind
1-B seldom has more than a few interests
1-C is unable to organize his ideas
1-D lacks the necessary time

1. Ⓐ Ⓑ Ⓒ Ⓓ

1-D The first sentence answers the question. It says that life is too short for one person to do many things well, which means the same thing as "there just isn't enough time."

2. Of the 300 cars owned in 1895, only four were manufactured in this country. Of the 100 million registered in 1973, most were manufactured in America.

Cars registered in this country in 1973

2-A were far in excess of those manufactured abroad in 1895
2-B were manufactured in the United States
2-C increased considerably over the preceding decade
2-D were largely of domestic construction

2. Ⓐ Ⓑ Ⓒ Ⓓ

2-D The main point of the paragraph is that by 1973 most cars in the U.S. were American-made cars. While choice A is also true, it misses the meaning of the paragraph. Choice B implies that *all* the cars were made in America, while the passage states that *most* cars were. Choice C is irrelevant.

DO NOT TURN THE PAGE UNTIL YOU ARE TOLD TO DO SO

PARAGRAPH COMPREHENSION

TIME: 13 Minutes—15 Questions

1. The indiscriminate or continual use of any drug without medical supervision is dangerous. Even drugs considered harmless may result in chronic poisoning if used for a period of years. Prescriptions should not be refilled without consulting your doctor. He prescribed a given amount because he wished to limit your use of the drug to a certain time. Never use a drug prescribed for someone else just because your symptoms appear similar. There may be differences, apparent to an expert but hidden from you, which indicate an entirely different ailment requiring different medication.

The paragraph best supports the statement that

1-A the use of drugs is very dangerous
1-B if a physician prescribes a drug it is safe to refill the prescription
1-C people with similar symptoms are usually suffering from the same ailment
1-D a drug considered harmless may be dangerous if taken over a long period of time without supervision

2. Formerly it was only unskilled labor that was shifted from place to place in the wake of industrial booms. Since so many business concerns have become nationwide in the fields they cover, the white-collar workers have been in a similar state of motion.

The growth of big business has resulted in

2-A a shifting supply of unskilled labor
2-B an increased tendency toward movement of workers
2-C an increased proportion of white-collar jobs
2-D the stabilization of industrial booms

3. In large organizations some standardized, simple, inexpensive method of giving employees information about company policies and rules, as well as specific instructions regarding their duties, is practically essential. This is the purpose of all office manuals of whatever type.

The paragraph best supports the statement that office manuals

3-A are all about the same
3-B should be simple enough for the average employee to understand
3-C are necessary to large organizations
3-D act as constant reminders to the employee of his duties

4. The Suggestion System is conducted to give thorough and understanding study to ideas presented by postal employees for promoting the welfare of postal personnel and for improving mail handling and other postal business; and to encourage and reward postal employees who think out, develop, and present acceptable ideas and plans. Through this system the talent and ability of postal employees are to be used for improving postal service and reducing expenses.

One purpose of the Suggestion System is to

4-A maintain a unit of experienced employees to plan and develop improvements
4-B obtain ideas that will help postal employees improve their work
4-C offer promotions to postal employees who suggest useful changes in service
4-D provide pay raises for employees who increase their output

5. It is wise to choose a duplicating machine that will do the work required with the greatest

efficiency and at the least cost. Users with a large volume of business need speedy machines that cost little to operate and are well made.

The paragraph best supports the statement that

5-A most users of duplicating machines prefer low operating cost to efficiency
5-B a well-built machine will outlast a cheap one
5-C a duplicating machine is not efficient unless it is sturdy
5-D a duplicating machine should be both efficient and economical

6. The X-ray has gone into business. Developed primarily to aid in diagnosing human ills, the machine now works in packing plants, in foundries, in service stations, and in a dozen ways contributes to precision and accuracy in industry.

The X-ray

6-A was first developed to aid business
6-B is being used to improve the functioning of industry
6-C is more accurate for packing plants than for foundries
6-D increases the output of such industries as service stations

7. The Federal investigator must direct his whole effort toward success in his work. If he wishes to succeed in each investigation, his work will be by no means easy, smooth, or peaceful; on the contrary, he will have to devote himself completely and continuously to a task that requires all his ability.

An investigator's success depends most upon

7-A ambition to advance rapidly in the service
7-B persistence in the face of difficulty
7-C training and experience
7-D willingness to obey orders without delay

8. Direct lighting is the least satisfactory lighting arrangement. The desk or ceiling light with a reflector which diffuses all the rays downward is sure to cause glare on the working surface.

Direct lighting is least satisfactory as a method of lighting chiefly because

8-A the light is diffused causing eye strain
8-B the shade on the individual desk lamp is not constructed along scientific lines
8-C the working surface is usually obscured by the glare
8-D direct lighting is injurious to the eyes

9. Unfortunately, specialization in industry creates workers who lack versatility. When a laborer is trained to perform only one task, he is almost entirely dependent for employment upon the demand for that particular skill. If anything happens to interrupt that demand he is unemployed.

The paragraph best supports the statement that

9-A the demand for labor of a particular type is constantly changing
9-B the average laborer is not capable of learning more than one task at a time
9-C some cases of unemployment are due to laborers' lack of versatility
9-D too much specialization is as dangerous as too little

10. Iron is used in making our bridges and skyscrapers, subways and steamships, railroads and automobiles, and nearly all kinds of machinery—besides millions of small articles varying from the farmer's scythe to the woman's needle.

The paragraph best supports the statement that iron

10-A is the most abundant of the metals
10-B has many different uses
10-C is the strongest of all metals
10-D is the only material used in building skyscrapers and bridges

11. The problem in adult education seems to be not the piling up of facts but practice in thinking.

The paragraph best supports the statement that

11-A educational methods for adults and young people should differ

11-B adults do not seem to retain new facts

11-C a well-educated adult is one who thinks but does not have a store of information

— 11-D adult education should stress ability to think

12. Since the government can spend only what it obtains from the people and this amount is ultimately limited by their capacity and willingness to pay taxes, it is very important that the people be given full information about the work of the government.

The paragraph best supports the statement that

12-A governmental employees should be trained not only in their own work, but also in how to perform the duties of other employees in their agency

— 12-B taxation by the government rests upon the consent of the people

12-C the release of full information on the work of the government will increase the efficiency of governmental operations

12-D the work of the government, in recent years, has been restricted because of reduced tax collections

13. Statutes to prevent and penalize adulteration of foods, and to provide for sanitary food preparation, are in force in every state. Such legislation has been upheld as proper under the police power of the state, since this legislation is obviously designed to promote the health and general welfare of the people.

The paragraph best supports the statement that

13-A the state provides for drastic measures to deal with violations of the pure food laws

13-B to make laws for the purpose of promoting the general health and general welfare of the people is a proper function of the state

13-C adulterated food is an outstanding menace to public health

13-D the right of the state to penalize adulteration of foods has never been questioned

14. "White collar" is a term used to describe one of the largest groups of workers in American industry and trade. It distinguishes those who work with the pencil and the mind from those who depend on their hands and the machine. It suggests occupations in which physical exertion and handling of materials are not primary features of the job.

"White collar" workers are

14-A not so strong physically as those who work with their hands

14-B those who supervise workers handling materials

14-C all whose work is entirely indoors

— 14-D not likely to use machines so much as are other groups of workers

15. Influenza, the flu, travels exactly as fast as man. In oxcart days its progress was slow. In 1918 man could girdle the globe in eight weeks, and that is exactly the time it took influenza to complete its encirclement of the earth. Today, by jets and air transport, man moves at higher speed. This modern speed makes influenza's advent unpredictable from day to day.

The purpose of this paragraph is to describe

15-A influenza around the world

15-B the world epidemic of influenza in 1918

15-C the unpredictability of influenza

15-D the effect of speed upon the spread of influenza

END OF PART 4

IF YOU FINISH BEFORE TIME IS UP, CHECK OVER YOUR WORK ON THIS PART ONLY. DO NOT GO BACK TO ANY PREVIOUS PART. DO NOT GO ON TO THE NEXT PART UNTIL YOU ARE TOLD TO DO SO.

PART 5

NUMERICAL OPERATIONS

The numerical operations part of your test battery consists of fifty very simple arithmetic questions which must be answered in only three minutes. Obviously, speed is a very important factor. You should not attempt to compute these answers using pencil and scratch paper. Instead, solve each problem in your head, then choose the correct answer from among the four choices and mark the letter of the correct answer on your answer sheet. If you are not sure of an answer, guess and go on to the next question. Do not skip any questions. You will most certainly not have time to go back to fill in. Since a wrong answer will not count against you, it cannot hurt to guess. Many people cannot complete all fifty questions in the three minutes allowed. Do not be upset if you cannot finish. Just answer as many questions as you can. Try these questions.

1. $6 + 8 =$

1-A 11
1-B 12
1-C 13
1-D 14

1. Ⓐ Ⓑ Ⓒ Ⓓ

1-D $6 + 8 = 14$

2. $5 - 3 =$

2-A 8
2-B 15
2-C 2
2-D 4

2. Ⓐ Ⓑ Ⓒ Ⓓ

2-C $5 - 3 = 2$

3. $4 \times 2 =$

3-A 6
3-B 8
3-C 16
3-D 2

3. Ⓐ Ⓑ Ⓒ Ⓓ

3-B $4 \times 2 = 8$

4. $12 \div 4 =$

4-A 3
4-B 8
4-C 16
4-D 2

4. Ⓐ Ⓑ Ⓒ Ⓓ

4-A $12 \div 4 = 3$

5. $9 \times 1 =$

5-A 0
5-B 10
5-C 1
5-D 9

5. Ⓐ Ⓑ Ⓒ Ⓓ

5-D $9 \times 1 = 9$

6. $6 + 2 =$

6-A 12
6-B 4
6-C 8
6-D 16

6. Ⓐ Ⓑ Ⓒ Ⓓ

6-C $6 + 2 = 8$

DO NOT TURN THE PAGE UNTIL YOU ARE TOLD TO DO SO

NUMERICAL OPERATIONS

TIME: 3 Minutes—50 Questions

1. 60 ÷ 10 =

1-A 5
1-B 6—
1-C 10
1-D 16

2. 5 + 2 =

2-A 3
2-B 6
2-C 7 —
2-D 9

3. 3 × 4 =

3-A 7
3-B 12 —
3-C 15
3-D 21

4. 8 − 6 =

4-A 12
4-B 5
4-C 4
4-D 2 —

5. 4 + 8 =

5-A 6
5-B 10
5-C 12 —
5-D 14

6. 6 × 8 =

6-A 24
6-B 48 —
6-C 42
6-D 36

7. 3 + 9 =

7-A 12 —
7-B 11
7-C 13
7-D 14

8. 7 + 8 =

8-A 12
8-B 15 —
8-C 17
8-D 19

9. 3 × 8 =

9-A 5
9-B 13
9-C 24 —
9-D 32

10. 16 ÷ 2 =

10-A 8 —
10-B 12
10-C 9
10-D 6

11. 7 − 2 =

11-A 5 —
11-B 9
11-C 14
11-D 7

12. 5 − 0 =

12-A 0
12-B 1
12-C 5 —
12-D 10

13. $6 \times 7 =$

13-A 13
13-B 24
13-C 27
13-D 42 —

14. $7 + 6 =$

14-A 11
14-B 13 —
14-C 14
14-D 21

15. $8 - 5 =$

15-A 13
15-B 11
15-C 4
15-D 3 —

16. $6 + 8 =$

16-A 2
16-B 10
16-C 12
16-D 14 —

17. $4 \times 6 =$

17-A 12
17-B 16
17-C 24 —
17-D 28

18. $3 + 3 =$

18-A 3
18-B 6 —
18-C 0
18-D 9

19. $2 - 1 =$

19-A 2
19-B 3
19-C 0
19-D 1 —

20. $4 \times 0 =$

20-A 4
20-B 1
20-C 16
20-D 0 —

21. $7 - 1 =$

21-A 6 —
21-B 7
21-C 8
21-D 0

22. $2 \times 3 =$

22-A 5
22-B 1
22-C 9 —
22-D 6 —

23. $9 - 7 =$

23-A 6
23-B 5
23-C 2 —
23-D 4

24. $6 + 8 =$

24-A 16
24-B 12
24-C 15
24-D 14 —

25. $10 \div 2 =$

25-A 2
25-B 5 —
25-C 20
25-D 12

26. $6 \times 3 =$

26-A 3
26-B 9
26-C 12
26-D 18 —

27. $5 + 9 =$

27-A 14 —
27-B 16
27-C 17
27-D 18

28. 7 + 7 =

    28-A 49
    28-B 77
    28-C 0
    28-D 14 —

29. 6 − 6 =

    29-A 0 —
    29-B 1
    29-C 6
    29-D 12

30. 9 × 6 =

    30-A 15
    30-B 54 —
    30-C 45
    30-D 72

31. 2 × 9 =

    31-A 17
    31-B 19
    31-C 18 —
    31-D 16

32. 7 + 3 =

    32-A 4
    32-B 10 —
    32-C 13
    32-D 11

33. 30 ÷ 3 =

    33-A 33
    33-B 11
    33-C 12
    33-D 10 —

34. 6 + 8 =

    34-A 14 —
    34-B 15
    34-C 17
    34-D 19

35. 9 + 2 =

    35-A 10
    35-B 7
    35-C 11 —
    35-D 12

36. 1 × 5 =

    36-A 5 —
    36-B 1
    36-C 6
    36-D 10

37. 3 + 6 =

    37-A 3
    37-B 8
    37-C 9 —
    37-D 18

38. 4 × 8 =

    38-A 24
    38-B 28
    38-C 32 —
    38-D 42

39. 5 + 5 =

    39-A 25
    39-B 10 —
    39-C 5
    39-D 1

40. 7 − 4 =

    40-A 11
    40-B 9
    40-C 6
    40-D 3 —

41. 8 + 9 =

    41-A 15
    41-B 17 —
    41-C 19
    41-D 21

42. 1 + 3 =

    42-A 1
    42-B 2
    42-C 3
    42-D 4 —

43. 2 × 7 =

    43-A 5
    43-B 9
    43-C 12
    43-D 14 —

44. 35 ÷ 7 =

44-A 12
44-B 7
44-C 6
44-D 5 —

45. 10 − 9 =

45-A 11
45-B 19
45-C 1 ⌒
45-D 0

46. 3 + 4 =

46-A 9
46-B 7 —
46-C 5
46-D 1

47. 8 − 6 =

47-A 2 —
47-B 4

47-C 12
47-D 14

48. 8 ÷ 2 =

48-A 6
48-B 16
48-C 10
48-D 4 —

49. 6 + 7 =

49-A 11
49-B 13 —
49-C 15
49-D 9

50. 9 + 1 =

50-A 8
50-B 9
50-C 10 —
50-D 11

END OF PART 5

DO NOT GO ON UNTIL YOU ARE TOLD TO DO SO

PART 6

CODING SPEED

The coding part of your exam is different from all other parts of the exam. Nothing that you have learned enters into your answering of these questions. Coding is a test of your memory, your eye-hand coordination and your working speed.

Before each set of questions you will find a "key." The key consists of ten words listed in alphabetical order. Each word has a four-digit code number assigned to it.

In the set of questions you will find the same ten words, scrambled and sometimes repeated. Following each word in the test are *five* answer choices in columns labelled "A" to "E." Each answer choice is a four-digit number. The answer choices are in ascending order; that is, the lowest number is always in column A, the next higher number is in column B, and so on to the highest number in column E. You must look at the word, find the correct code number among the choices and mark on your answer sheet the letter of the column in which you found the correct code number.

On the actual examination you must work very quickly. You have only seven minutes in which to try to answer eighty-four questions. Use the sample questions that follow to develop a system that works for you—memorization, some sort of word-number association, a mathematical formula or any private method that helps you work up speed and accuracy. Many people cannot finish this part in the time allowed. Do not be upset if you cannot finish. Just do your best. Try these questions.

Key

band 2241	dog 1715	nail 4462
branch 5016	gravy 3230	orange 7096
castle 8317	hot 2046	wife 9812
	mare 6735	

Answers

		A	B	C	D	E	
1.	castle	2046	4462	6735	8317	9812	1. Ⓐ Ⓑ Ⓒ Ⓓ Ⓔ
2.	hot	2046	2241	5016	6735	8317	2. Ⓐ Ⓑ Ⓒ Ⓓ Ⓔ
3.	mare	1715	3230	6735	7096	9812	3. Ⓐ Ⓑ Ⓒ Ⓓ Ⓔ
4.	gravy	2241	3230	4462	6735	8317	4. Ⓐ Ⓑ Ⓒ Ⓓ Ⓔ
5.	orange	1715	5016	6735	7096	9812	5. Ⓐ Ⓑ Ⓒ Ⓓ Ⓔ
6.	branch	2241	4462	5016	6735	7096	6. Ⓐ Ⓑ Ⓒ Ⓓ Ⓔ
7.	wife	3230	5016	7096	8317	9812	7. Ⓐ Ⓑ Ⓒ Ⓓ Ⓔ
8.	band	2241	4462	5016	6735	8317	8. Ⓐ Ⓑ Ⓒ Ⓓ Ⓔ
9.	dog	1715	2046	2241	5016	7096	9. Ⓐ Ⓑ Ⓒ Ⓓ Ⓔ
10.	nail	2046	4462	6735	8317	9812	10. Ⓐ Ⓑ Ⓒ Ⓓ Ⓔ
11.	orange	3230	5016	6735	7096	8317	11. Ⓐ Ⓑ Ⓒ Ⓓ Ⓔ
12.	branch	2046	2241	3230	4462	5016	12. Ⓐ Ⓑ Ⓒ Ⓓ Ⓔ

The correct answers are:

1-D	4-B	7-E	10-B
2-A	5-D	8-A	11-D
3-C	6-C	9-A	12-E

Key

cat 3382	empty 3571	oil 8513
cough 5842	fudge 4002	spoon 7975
dime 9186	game 8934	white 6300
	heart 1010	

Answers

		A	B	C	D	E	
13.	fudge	1010	3382	4002	8934	9186	13. Ⓐ Ⓑ © Ⓓ Ⓔ
14.	cough	3571	5842	6300	7975	8513	14. Ⓐ Ⓑ © Ⓓ Ⓔ
15.	white	4002	5842	6300	8513	9186	15. Ⓐ Ⓑ © Ⓓ Ⓔ
16.	spoon	3382	3571	5842	6300	7975	16. Ⓐ Ⓑ © Ⓓ Ⓔ
17.	cat	1010	3382	4002	5842	9186	17. Ⓐ Ⓑ © Ⓓ Ⓔ
18.	oil	3571	7975	8513	8934	9186	18. Ⓐ Ⓑ © Ⓓ Ⓔ
19.	heart	1010	3382	3571	7975	8934	19. Ⓐ Ⓑ © Ⓓ Ⓔ
20.	dime	3382	3571	4002	8513	9186	20. Ⓐ Ⓑ © Ⓓ Ⓔ
21.	empty	3571	5842	6300	8513	8934	21. Ⓐ Ⓑ © Ⓓ Ⓔ
22.	game	3382	4002	5842	8934	9186	22. Ⓐ Ⓑ © Ⓓ Ⓔ
23.	cough	1010	4002	5842	6300	7975	23. Ⓐ Ⓑ © Ⓓ Ⓔ
24.	empty	1010	3382	3571	5842	8513	24. Ⓐ Ⓑ © Ⓓ Ⓔ

The correct answers are:

13-C	16-E	19-A	22-D
14-B	17-B	20-E	23-C
15-C	18-C	21-A	24-C

DO NOT TURN THE PAGE UNTIL YOU ARE TOLD TO DO SO

CODING SPEED

TIME: 7 Minutes—84 Questions

Key

button	5266	flu	3838	mail	6234
chop	1817	gold	8351	pot	7007
dawn	9745	iris	4658	puppy	6606
		love	2456		

Answers

		A	B	C	D	E
1.	button	2456	4658	5266	6234	8351
2.	puppy	1817	2456	5266	6234	6606
3.	gold	1817	3838	6234	8351	9745
4.	mail	2456	4658	5266	6234	8351
5.	flu	3838	5266	6234	6606	9745
6.	iris	2456	4658	5266	6234	8351
7.	pot	3838	5266	6606	7007	9745
8.	chop	1817	3838	6234	6606	8351
9.	love	2456	4658	5266	6234	9745
10.	iris	1817	3838	4658	6234	7007
11.	dawn	2456	3838	6234	6606	9745
12.	mail	2456	4658	6234	8351	9745

Key

blue	5913	food	1238	roast	4650
clown	3761	hat	8884	toe	7277
dust	9009	lamp	2212	wish	6702
		money	8648		

Answers

		A	B	C	D	E
13.	clown	1238	2212	3761	8884	9009
14.	wish	3761	4650	5913	6702	7277
15.	roast	2212	4650	6702	8648	8884
16.	blue	1238	2212	3761	4650	5913
17.	roast	1238	3761	4650	7277	8884
18.	dust	3761	5913	6702	8648	9009
19.	food	1238	2212	4650	6702	8648
20.	toe	4650	5913	6702	7277	8884
21.	lamp	2212	3761	6702	8648	8884
22.	money	4650	5913	8648	8884	9009
23.	clown	3761	4650	6702	7277	9009
24.	hat	1238	2212	5913	8648	8884

Key

army 9234	land 1620	paint 7677
coast 4532	line 1854	rug 5600
disc 6957	man 3002	test 8406
	pain 2610	

Answers

		A	B	C	D	E
25.	disc	1620	3002	5600	6957	8406
26.	paint	1854	2610	4532	6957	7677
27.	line	1620	1854	2610	3002	5600
28.	test	1854	4532	6957	8406	9234
29.	pain	2610	3002	5600	7677	8406
30.	army	1620	2610	3002	6957	9234
31.	rug	4532	5600	6957	8406	9234
32.	man	3002	4532	6957	7677	8406
33.	paint	1620	2610	7677	8406	9234
34.	coast	2610	3002	4532	5600	6957
35.	land	1620	1854	2610	3002	5600
36.	rug	2610	4532	5600	6957	9234

Key

coach 4589	gun 1118	root 6943
coal 9260	lunch 2024	stable 3377
eagle 5583	marble 6874	top 7337
	oven 1418	

Answers

		A	B	C	D	E
37.	marble	2024	4589	5583	6874	6943
38.	stable	1418	3377	5583	7337	9260
39.	eagle	1118	2024	3377	5583	6874
40.	lunch	1118	1418	2024	6943	9260
41.	oven	1418	3377	4589	6943	7337
42.	coal	2024	4589	6874	6943	9260
43.	root	5583	6874	6943	7337	9260
44.	coach	1118	2024	3377	4589	6874
45.	top	1418	3377	5583	6943	7337
46.	gun	1118	1418	4589	7337	9260
47.	eagle	2024	3377	5583	6943	7337
48.	root	1418	2024	6943	7337	9260

Key

angel	7717	flood	5846	llama	2573
brick	1492	gown	3232	nut	9089
eye	6943	ink	4921	red	5487
		joke	8614		

Answers

		A	B	C	D	E
49.	flood	1492	4921	5487	5846	6943
50.	gown	2573	3232	6943	8614	9089
51.	joke	1492	4921	5846	7717	8614
52.	nut	1492	2573	3232	8614	9089
53.	angel	2573	4921	6943	7717	8614
54.	ink	1492	4921	6943	7715	8614
55.	red	1492	4912	5487	5846	6943
56.	eye	4921	6943	7717	8614	9089
57.	brick	1492	4912	5846	6943	8614
58.	llama	2573	3232	4921	6943	9089
59.	eye	1492	2573	3232	5846	6943
60.	ink	2573	3232	4921	7717	8614

Key

art	2679	flag	4855	nation	5897
basket	4562	gas	1499	nature	7004
crust	9911	link	3964	razor	8282
		music	6242		

Answers

		A	B	C	D	E
61.	basket	1499	4562	4855	5897	6242
62.	nation	1499	2679	3964	4855	5897
63.	music	4562	6242	7004	8282	9911
64.	nature	2679	3964	4855	6242	7004
65.	gas	1499	3964	4562	4855	9911
66.	link	1499	2679	3964	5897	6242
67.	flag	4562	4855	5897	6242	8282
68.	razor	2679	4562	6242	8282	9911
69.	art	2679	3964	4855	5897	6242
70.	crust	1499	4562	4855	7004	9911
71.	nature	2679	5897	7004	8282	9911
72.	flag	1499	2679	3964	4562	4855

Key

bell	5458	echo	1978	jewel	6877
cable	1058	fuss	4363	mug	7613
dash	4844	height	2984	tub	3439
		iron	9100		

Answers

		A	B	C	D	E
73.	height	1058	1978	2984	7613	9100
74.	jewel	1978	4844	5458	6877	7613
75.	bell	2984	3439	4363	4844	5458
76.	dash	2984	3439	4363	4844	6877
77.	cable	1058	1978	6877	7613	9100
78.	fuss	3439	4363	4844	5458	7613
79.	mug	2984	4363	5458	6877	7613
80.	echo	1978	2984	5458	7613	9100
81.	tub	3439	4363	4844	6877	7613
82.	iron	1058	1978	4363	7613	9100
83.	bell	1978	2984	5458	6877	7613
84.	dash	4363	4844	5458	7613	9100

END OF PART 6

IF YOU FINISH BEFORE TIME IS UP, CHECK TO BE SURE THAT ALL YOUR ANSWERS ARE CLEARLY MARKED. DO NOT RETURN TO ANY PREVIOUS PART. DO NOT GO ON TO THE NEXT PART UNTIL YOU ARE TOLD TO DO SO.

AUTO & SHOP INFORMATION

The auto and shop information questions test your knowledge and understanding of automobiles and of tools and shop practices. The answers to many questions come straight from your life experience. However, if this is not your area of interest, there will be questions to which you do not know the answer. Make the most sensible guess. Answer all questions. Mark the letter of your choice on your answer sheet. Try these questions.

1. A green puddle under the front end of a car means that the car is losing

    1-A power steering fluid
    1-B antifreeze
    1-C transmission fluid
    1-D crankcase oil

    1. Ⓐ Ⓑ Ⓒ Ⓓ

1-B ANTIFREEZE is green. Power steering fluid (A) and transmission fluid (C) are pink. Crankcase oil (D) is brown.

2. The probable reason why a moving car with power steering might suddenly become hard to steer is that

    2-A the emergency brake is on
    2-B the wheels are out of alignment
    2-C transmission belts are stretched
    2-D the engine has stalled

    2. Ⓐ Ⓑ Ⓒ Ⓓ

2-D Power steering is powered by the car's engine. If the engine STALLS, the power assistance vanishes and the car becomes very difficult to steer. The car might be hard to steer if the emergency brake was on (A), but this would be noticed at the outset of a trip, not suddenly after the car had been moving. Out of alignment wheels (B) also affect steering, but the effect is constant, not sudden. Transmission (C) has nothing to do with steering.

3.

The tool above is a

    3-A screw
    3-B screwdriver
    3-C drill bit
    3-D corkscrew

    3. Ⓐ Ⓑ Ⓒ Ⓓ

3-C The tool is a DRILL BIT. The smooth end is inserted into the drill chuck and is tightened so that it is very secure. When the drill motor goes, the bit turns very fast and drills holes wherever it is applied.

4. Wood screws properly used as compared to nails properly used

    4-A are easier to install
    4-B generally hold better
    4-C are easier to drive flush with surface
    4-D are more likely to split the wood

    4. Ⓐ Ⓑ Ⓒ Ⓓ

4-B Wood screws are usually *more* difficult to install than are nails, but they are often preferable because they generally HOLD BETTER and are *less* likely to split the wood.

DO NOT TURN THE PAGE UNTIL YOU ARE TOLD TO DO SO

AUTO & SHOP INFORMATION

TIME: 11 Minutes—25 Questions

1. An engine, such as is most often used in automobiles, is called a(n)

   1-A diesel engine
   1-B external-combustion engine
   1-C internal-combustion engine
   1-D three cycle engine

2. The most important rule for a driver to remember in the care of an automobile battery is to

   2-A make certain that the points are properly adjusted in the spark plugs
   2-B burn the headlights or play the radio, occasionally, while the ignition is turned on
   2-C have the battery discharged at regular intervals, weekly in the winter, bi-weekly in the summer
   2-D keep the level of the liquid above the plates

3. Cam ground pistons are used primarily because

   3-A they can be used in badly worn engines without reboring the cylinders
   3-B their use increases the compression ratio
   3-C their use aids in the lubrication of the cylinder walls
   3-D they eliminate piston slap in engine warm-up and permit expansion

4. When the level of the liquid in a battery gets too low, it is necessary to put in some more

   4-A battery acid
   4-B hydroxide
   4-C water
   4-D antifreeze

5. The headlights to automobiles are found to be connected ordinarily in

   5-A parallel
   5-B series
   5-C diagonal
   5-D perpendicular

6. When painting, nail holes and cracks should be

   6-A filled with putty before starting
   6-B filled with putty after the priming coat is applied
   6-C filled with paint by careful working
   6-D ignored

7. Paint is "thinned" with

   7-A linseed oil
   7-B varnish
   7-C turpentine
   7-D gasoline

8.

   The tool shown above is used to

   8-A set nails
   8-B drill holes in concrete
   8-C cut a brick accurately
   8-D centerpunch for holes

9. If the head of a hammer has become loose on the handle, it should properly be tightened by

   9-A driving the handle further into the head
   9-B driving a nail alongside the present wedge
   9-C using a slightly larger wedge
   9-D soaking the handle in water

10. The type of screwdriver that will develop the greatest turning force is a

   10-A screwdriver-bit and brace
   10-B straight handle with ratchet
   10-C standard straight handle
   10-D spiral push-type

11. Glazier's points are used to

   11-A hold glass in wooden window sash
   11-B scratch glass so that it can be broken to size
   11-C force putty into narrow spaces between glass and sash
   11-D remove broken glass from a pane

12.

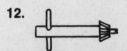

   The tool pictured above is a

   12-A lug wrench
   12-B star drill
   12-C lead anchor
   12-D chuck key

13. A good lubricant for locks is

   13-A graphite
   13-B grease
   13-C mineral oil
   13-D motor oil

14. A fuel injection system on an automobile engine eliminates the necessity for

   14-A a manifold
   14-B a carburetor
   14-C spark plugs
   14-D a distributor

15. Setting the spark plug gap opening closer than normally required would probably result in

   15-A smoother idling and increase in top engine speed
   15-B rougher idling and decrease in top engine speed
   15-C smoother idling and decrease in top engine speed
   15-D rougher idling and increase in top engine speed

16. What forces fuel from the carburetor into the cylinder?

   16-A the fuel pump
   16-B atmospheric pressure
   16-C temperature difference
   16-D the distributor

17. A mechanic sets the proper electrode gap on a sparkplug most accurately if he uses a

   17-A dial gauge
   17-B round wire feeler gauge
   17-C square wire feeler gauge
   17-D conventional flat feeler gauge

18. Upon the complete loss of oil pressure while a car is in operation it is best that the car be

   18-A pulled over to the side of the road and the engine stopped immediately for inspection
   18-B pulled over to the side of the road, and a repair truck called to install a new oil pump
   18-C driven a few miles to your favorite garage
   18-D driven as usual for the entire day and be dropped off at the garage in the evening

19. Which of the saws is used to make curved cuts?

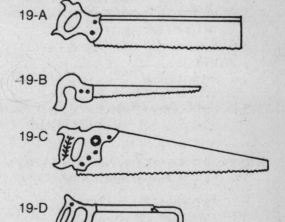

20.

The tool shown above is used to measure

20-A clearances
20-B wire thickness
20-C inside slots
20-D screw pitch

21. "Blistering" is generally caused by applying paint

21-A over a primer that has not completely dried
21-B containing an improper binder for the pigment
21-C that has been thinned too much
21-D over a surface that has excessive moisture

22. A 6-point saw is one which

22-A weighs 6 ounces per foot
22-B is made of no. 6 gauge steel
22-C has 6 teeth per inch
22-D has 6 styles of teeth for universal work

23. Alcohol is put into the radiator of an automobile in cold weather because it

23-A lowers the boiling point of the mixture
23-B lowers the freezing point of the mixture

23-C raises the boiling point of the mixture
23-D raises the freezing point of the mixture

24. The carpenter's "hand screw" is

24-A

24-B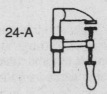

24-C

24-D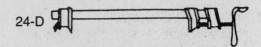

25. Of the following, the best tool to use to make a hole in a coping stone is a

25-A star drill
25-B coping saw
25-C pneumatic grinder
25-D diamond wheel dresser

END OF PART 7

IF YOU FINISH BEFORE TIME IS UP, CHECK OVER YOUR WORK ON THIS PART ONLY. DO NOT RETURN TO ANY PREVIOUS PART. DO NOT GO ON UNTIL YOU ARE TOLD TO DO SO.

PART 8

MATHEMATICS KNOWLEDGE

To solve the problems in this part, you must draw upon your knowledge of high school mathematics. The problems require you to use simple algebra and geometry along with arithmetic skills and reasoning power. Some questions can be answered in your head. Others will require the use of scratch paper. If you use scratch paper for your calculations, be sure to mark the letter of the correct answer on your answer sheet. Try these questions.

1. A square measures 8 inches on one side. By how much will the area be increased if its length is increased by 4 inches and its width decreased by 2 inches?

1-A   14 sq. in.
1-B   12 sq. in.
1-C   10 sq. in.
1-D   8 sq. in.

1. Ⓐ Ⓑ Ⓒ Ⓓ

1-D Area = length × width
Area of square = 8 × 8 = 64 sq. in.
Area of rectangle = (8 + 4) (8 − 2) = 12 × 6 = 72 sq. in.
72 − 64 = 8 sq. in.

2. 1% of 8 −

2-A   8
2-B   .8
2-C   .08
2-D   .008

2. Ⓐ Ⓑ Ⓒ Ⓓ

2-C To remove a % sign, divide the number by 100.
Thus, 1% = 1/100 = .01.
1% of 8 is the same as 1% times 8 = .01 × 8 = .08

3. $(3 + 4)^3 =$

3-A   21
3-B   91

3-C   343
3-D   490

3. Ⓐ Ⓑ Ⓒ Ⓓ

3-C First perform the operation within the parentheses. To cube a number, multiply it by itself two times.

$$(3 + 4)^3 = (7)^3 = 7 \times 7 \times 7 = 343$$

4. Aluminum bronze consists of copper and aluminum, usually in the ratio of 10:1 by weight. If an object made of this alloy weighs 77 pounds, how many pounds of aluminum does it contain?

4-A   7.7
4-B   7.0
4-C   70.0
4-D   10

4. Ⓐ Ⓑ Ⓒ Ⓓ

4-B Copper and aluminum in the ratio of 10:1 means 10 parts copper to 1 part aluminum.

Let x = weight of aluminum
Then 10 x = weight of copper
10x + x = 77
11x = 77
x = 7

DO NOT TURN THE PAGE UNTIL YOU ARE TOLD TO DO SO

MATHEMATICS KNOWLEDGE

TIME: 24 Minutes—25 Questions

1. A box contains 3 black, 4 red, and 5 white marbles. If one marble is to be picked at random, what is the probability that it will be red?

   1-A 1/5
   1-B 1/2
   1-C 1/3
   1-D 1/4

2. 36 yards and 12 feet divided by 3 =

   2-A 40 ft.
   2-B 124 ft.
   2-C 12¼ yds.
   2-D 12 yds.

3. If the circumference of a circle has the same numbered value as its area, then the radius of the circle must be

   3-A 1
   3-B 5
   3-C 2
   3-D 0

4. If $A^2 + B^2 = A^2 + X^2$, then B equals

   4-A X
   4-B $X^2 - 2A^2$
   4-C A
   4-D $A^2 + X^2$

5. If 5 pints of water are needed to water each square foot of lawn, the minimum gallons of water needed for a lawn 8′ by 12′ is

   5-A 5
   5-B 20
   5-C 40
   5-D 60

6. What fraction of 63 is $\frac{2}{7}$ of 21?

6-A $\frac{1}{42}$
6-B $\frac{7}{6}$
6-C $\frac{2}{21}$
6-D $\frac{1}{3}$

7. $\sqrt{960}$ is a number between

   7-A 20 and 30
   7-B 60 and 70
   7-C 80 and 90
   7-D 30 and 40

8. A man has T dollars to invest. After he invests $1,000 how much money does he have remaining?

   8-A T + 1000
   8-B T − 1000
   8-C 1000 − T
   8-D 1000T

9. 25 is what percent of 5?

   9-A 5
   9-B 500
   9-C 20
   9-D 50

10. How many pints are equal to 2 gallons?

    10-A 8
    10-B 16
    10-C 4
    10-D 24

11. A rectangular field is 900 yds. by 240 yds. What is the largest number of rectangular lots 120 yds. by 60 yds. that it can be divided into?

    11-A 20
    11-B 60

11-C 30
11-D 40

12. $9\overline{)111111111}$ =

12-A 12345678
12-B 11111119
12-C 11191119
12-D 12345679

13. A boy has 5 pairs of slacks, and 3 sport jackets. How many different combinations can he wear?

13-A 3
13-B 5
13-C 8
13-D 15

14. If a = 3, then $a^a \cdot a$ =

14-A 9
14-B 51
14-C 18
14-D 81

15. What is the correct time if the hour hand is exactly $\frac{2}{3}$ of the way between 5 and 6?

15-A 5:25
15-B 5:40
15-C 5:30
15-D 5:45

16. To find the radius of a circle whose circumference is 60 inches

16-A multiply 60 by π
16-B divide 60 by 2π
16-C divide 30 by 2π
16-D divide 60 by π and extract the square root of the result

17. (3 + 2)(6 − 2)(7 + 1) = (4 + 4)(x). What is the value of x?

17-A 13 + 2
17-B 14 + 4
17-C 4 + 15
17-D 8 + 12

18. How many of the numbers between 100 and 300 begin or end with 2?

18-A 40
18-B 180
18-C 100
18-D 110

19. The pages of a typewritten report are numbered from 1 to 100 by hand. How many times will it be necessary to write the number 5?

19-A 10
19-B 11
19-C 12
19-D 20

20. A certain highway intersection has had A accidents over a ten-year period, resulting in B deaths. What is the yearly average death rate for the intersection?

20-A A + B − 10
20-B $\dfrac{B}{10}$
20-C $10 - \dfrac{A}{B}$
20-D $\dfrac{A}{10}$

21. When 5.1 is divided by 0.017 the quotient is

21-A 30
21-B 300
21-C 3,000
21-D 30,000

22. The area of the figure shown can be determined by the formula

22-A ac ÷ b
22-B $\frac{1}{2}$bh
22-C bc ÷ a
22-D bh²

23. The figure on the right is a

23-A hexagon
23-B octagon
23-C pentagon
23-D decahedron

24. If 9 is 9% of x, then x =

    24-A .01
    24-B 100
    24-C 1
    24-D 9

25. Angle ABD is

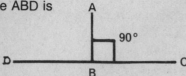

    25-A a straight angle and contains 180°
    25-B an acute angle and contains 35°
    25-C a right angle and contains 90°
    25-D a right angle and contains 45°

END OF PART 8

IF YOU FINISH BEFORE THE TIME IS UP, MAKE CERTAIN THAT YOU HAVE MARKED ALL YOUR ANSWERS ON THE ANSWER SHEET. THEN CHECK OVER YOUR WORK ON THIS PART ONLY. DO NOT GO BACK TO ANY PREVIOUS PART. DO NOT GO ON UNTIL YOU ARE TOLD TO DO SO.

MECHANICAL COMPREHENSION

Part 9 consists of questions about your understanding of general mechanical and physical principles. Your understanding of these principles will come from your own observations, from experience in working with mechanical devices and from your reading and school courses. Answer all the questions as best you can, marking the letter of your choice on your answer sheet. Try these questions.

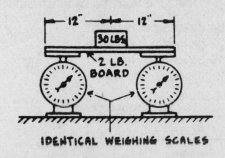

IDENTICAL WEIGHING SCALES

The weight held by the board and placed on the two identical scales will cause *each* scale to read

1-A   8 lbs.
1-B   16 lbs.
1-C   15 lbs.
1-D   32 lbs.

1. Ⓐ Ⓑ Ⓒ Ⓓ

1-B Since the 32 total pounds (30-lb. weight plus 2-lb. board) are exactly evenly distributed between the two scales, each scale is supporting exactly one half of the weight. Hence, each scale will read 16 pounds.

2.

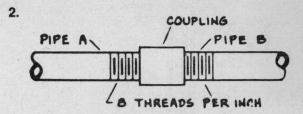

If pipe A is held in a vise and pipe B is turned ten revolutions with a wrench, the overall length of the pipes and coupling will decrease

2-A $\frac{5}{8}$ inch
2-B $2\frac{1}{2}$ inches
2-C $1\frac{1}{4}$ inches
2-D $3\frac{3}{4}$ inches

2. Ⓐ Ⓑ Ⓒ Ⓓ

2-C The overall length of pipes and coupling could decrease or increase, depending upon the direction in which pipe B is turned. However, as stated in this question, pipe B is turned so as to disappear into the coupling. Since there are 8 threads to the inch, eight complete revolutions of the pipe would shorten the pipes and coupling by one inch. An additional two turns, for a total of ten, would shorten the pipes and coupling by an additional two-eighths or one-fourth of an inch.

DO NOT TURN THE PAGE UNTIL YOU ARE TOLD TO DO SO

MECHANICAL COMPREHENSION

TIME: 19 Minutes—25 Questions

1.

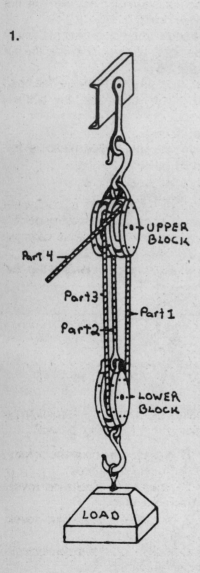

When a load is hoisted by means of the tackle shown above, the part that remains stationary is

1-A   the load
1-B   the lower block
1-C   the lower hook
1-D   the upper block

2.

Eight gallons of water per minute are flowing at a given time from the one-inch outlet in the tank shown. What is the amount of water flowing at that time from the two-inch outlet?

2-A   64 gallons per minute
2-B   32 gallons per minute
2-C   16 gallons per minute
2-D   2 gallons per minute

3.

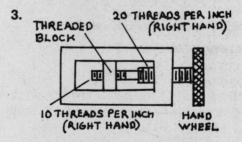

In the figure above, the threaded block can slide in the slot but cannot revolve. If the hand wheel is turned 20 revolutions clockwise, the threaded block will move

3-A   one inch to the left
3-B $\frac{1}{2}$ inch to the left
3-C   one inch to the right
3-D $\frac{1}{2}$ inch to the right

4. Automatic operation of a sump pump is controlled by the

4-A   pneumatic switch
4-B   float
4-C   foot valve
4-D   centrifugal driving unit

5.

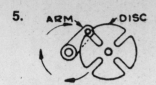

The figure above shows a slotted disc turned by a pin on a rotating arm. One revolution of the arm turns the disc

5-A   1/4 turn
5-B   1/2 turn
5-C   3/4 turn
5-D   one complete turn

6.

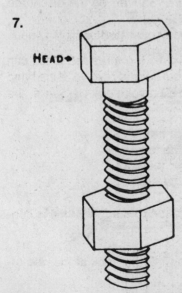

The tank "T" is to be raised as shown by attaching the pull rope to a truck. If the tank is to be raised ten feet, the truck will have to move

6-A   20 feet
6-B   40 feet
6-C   30 feet
6-D   50 feet

7.

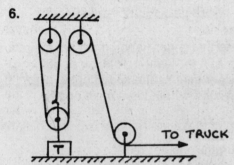

Referring to the figure below, which one of the following statements is true?

7-A   If the nut is held stationary and the head turned clockwise, the bolt will move down.
7-B   If the head of the bolt is held stationary and the nut is turned clockwise, the nut will move down.
7-C   If the head of the bolt is held stationary and the nut is turned clockwise, the nut will move up.
7-D   If the nut is held stationary and the head turned counter-clockwise, the bolt will move up.

8. Condensation on cold water pipes is frequently prevented by

8-A   insulating the pipe
8-B   keeping the temperature of cold water at least 10° above the freezing point
8-C   keeping the cold water lines near the hot water lines
8-D   oiling or greasing the outside of the pipe

9.

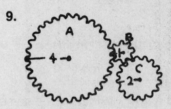

If gear A makes one clockwise revolution per minute, which of the following is true?

9-A   Gear B makes one counterclockwise revolution every 4 minutes.
9-B   Gear C makes two clockwise revolutions every minute.
9-C   Gear B makes four clockwise revolutions every minute.
9-D   Gear C makes one counterclockwise revolution every 8 minutes.

10.

In the case of the standard flanged pipe at 10, the maximum angle through which it would be necessary to rotate the pipe in order to line up the holes is

10-A 22.5 degrees
10-B 45 degrees
10-C 30 degrees
10-D 60 degrees

11. With the same water pressure, the amount of water that can be carried by a 2-inch pipe as compared with a 1-inch pipe is

11-A twice as much
11-B 3 times as much
11-C 3½ times as much
11-D 4 times as much

12.

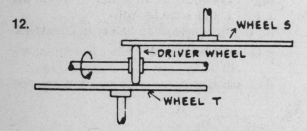

With the wheels in the position shown

12-A wheels S and T will rotate in opposite directions
12-B wheels S and T will rotate at the same speed
12-C wheels S and T will rotate in the same direction
12-D wheel S will rotate at exactly the same speed as the driver wheel

13.

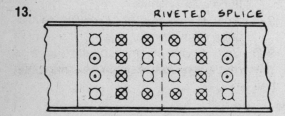

In the structural steel splice the different types of rivets are shown by different symbols. The number of different types of rivets is

13-A 6
13-B 4
13-C 5
13-D 3

14. The main purpose of expansion joints in steam lines is to

14-A provide for changes in length of heated pipe
14-B allow for connection of additional radiators
14-C provide locations for valves
14-D reduce breakage of pipe due to minor movement of the building frame

15. Assume that a gear and pinion have a ratio of 3 to 1. If the gear is rotating at 300 revolutions per minute, the speed of the pinion in revolutions per minute is most nearly

15-A 100
15-B 900
15-C 300
15-D 1800

16. A characteristic of a rotary pump is

16-A a rapidly rotating impeller moves the liquid through the discharge piping
16-B two gears, meshed together and revolving in opposite directions, move the liquid to the discharge pipe
16-C valves are required on the discharge side of the pump
16-D it is usually operated at high speeds up to 3600 rpm

17.

If water is flowing into the tank at the rate of

120 gallons per hour and flowing out of the tank at a constant rate of one gallon per minute, the water level in the tank will

17-A rise 1 gallon per minute
17-B rise 2 gallons per minute
17-C fall 2 gallons per minute
17-D fall 1 gallon per minute

18. The best reason for having gaskets on manholes of a boiler is to

18-A prevent leakage from the boiler
18-B provide an emergency exit for excessive steam pressure
18-C provide easy access to the boiler for cleaning
18-D prevent corrosion at the manholes

19. The symbol ℄ 1.5 on a drawing means:

19-A load center
19-B combination angle
19-C clearance limit
19-D center line

20.

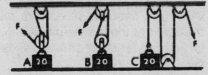

Which pulley arrangement requires the least force at F in order to lift the weight?

20-A A
20-B B
20-C C
20-D All three require the same force

21. In order to stop a faucet from dripping, your first act should be to replace the

21-A cap nut
21-B seat
21-C washer
21-D spindle

22.

If the block on which the lever is resting is moved closer to the brick

22-A the brick will be easier to lift and will be lifted higher
22-B the brick will be harder to lift and will be lifted higher
22-C the brick will be easier to lift but will not be lifted as high
22-D the brick will be harder to lift and will not be lifted as high

23.

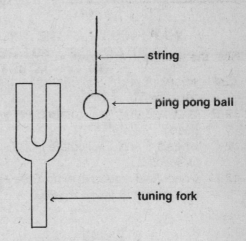

When the tuning fork is struck, the ping pong ball will

23-A remain stationary
23-B bounce up and down
23-C hit the tuning fork
23-D swing away from the tuning fork

24.

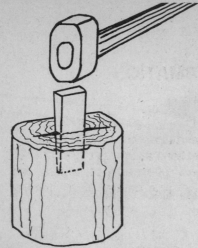

The simple machine pictured above is a form of

24-A   inclined plane
24-B   pulley
24-C   spur gear
24-D   torque

25.

If both cyclists pedal at the same rate on the same surface, the cyclist in front will

25-A   travel at the same speed as the cyclist behind
25-B   move faster than the cyclist behind
25-C   move more slowly than the other cyclist
25-D   have greater difficulty steering

END OF PART 9

IF YOU FINISH BEFORE TIME IS UP, CHECK OVER YOUR WORK ON THIS PART ONLY. DO NOT RETURN TO ANY PREVIOUS PART. DO NOT GO ON UNTIL YOU ARE TOLD TO DO SO.

PART 10

ELECTRONICS INFORMATION

The questions in this part test your knowledge and understanding of electricity, radio and electronics. To answer some of the questions all you need is common sense. Other questions can be answered on the basis of experience, courses and reading. Answer all the questions. Mark the letter of your answer on the answer sheet. Try these questions.

1. The fuse of a certain circuit has blown and is replaced with a fuse of the same rating which also blows when the switch is closed. In this case

    1-A a fuse of higher current rating should be used
    1-B a fuse of higher voltage rating should be used
    1-C the fuse should be temporarily replaced by a heavy piece of wire
    1-D the circuit should be checked

    1. Ⓐ Ⓑ Ⓒ Ⓓ

1-D The purpose of a fuse is to protect a circuit from overheating through overloading or through the action of a malfunctioning appliance on that circuit. When a fuse burns out, the first test is to try a fresh fuse. It is always possible that the first fuse simply burned out from old age. If the second fuse blows immediately, assuming the fuses were of current rating for that circuit, a heavier, higher rated fuse should NEVER be substituted, nor should the circuit be closed with wire or a penny. The blowing of the fuse is a warning of trouble on the circuit. The circuit must be carefully checked for overload, appliances in poor condition and frayed wires.

2. The one of the following which could *not* be correctly used in describing a toggle switch is

    2-A single-hole mounting
    2-B slow-acting
    2-C three-way
    2-D double-pole

2. Ⓐ Ⓑ Ⓒ Ⓓ

2-B A toggle switch is an ordinary light switch, like the ones you find on your walls at home. The method of mounting a toggle switch depends upon the manufacture of the switch and upon the number of switches in the unit. Toggle switches come in great variety, some controlling auxiliary outlets like those in bathroom fixtures, some sharing control of the same fixture with another switch in another location. The one characteristic which IS TRUE of all toggle switches is that they are *fast* acting. There is no time lag. You flip the switch, and the light is on.

3. A piece of electrical equipment that serves the same purpose as a fuse is a

    3-A transformer
    3-B generator
    3-C switch
    3-D circuit breaker

    3. Ⓐ Ⓑ Ⓒ Ⓓ

3-D In new construction or in the upgrading of old electrical installations, a breaker box is substituted for a fuse box. The circuit breakers serve exactly the same function as a fuse. If a circuit becomes overloaded for any reason, the breaker will "trip" and break the circuit. If a circuit breaker "trips" the circuit must be checked. There is no possibility of a "tired" fuse. Use of a circuit breaker avoids the possibility of running out of fuses. It also makes it impossible to substitute a higher rated fuse or a copper penny and to thus lose the protection of the fuse.

DO NOT TURN THE PAGE UNTIL YOU ARE TOLD TO DO SO.

ELECTRONICS INFORMATION

TIME: 9 Minutes—20 Questions

1. In lights controlled by three-way switches, the switches should be treated and put in as

   1-A flush switches
   1-B single pole switches
   1-C three double pole switches
   1-D three pole switches

2. An electrician should consider all electrical equipment "alive" unless he definitely knows otherwise. The main reason for this practice is to avoid

   2-A doing unnecessary work
   2-B energizing the wrong circuit
   2-C personal injury
   2-D de-energizing a live circuit

3.

   1   2   3   4

   The shape of nut most commonly used on electrical terminals is

   3-A 1
   3-B 2
   3-C 3
   3-D 4

4.

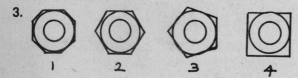

GENERATOR   LAMPS

EACH LAMP TAKES 1 AMPERE

   The current in the wire at the point indicated by the arrow is

   4-A 1 ampere
   4-B 2 amperes
   4-C 3 amperes
   4-D 4 amperes

5.

   The reading of the kilowatt-hour meter is

   5-A 9672
   5-B 1779
   5-C 2770
   5-D 0762

6.

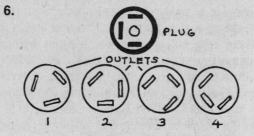

   The outlet that will accept the plug is

   6-A 1
   6-B 2
   6-C 3
   6-D 4

7. The following equipment is required for a "2-line return-call" electric bell circuit:

   7-A 2 bells, 2 metallic lines, 2 ordinary push buttons, and one set of batteries

7-B 2 bells, 2 metallic lines, 2 return-call push buttons and 2 sets of batteries

7-C 2 bells, 2 metallic lines, 2 return-call push buttons and one set of batteries

7-D 2 bells, 2 metallic lines, one ordinary push button, one return-call push button and one set of batteries

8. To determine directly whether all finished wire installations possess resistance between conductors, and between conductors and ground, use

8-A clamps
8-B set screws
8-C shields
8-D megger

9. Locknuts are frequently used in making electrical connections on terminal boards. The purpose of the locknuts is to

9-A eliminate the use of flat washers
9-B prevent unauthorized personnel from tampering with the connections
9-C keep the connections from loosening through vibration
9-D increase the contact area at the connection point

10. Low Potential is a trade term which refers to

10-A 700 volts
10-B 600 volts or less
10-C 1200 volts
10-D 900 volts

11. The three elements of a transistor are

11-A collector, base, emitter
11-B collector, grid, cathode
11-C plate, grid, emitter
11-D plate, base, cathode

12.

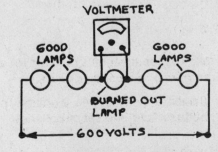

The reading of the voltmeter should be

12-A 600
12-B 300
12-C 120
12-D zero

13.

The reading of the kilowatt-hour meter is

13-A 7972
13-B 1786
13-C 2786
13-D 6872

14.

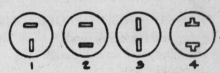

The convenience outlet that is known as *polarized* outlet is number

14-A 1
14-B 2
14-C 3
14-D 4

15. An alternator is

15-A an a.c. generator
15-B a frequency meter
15-C a ground detector device
15-D a choke coil

16. The term which is NOT applicable in describing the *construction* of a microphone is

16-A dynamic
16-B carbon
16-C crystal
16-D feedback

17. In order to control a lamp from two different positions it is necessary to use

17-A two single pole switches

17-B one single pole switch and one four way switch

17-C two three-way switches

17-D one single pole switch and two four way switches

18. When the electric refrigerator in a certain household kitchen starts up, the kitchen light at first dims down considerably and then it increases somewhat in brightness while the refrigerator motor is running; the light finally returns to full brightness when the refrigerator shuts off. This behavior of the light shows that most likely the

18-A circuit wires are too small

18-B refrigerator motor is defective

18-C circuit fuse is too small

18-D kitchen lamp is too large

19. Rosin is a material generally used

19-A in batteries

19-B for high voltage insulation

19-C as a dielectric

19-D as a soldering flux

20. A compound motor usually has

20-A only a shunt field

20-B both a shunt and a series field

20-C only a series field

20-D no brushes

END OF EXAMINATION

IF YOU FINISH BEFORE TIME IS UP, CHECK YOUR WORK ON THIS PART ONLY. DO NOT GO BACK TO ANY PREVIOUS PART.

CORRECT ANSWERS—THIRD MODEL EXAM

PART 1—GENERAL SCIENCE

1. C	5. B	8. D	11. B	14. C	17. D	20. C	23. C
2. C	6. D	9. C	12. B	15. D	18. C	21. C	24. B
3. B	7. D	10. B	13. A	16. D	19. D	22. B	25. B
4. A							

PART 2—ARITHMETIC REASONING

1. A	5. D	9. C	13. B	17. C	21. C	25. B	28. D
2. D	6. B	10. A	14. B	18. D	22. A	26. D	29. C
3. C	7. D	11. C	15. C	19. B	23. D	27. C	30. D
4. D	8. A	12. C	16. C	20. D	24. A		

PART 3—WORD KNOWLEDGE

1. B	6. D	11. B	16. C	20. B	24. C	28. C	32. C
2. D	7. B	12. B	17. B	21. D	25. A	29. B	33. D
3. C	8. B	13. C	18. B	22. C	26. D	30. C	34. D
4. D	9. A	14. C	19. B	23. C	27. B	31. B	35. C
5. D	10. D	15. A					

PART 4—PARAGRAPH COMPREHENSION

1. D	3. C	5. D	7. B	9. C	11. D	13. B	15. D
2. B	4. B	6. B	8. C	10. B	12. B	14. D	

PART 5—NUMERICAL OPERATIONS

1. B	8. B	15. D	21. A	27. A	33. D	39. B	45. C
2. C	9. C	16. D	22. D	28. D	34. A	40. D	46. B
3. B	10. A	17. C	23. C	29. A	35. C	41. B	47. A
4. D	11. A	18. B	24. D	30. B	36. A	42. D	48. D
5. C	12. C	19. D	25. B	31. C	37. C	43. D	49. B
6. B	13. D	20. D	26. D	32. B	38. C	44. D	50. C
7. A	14. B						

PART 6—CODING SPEED

1. C	12. C	23. A	34. C	45. E	55. C	65. A	75. E
2. E	13. C	24. E	35. A	46. A	56. B	66. C	76. D
3. D	14. D	25. D	36. C	47. C	57. A	67. B	77. A
4. D	15. B	26. E	37. D	48. C	58. A	68. D	78. B
5. A	16. E	27. B	38. B	49. D	59. E	69. A	79. E
6. B	17. C	28. D	39. D	50. B	60. C	70. E	80. A
7. D	18. E	29. A	40. C	51. E	61. B	71. C	81. A
8. A	19. A	30. E	41. A	52. E	62. E	72. E	82. E
9. A	20. D	31. B	42. E	53. D	63. B	73. C	83. C
10. C	21. A	32. A	43. C	54. B	64. E	74. D	84. B
11. E	22. C	33. C	44. D				

PART 7—AUTO & SHOP INFORMATION

1. C	5. A	8. B	11. A	14. B	17. B	20. D	23. B
2. D	6. B	9. C	12. D	15. D	18. A	21. D	24. B
3. D	7. C	10. A	13. A	16. B	19. B	22. C	25. A
4. C							

PART 8—MATHEMATICS KNOWLEDGE

1. C	5. D	8. B	11. C	14. D	17. D	20. B	23. B
2. A	6. C	9. B	12. D	15. B	18. D	21. B	24. B
3. A	7. D	10. B	13. D	16. B	19. D	22. B	25. C
4. A							

PART 9—MECHANICAL COMPREHENSION

1. D	5. A	8. A	11. D	14. A	17. A	20. A	23. D
2. B	6. C	9. B	12. C	15. B	18. A	21. C	24. A
3. C	7. C	10. A	13. B	16. B	19. D	22. C	25. B
4. B							

PART 10—ELECTRONICS INFORMATION

1. B	4. B	7. B	10. B	13. D	15. A	17. C	19. D
2. C	5. A	8. D	11. A	14. A	16. D	18. A	20. B
3. B	6. C	9. C	12. A				

SCORE SHEET—THIRD MODEL EXAM

PART	NUMBER CORRECT		NUMBER OF QUESTIONS	
GENERAL SCIENCE	16	÷ 25 =	9	× 100 = 90 %
ARITHMETIC REASONING	10	÷ 30 =	3	× 100 = 83 %
WORD KNOWLEDGE	30	÷ 35 =	36	× 100 = 1.87 %
PARAGRAPH COMPREHENSION	14	÷ 15 =	1	× 100 = 100 %
NUMERICAL OPERATIONS		÷ 50 =		× 100 = %
CODING SPEED		÷ 84 =		× 100 = %
AUTO & SHOP INFORMATION		÷ 25 =		× 100 = %
MATHEMATICS KNOWLEDGE		÷ 25 =		× 100 = %
MECHANICAL COMPREHENSION		÷ 25 =		× 100 = %
ELECTRONICS INFORMATION		÷ 20 =		× 100 = %
TOTAL		÷ 334 =		× 100 = %

PROGRESS CHART

	Exam I	Exam II	Exam III
GENERAL SCIENCE	%	%	%
ARITHMETIC REASONING	%	%	%
WORD KNOWLEDGE	%	%	%
PARAGRAPH COMPREHENSION	%	%	%
NUMERICAL OPERATIONS	%	%	%
CODING SPEED	%	%	%
AUTO & SHOP INFORMATION	%	%	%
MATHEMATICS KNOWLEDGE	%	%	%
MECHANICAL COMPREHENSION	%	%	%
ELECTRONICS INFORMATION	%	%	%
TOTAL	%	%	%

WHAT ABOUT ASVAB-5?

ASVAB-5 is the high school version of the ASVAB exam. At one time, ASVAB-5 was the only exam administered both to military recruits and to high school students. With the development of the newer exam, described in this book up to this point, ASVAB-5 has been limited to use in the high school testing program. The testing program is widely used in high schools as an aid to vocational counseling. The high school counselor may request this service, and, free of charge, military personnel will administer the exam and assist with its interpretation. The Military Enlistment Processing Command has prepared charts and tables which help the counselor to compare the student's scores on each part with those of other high school students and with those of military men successful in the various training areas. The pattern of subscores—individual part scores and combined scores of certain parts—helps to define a student's areas of interest, aptitude and ability. This information is useful whether the student is considering a military or a civilian career. With the information provided by the student's ASVAB-5 scores and pattern of scores, the school counselor can be of greater assistance in helping the student to establish realistic goals and to choose the best path for attaining them.

A student who has taken ASVAB-5 in high school does not have to take another exam should he or she choose to enter the Air Force right after graduation. Although versions of the exam differ slightly, the information they give is comparable and the Air Force is able to interpret ASVAB-5 scores for its own purposes.

If you are still in high school and are planning a military career, try the full-length specimen ASVAB-5 that follows. Carefully follow all directions and time limits. Score yourself and compare your scores on this exam with your scores on the three model exams you did earlier in the book. If you find that you are happier with General Information, Attention to Detail and Space Perception than you are with Paragraph Comprehension and Coding Speed, then you might discuss with your counselor the possibility of taking ASVAB-5 in school. On the other hand, you are *not required* to offer ASVAB-5 scores even though you are still in high school. If you prefer the newer exam, you may take it as well, and offer its scores for training school placement. Follow your recruiter's instructions. He/she will direct you to the enlistment testing center for your area and will tell you when to report for testing.

If you are no longer in high school, you cannot take ASVAB-5. We suggest that you just skip over General Information, Attention to Detail and Space Perception, none of which will appear on your exam. However, we do recommend that you answer all the remaining questions in the Specimen ASVAB-5. These questions are similar to questions on the exam you will take, and answering them will give you valuable extra practice.

SPECIMEN ASVAB-5

ANSWER SHEET—SPECIMEN ASVAB-5

PART 1—GENERAL INFORMATION

1 Ⓐ Ⓑ Ⓒ Ⓓ   6 Ⓐ Ⓑ Ⓒ Ⓓ   11 Ⓐ Ⓑ Ⓒ Ⓓ   16 Ⓐ Ⓑ Ⓒ Ⓓ

2 Ⓐ Ⓑ Ⓒ Ⓓ   7 Ⓐ Ⓑ Ⓒ Ⓓ   12 Ⓐ Ⓑ Ⓒ Ⓓ   17 Ⓐ Ⓑ Ⓒ Ⓓ

3 Ⓐ Ⓑ Ⓒ Ⓓ   8 Ⓐ Ⓑ Ⓒ Ⓓ   13 Ⓐ Ⓑ Ⓒ Ⓓ   18 Ⓐ Ⓑ Ⓒ Ⓓ

4 Ⓐ Ⓑ Ⓒ Ⓓ   9 Ⓐ Ⓑ Ⓒ Ⓓ   14 Ⓐ Ⓑ Ⓒ Ⓓ   19 Ⓐ Ⓑ Ⓒ Ⓓ

5 Ⓐ Ⓑ Ⓒ Ⓓ   10 Ⓐ Ⓑ Ⓒ Ⓓ   15 Ⓐ Ⓑ Ⓒ Ⓓ   20 Ⓐ Ⓑ Ⓒ Ⓓ

PART 2—NUMERICAL OPERATIONS

21 Ⓐ Ⓑ Ⓒ Ⓓ   31 Ⓐ Ⓑ Ⓒ Ⓓ   41 Ⓐ Ⓑ Ⓒ Ⓓ   51 Ⓐ Ⓑ Ⓒ Ⓓ   61 Ⓐ Ⓑ Ⓒ Ⓓ

22 Ⓐ Ⓑ Ⓒ Ⓓ   32 Ⓐ Ⓑ Ⓒ Ⓓ   42 Ⓐ Ⓑ Ⓒ Ⓓ   52 Ⓐ Ⓑ Ⓒ Ⓓ   62 Ⓐ Ⓑ Ⓒ Ⓓ

23 Ⓐ Ⓑ Ⓒ Ⓓ   33 Ⓐ Ⓑ Ⓒ Ⓓ   43 Ⓐ Ⓑ Ⓒ Ⓓ   53 Ⓐ Ⓑ Ⓒ Ⓓ   63 Ⓐ Ⓑ Ⓒ Ⓓ

24 Ⓐ Ⓑ Ⓒ Ⓓ   34 Ⓐ Ⓑ Ⓒ Ⓓ   44 Ⓐ Ⓑ Ⓒ Ⓓ   54 Ⓐ Ⓑ Ⓒ Ⓓ   64 Ⓐ Ⓑ Ⓒ Ⓓ

25 Ⓐ Ⓑ Ⓒ Ⓓ   35 Ⓐ Ⓑ Ⓒ Ⓓ   45 Ⓐ Ⓑ Ⓒ Ⓓ   55 Ⓐ Ⓑ Ⓒ Ⓓ   65 Ⓐ Ⓑ Ⓒ Ⓓ

26 Ⓐ Ⓑ Ⓒ Ⓓ   36 Ⓐ Ⓑ Ⓒ Ⓓ   46 Ⓐ Ⓑ Ⓒ Ⓓ   56 Ⓐ Ⓑ Ⓒ Ⓓ

66 Ⓐ Ⓑ Ⓒ Ⓓ

27 Ⓐ Ⓑ Ⓒ Ⓓ   37 Ⓐ Ⓑ Ⓒ Ⓓ   47 Ⓐ Ⓑ Ⓒ Ⓓ   57 Ⓐ Ⓑ Ⓒ Ⓓ   67 Ⓐ Ⓑ Ⓒ Ⓓ

28 Ⓐ Ⓑ Ⓒ Ⓓ   38 Ⓐ Ⓑ Ⓒ Ⓓ   48 Ⓐ Ⓑ Ⓒ Ⓓ   58 Ⓐ Ⓑ Ⓒ Ⓓ   68 Ⓐ Ⓑ Ⓒ Ⓓ

29 Ⓐ Ⓑ Ⓒ Ⓓ   39 Ⓐ Ⓑ Ⓒ Ⓓ   49 Ⓐ Ⓑ Ⓒ Ⓓ   59 Ⓐ Ⓑ Ⓒ Ⓓ   69 Ⓐ Ⓑ Ⓒ Ⓓ

30 Ⓐ Ⓑ Ⓒ Ⓓ   40 Ⓐ Ⓑ Ⓒ Ⓓ   50 Ⓐ Ⓑ Ⓒ Ⓓ   60 Ⓐ Ⓑ Ⓒ Ⓓ   70 Ⓐ Ⓑ Ⓒ Ⓓ

PART 3—ATTENTION TO DETAIL

71 ⑪ ⑫ ⑬ ⑭ ⑮   77 ⑪ ⑫ ⑬ ⑭ ⑮   83 ⑪ ⑫ ⑬ ⑭ ⑮   89 ⑪ ⑫ ⑬ ⑭ ⑮   95 ⑪ ⑫ ⑬ ⑭ ⑮

72 ⑪ ⑫ ⑬ ⑭ ⑮   78 ⑪ ⑫ ⑬ ⑭ ⑮   84 ⑪ ⑫ ⑬ ⑭ ⑮   90 ⑪ ⑫ ⑬ ⑭ ⑮   96 ⑪ ⑫ ⑬ ⑭ ⑮

73 ⑪ ⑫ ⑬ ⑭ ⑮   79 ⑪ ⑫ ⑬ ⑭ ⑮   85 ⑪ ⑫ ⑬ ⑭ ⑮   91 ⑪ ⑫ ⑬ ⑭ ⑮   97 ⑪ ⑫ ⑬ ⑭ ⑮

74 ⑪ ⑫ ⑬ ⑭ ⑮   80 ⑪ ⑫ ⑬ ⑭ ⑮   86 ⑪ ⑫ ⑬ ⑭ ⑮   92 ⑪ ⑫ ⑬ ⑭ ⑮   98 ⑪ ⑫ ⑬ ⑭ ⑮

75 ⑪ ⑫ ⑬ ⑭ ⑮   81 ⑪ ⑫ ⑬ ⑭ ⑮   87 ⑪ ⑫ ⑬ ⑭ ⑮   93 ⑪ ⑫ ⑬ ⑭ ⑮   99 ⑪ ⑫ ⑬ ⑭ ⑮

76 ⑪ ⑫ ⑬ ⑭ ⑮   82 ⑪ ⑫ ⑬ ⑭ ⑮   88 ⑪ ⑫ ⑬ ⑭ ⑮   94 ⑪ ⑫ ⑬ ⑭ ⑮   100 ⑪ ⑫ ⑬ ⑭ ⑮

PART 4—WORD KNOWLEDGE

1 Ⓐ Ⓑ Ⓒ Ⓓ	7 Ⓐ Ⓑ Ⓒ Ⓓ	13 Ⓐ Ⓑ Ⓒ Ⓓ	19 Ⓐ Ⓑ Ⓒ Ⓓ	25 Ⓐ Ⓑ Ⓒ Ⓓ
2 Ⓐ Ⓑ Ⓒ Ⓓ	8 Ⓐ Ⓑ Ⓒ Ⓓ	14 Ⓐ Ⓑ Ⓒ Ⓓ	20 Ⓐ Ⓑ Ⓒ Ⓓ	26 Ⓐ Ⓑ Ⓒ Ⓓ
3 Ⓐ Ⓑ Ⓒ Ⓓ	9 Ⓐ Ⓑ Ⓒ Ⓓ	15 Ⓐ Ⓑ Ⓒ Ⓓ	21 Ⓐ Ⓑ Ⓒ Ⓓ	27 Ⓐ Ⓑ Ⓒ Ⓓ
4 Ⓐ Ⓑ Ⓒ Ⓓ	10 Ⓐ Ⓑ Ⓒ Ⓓ	16 Ⓐ Ⓑ Ⓒ Ⓓ	22 Ⓐ Ⓑ Ⓒ Ⓓ	28 Ⓐ Ⓑ Ⓒ Ⓓ
5 Ⓐ Ⓑ Ⓒ Ⓓ	11 Ⓐ Ⓑ Ⓒ Ⓓ	17 Ⓐ Ⓑ Ⓒ Ⓓ	23 Ⓐ Ⓑ Ⓒ Ⓓ	29 Ⓐ Ⓑ Ⓒ Ⓓ
6 Ⓐ Ⓑ Ⓒ Ⓓ	12 Ⓐ Ⓑ Ⓒ Ⓓ	18 Ⓐ Ⓑ Ⓒ Ⓓ	24 Ⓐ Ⓑ Ⓒ Ⓓ	30 Ⓐ Ⓑ Ⓒ Ⓓ

PART 5—ARITHMETIC REASONING

31 Ⓐ Ⓑ Ⓒ Ⓓ	35 Ⓐ Ⓑ Ⓒ Ⓓ	39 Ⓐ Ⓑ Ⓒ Ⓓ	43 Ⓐ Ⓑ Ⓒ Ⓓ	47 Ⓐ Ⓑ Ⓒ Ⓓ
32 Ⓐ Ⓑ Ⓒ Ⓓ	36 Ⓐ Ⓑ Ⓒ Ⓓ	40 Ⓐ Ⓑ Ⓒ Ⓓ	44 Ⓐ Ⓑ Ⓒ Ⓓ	48 Ⓐ Ⓑ Ⓒ Ⓓ
33 Ⓐ Ⓑ Ⓒ Ⓓ	37 Ⓐ Ⓑ Ⓒ Ⓓ	41 Ⓐ Ⓑ Ⓒ Ⓓ	45 Ⓐ Ⓑ Ⓒ Ⓓ	49 Ⓐ Ⓑ Ⓒ Ⓓ
34 Ⓐ Ⓑ Ⓒ Ⓓ	38 Ⓐ Ⓑ Ⓒ Ⓓ	42 Ⓐ Ⓑ Ⓒ Ⓓ	46 Ⓐ Ⓑ Ⓒ Ⓓ	50 Ⓐ Ⓑ Ⓒ Ⓓ

PART 6—SPACE PERCEPTION

51 Ⓐ Ⓑ Ⓒ Ⓓ	55 Ⓐ Ⓑ Ⓒ Ⓓ	59 Ⓐ Ⓑ Ⓒ Ⓓ	63 Ⓐ Ⓑ Ⓒ Ⓓ	67 Ⓐ Ⓑ Ⓒ Ⓓ
52 Ⓐ Ⓑ Ⓒ Ⓓ	56 Ⓐ Ⓑ Ⓒ Ⓓ	60 Ⓐ Ⓑ Ⓒ Ⓓ	64 Ⓐ Ⓑ Ⓒ Ⓓ	68 Ⓐ Ⓑ Ⓒ Ⓓ
53 Ⓐ Ⓑ Ⓒ Ⓓ	57 Ⓐ Ⓑ Ⓒ Ⓓ	61 Ⓐ Ⓑ Ⓒ Ⓓ	65 Ⓐ Ⓑ Ⓒ Ⓓ	69 Ⓐ Ⓑ Ⓒ Ⓓ
54 Ⓐ Ⓑ Ⓒ Ⓓ	58 Ⓐ Ⓑ Ⓒ Ⓓ	62 Ⓐ Ⓑ Ⓒ Ⓓ	66 Ⓐ Ⓑ Ⓒ Ⓓ	70 Ⓐ Ⓑ Ⓒ Ⓓ

PART 7—MATHEMATICS KNOWLEDGE

71 Ⓐ Ⓑ Ⓒ Ⓓ	75 Ⓐ Ⓑ Ⓒ Ⓓ	79 Ⓐ Ⓑ Ⓒ Ⓓ	83 Ⓐ Ⓑ Ⓒ Ⓓ	87 Ⓐ Ⓑ Ⓒ Ⓓ
72 Ⓐ Ⓑ Ⓒ Ⓓ	76 Ⓐ Ⓑ Ⓒ Ⓓ	80 Ⓐ Ⓑ Ⓒ Ⓓ	84 Ⓐ Ⓑ Ⓒ Ⓓ	88 Ⓐ Ⓑ Ⓒ Ⓓ
73 Ⓐ Ⓑ Ⓒ Ⓓ	77 Ⓐ Ⓑ Ⓒ Ⓓ	81 Ⓐ Ⓑ Ⓒ Ⓓ	85 Ⓐ Ⓑ Ⓒ Ⓓ	89 Ⓐ Ⓑ Ⓒ Ⓓ
74 Ⓐ Ⓑ Ⓒ Ⓓ	78 Ⓐ Ⓑ Ⓒ Ⓓ	82 Ⓐ Ⓑ Ⓒ Ⓓ	86 Ⓐ Ⓑ Ⓒ Ⓓ	90 Ⓐ Ⓑ Ⓒ Ⓓ

PART 8—ELECTRONICS INFORMATION

91 Ⓐ Ⓑ Ⓒ Ⓓ   97 Ⓐ Ⓑ Ⓒ Ⓓ   103 Ⓐ Ⓑ Ⓒ Ⓓ   109 Ⓐ Ⓑ Ⓒ Ⓓ   115 Ⓐ Ⓑ Ⓒ Ⓓ

92 Ⓐ Ⓑ Ⓒ Ⓓ   98 Ⓐ Ⓑ Ⓒ Ⓓ   104 Ⓐ Ⓑ Ⓒ Ⓓ   110 Ⓐ Ⓑ Ⓒ Ⓓ   116 Ⓐ Ⓑ Ⓒ Ⓓ

93 Ⓐ Ⓑ Ⓒ Ⓓ   99 Ⓐ Ⓑ Ⓒ Ⓓ   105 Ⓐ Ⓑ Ⓒ Ⓓ   111 Ⓐ Ⓑ Ⓒ Ⓓ   117 Ⓐ Ⓑ Ⓒ Ⓓ

94 Ⓐ Ⓑ Ⓒ Ⓓ   100 Ⓐ Ⓑ Ⓒ Ⓓ   106 Ⓐ Ⓑ Ⓒ Ⓓ   112 Ⓐ Ⓑ Ⓒ Ⓓ   118 Ⓐ Ⓑ Ⓒ Ⓓ

95 Ⓐ Ⓑ Ⓒ Ⓓ   101 Ⓐ Ⓑ Ⓒ Ⓓ   107 Ⓐ Ⓑ Ⓒ Ⓓ   113 Ⓐ Ⓑ Ⓒ Ⓓ   119 Ⓐ Ⓑ Ⓒ Ⓓ

96 Ⓐ Ⓑ Ⓒ Ⓓ   102 Ⓐ Ⓑ Ⓒ Ⓓ   108 Ⓐ Ⓑ Ⓒ Ⓓ   114 Ⓐ Ⓑ Ⓒ Ⓓ   120 Ⓐ Ⓑ Ⓒ Ⓓ

PART 9—MECHANICAL COMPREHENSION

121 Ⓐ Ⓑ Ⓒ Ⓓ   125 Ⓐ Ⓑ Ⓒ Ⓓ   129 Ⓐ Ⓑ Ⓒ Ⓓ   133 Ⓐ Ⓑ Ⓒ Ⓓ   137 Ⓐ Ⓑ Ⓒ Ⓓ

122 Ⓐ Ⓑ Ⓒ Ⓓ   126 Ⓐ Ⓑ Ⓒ Ⓓ   130 Ⓐ Ⓑ Ⓒ Ⓓ   134 Ⓐ Ⓑ Ⓒ Ⓓ   138 Ⓐ Ⓑ Ⓒ Ⓓ

123 Ⓐ Ⓑ Ⓒ Ⓓ   127 Ⓐ Ⓑ Ⓒ Ⓓ   131 Ⓐ Ⓑ Ⓒ Ⓓ   135 Ⓐ Ⓑ Ⓒ Ⓓ   139 Ⓐ Ⓑ Ⓒ Ⓓ

124 Ⓐ Ⓑ Ⓒ Ⓓ   128 Ⓐ Ⓑ Ⓒ Ⓓ   132 Ⓐ Ⓑ Ⓒ Ⓓ   136 Ⓐ Ⓑ Ⓒ Ⓓ   140 Ⓐ Ⓑ Ⓒ Ⓓ

PART 10—GENERAL SCIENCE

141 Ⓐ Ⓑ Ⓒ Ⓓ   145 Ⓐ Ⓑ Ⓒ Ⓓ   149 Ⓐ Ⓑ Ⓒ Ⓓ   153 Ⓐ Ⓑ Ⓒ Ⓓ   157 Ⓐ Ⓑ Ⓒ Ⓓ

142 Ⓐ Ⓑ Ⓒ Ⓓ   146 Ⓐ Ⓑ Ⓒ Ⓓ   150 Ⓐ Ⓑ Ⓒ Ⓓ   154 Ⓐ Ⓑ Ⓒ Ⓓ   158 Ⓐ Ⓑ Ⓒ Ⓓ

143 Ⓐ Ⓑ Ⓒ Ⓓ   147 Ⓐ Ⓑ Ⓒ Ⓓ   151 Ⓐ Ⓑ Ⓒ Ⓓ   155 Ⓐ Ⓑ Ⓒ Ⓓ   159 Ⓐ Ⓑ Ⓒ Ⓓ

144 Ⓐ Ⓑ Ⓒ Ⓓ   148 Ⓐ Ⓑ Ⓒ Ⓓ   152 Ⓐ Ⓑ Ⓒ Ⓓ   156 Ⓐ Ⓑ Ⓒ Ⓓ   160 Ⓐ Ⓑ Ⓒ Ⓓ

PART 11—SHOP INFORMATION

161 Ⓐ Ⓑ Ⓒ Ⓓ   165 Ⓐ Ⓑ Ⓒ Ⓓ   169 Ⓐ Ⓑ Ⓒ Ⓓ   173 Ⓐ Ⓑ Ⓒ Ⓓ   177 Ⓐ Ⓑ Ⓒ Ⓓ

162 Ⓐ Ⓑ Ⓒ Ⓓ   166 Ⓐ Ⓑ Ⓒ Ⓓ   170 Ⓐ Ⓑ Ⓒ Ⓓ   174 Ⓐ Ⓑ Ⓒ Ⓓ   178 Ⓐ Ⓑ Ⓒ Ⓓ

163 Ⓐ Ⓑ Ⓒ Ⓓ   167 Ⓐ Ⓑ Ⓒ Ⓓ   171 Ⓐ Ⓑ Ⓒ Ⓓ   175 Ⓐ Ⓑ Ⓒ Ⓓ   179 Ⓐ Ⓑ Ⓒ Ⓓ

164 Ⓐ Ⓑ Ⓒ Ⓓ   168 Ⓐ Ⓑ Ⓒ Ⓓ   172 Ⓐ Ⓑ Ⓒ Ⓓ   176 Ⓐ Ⓑ Ⓒ Ⓓ   180 Ⓐ Ⓑ Ⓒ Ⓓ

PART 12—AUTOMOTIVE INFORMATION

181 Ⓐ Ⓑ Ⓒ Ⓓ   185 Ⓐ Ⓑ Ⓒ Ⓓ   189 Ⓐ Ⓑ Ⓒ Ⓓ   193 Ⓐ Ⓑ Ⓒ Ⓓ   197 Ⓐ Ⓑ Ⓒ Ⓓ

182 Ⓐ Ⓑ Ⓒ Ⓓ   186 Ⓐ Ⓑ Ⓒ Ⓓ   190 Ⓐ Ⓑ Ⓒ Ⓓ   194 Ⓐ Ⓑ Ⓒ Ⓓ   198 Ⓐ Ⓑ Ⓒ Ⓓ

183 Ⓐ Ⓑ Ⓒ Ⓓ   187 Ⓐ Ⓑ Ⓒ Ⓓ   191 Ⓐ Ⓑ Ⓒ Ⓓ   195 Ⓐ Ⓑ Ⓒ Ⓓ   199 Ⓐ Ⓑ Ⓒ Ⓓ

184 Ⓐ Ⓑ Ⓒ Ⓓ   188 Ⓐ Ⓑ Ⓒ Ⓓ   192 Ⓐ Ⓑ Ⓒ Ⓓ   196 Ⓐ Ⓑ Ⓒ Ⓓ   200 Ⓐ Ⓑ Ⓒ Ⓓ

PART 1

GENERAL INFORMATION

TIME: 7 Minutes. 20 Questions.

This is a test to find out how much you know about different kinds of things. Pick the best answer for each question, then blacken the space on your separate answer form which has the same number and letter as your choice.

1. A rose is a kind of
   1-A   animal.
   1-B   bird.
   1-C   flower.
   1-D   fish.

2. An ally of the United States during WWII was
   2-A   Japan.
   2-B   Germany.
   2-C   Italy.
   2-D   Great Britain.

3. How many degrees apart are the foul lines on a baseball field?
   3-A   60°
   3-B   90°
   3-C   120°
   3-D   180°

4. For which of the following taxes was it necessary to amend the US Constitution?
   4-A   Income.
   4-B   Sales.
   4-C   Liquor.
   4-D   Tobacco.

5. Picasso was a famous
   5-A   poet.
   5-B   painter.
   5-C   philosopher.
   5-D   soldier.

6. Which one of the following states does **not** border Canada?
   6-A   Washington.
   6-B   Idaho.
   6-C   Wyoming.
   6-D   New York.

7. The Rosetta stone provided the key for translating
   7-A   The Mosaic Tablets.
   7-B   Babylonian Cuneiform.
   7-C   New Testament Papyri.
   7-D   Egyptian Hieroglyphs.

8. A women writer famous for her books about China is
   8-A   Pearl Buck.
   8-B   Ellen Glasgow.
   8-C   Willa Cather.
   8-D   Edith Wharton.

9. During the period from 1963 to 1974 which collegiate basketball team won the most NCAA titles?
   9-A   North Carolina State University.
   9-B   Marquette University.
   9-C   University of California at Los Angeles.
   9-D   University of Houston.

10. Which flower below is grown from a bulb?

10-A   Petunia.
10-B   Cosmos.
10-C   Gladiola.
10-D   Poppy.

11. A fabric woven from smooth surface yarn spun from long, stapled wool is

11-A   Gingham.
11-B   Convert Cloth.
11-C   Worsted.
11-D   Shetland Tweed.

12. Which city below has a Spanish name?

12-A   New Orleans.
12-B   Sault Ste. Marie.
12-C   Seattle.
12-D   Monterey.

13. A coarse acid bread made of unbolted rye is called

13-A   Black bread.
13-B   Pumpernickel.
13-C   French bread.
13-D   Vienna bread.

14. Citrus fruits include

14-A   Apples.
14-B   Bananas.
14-C   Oranges.
14-D   Peaches.

15. Margaret Chase Smith is a noted

15-A   Interior decorator.
15-B   Political figure.
15-C   Business executive.
15-D   Television commentator.

16. Cork is obtained from

16-A   An animal skeleton.
16-B   A tree.
16-C   A mineral.
16-D   A deep-sea plant.

17. The author of the Pulitzer prize winning play "Death of a Salesman" is

17-A   Arthur Miller.
17-B   Henry Miller.
17-C   Sidney Miller.
17-D   Mitchell Miller.

18. The state which has the smallest area is

18-A   Nevada.
18-B   Rhode Island.
18-C   Connecticut.
18-D   Delaware.

19. A man of the Renaissance who worked in many fields of art and science was

19-A   Niccolo Machiavelli.
19-B   Sir Thomas More.
19-C   Erasmus.
19-D   Francis Bacon.

20. In the United Nations, one difference between the General Assembly and the Security Council is that the General Assembly

20-A   Permits use of the veto.
20-B   Includes Communist China.
20-C   Does not deal with military matters.
20-D   Gives more power to the smaller nations.

STOP!

IF YOU FINISH THIS PART BEFORE THE TIME IS UP, CHECK OVER YOUR WORK ON THIS PART ONLY. DO NOT GO ON UNTIL YOU ARE TOLD TO DO SO.

PART 2

NUMERICAL OPERATIONS

TIME: 3 Minutes. 50 Questions.

This is a test to see how rapidly and accurately you can do arithmetic problems. Each problem is followed by four answers, only one of which is correct. Decide which answer is correct, then blacken the space on your answer form which has the same number and letter as your choice.

This is a speed test, so work as fast as you can without making mistakes. Do each problem as it comes. If you finish before time is up, go back and check your work.

21. 2 + 3 =
- 21-A 1
- 21-B 4
- 21-C 5
- 21-D 6

22. 8 − 5 =
- 22-A 3
- 22-B 1
- 22-C 4
- 22-D 2

23. 9 ÷ 3 =
- 23-A 2
- 23-B 3
- 23-C 6
- 23-D 4

24. 4 × 2 =
- 24-A 2
- 24-B 4
- 24-C 6
- 24-D 8

25. 7 − 3 =
- 25-A 5
- 25-B 3
- 25-C 2
- 25-D 4

26. 9 + 1 =
- 26-A 10
- 26-B 8
- 26-C 2
- 26-D 7

27. 8 − 4 =
- 27-A 4
- 27-B 12
- 27-C 10
- 27-D 2

28. 2 × 8 =
- 28-A 10
- 28-B 6
- 28-C 16
- 28-D 4

29. 9 − 6 =
- 29-A 1
- 29-B 2
- 29-C 3
- 29-D 4

30. 3 − 2 =
- 30-A 1
- 30-B 2
- 30-C 3
- 30-D 4

31. 1 − 1 =
- 31-A 2
- 31-B 3
- 31-C 0
- 31-D 1

32. 2 × 9 =
- 32-A 16
- 32-B 17
- 32-C 18
- 32-D 20

33. 9 + 3 =
- 33-A 3
- 33-B 7
- 33-C 11
- 33-D 12

34. 8 + 6 =
- 34-A 2
- 34-B 10
- 34-C 12
- 34-D 14

35. 9 − 4 =
- 35-A 3
- 35-B 5
- 35-C 6
- 35-D 7

36. 10 ÷ 2 =
- 36-A 8
- 36-B 7
- 36-C 6
- 36-D 5

37. 7 − 2 =
- 37-A 5
- 37-B 7
- 37-C 9
- 37-D 10

38. 3 − 3 =
- 38-A 0
- 38-B 5
- 38-C 6
- 38-D 9

39. 4 − 3 =
- 39-A 0
- 39-B 1
- 39-C 2
- 39-D 4

40. 8 − 3 =
- 40-A 3
- 40-B 4
- 40-C 5
- 40-D 6

41. 7 × 4 =
- 41-A 28
- 41-B 30
- 41-C 32
- 41-D 34

42. 5 + 8 =
- 42-A 3
- 42-B 7
- 42-C 12
- 42-D 13

43. 20 ÷ 2 =
- 43-A 6
- 43-B 8
- 43-C 10
- 43-D 12

44. 15 − 7 =
- 44-A 5
- 44-B 8
- 44-C 10
- 44-D 12

45. 6 ÷ 2 =

    45-A 3
    45-B 4
    45-C 5
    45-D 8

46. 9 − 1 =

    46-A 2
    46-B 5
    46-C 6
    46-D 8

47. 10 − 2 =

    47-A 8
    47-B 7
    47-C 5
    47-D 4

48. 1 + 6 =

    48-A 5
    48-B 7
    48-C 8
    48-D 9

49. 4 × 5 =

    49-A 8
    49-B 10
    49-C 16
    49-D 20

50. 7 − 7 =

    50-A 14
    50-B 10
    50-C 1
    50-D 0

51. 5 + 5 =

    51-A 0
    51-B 10
    51-C 15
    51-D 20

52. 5 × 3 =

    52-A 8
    52-B 10
    52-C 13
    52-D 15

53. 16 ÷ 4 =

    53-A 2
    53-B 4
    53-C 6
    53-D 7

54. 7 + 9 =

    54-A 2
    54-B 13
    54-C 16
    54-D 18

55. 5 × 5 =

    55-A 10
    55-B 15
    55-C 20
    55-D 25

56. 4 − 3 =

    56-A 1
    56-B 5
    56-C 7
    56-D 9

57. 7 + 3 =

    57-A 4
    57-B 5
    57-C 9
    57-D 10

58. 9 + 3 =

    58-A 3
    58-B 6
    58-C 12
    58-D 13

59. 6 + 4 =

    59-A 10
    59-B 12
    59-C 14
    59-D 16

60. 10 + 2 =

    60-A 4
    60-B 5
    60-C 8
    60-D 12

61. 2 + 8 =

    61-A 6
    61-B 8
    61-C 10
    61-D 12

62. 8 − 2 =

    62-A 4
    62-B 6
    62-C 8
    62-D 10

63. 2 + 2 =

    63-A 4
    63-B 5
    63-C 6
    63-D 8

64. 3 × 5 =

    64-A 8
    64-B 10
    64-C 12
    64-D 15

65. 25 ÷ 5 =

    65-A 4
    65-B 5
    65-C 6
    65-D 7

66. 30 ÷ 5 =

    66-A 5
    66-B 6
    66-C 7
    66-D 8

67. 7 + 5 =

    67-A 12
    67-B 13
    67-C 14
    67-D 15

68. 3 × 6 =

    68-A 3
    68-B 9
    68-C 15
    68-D 18

69. 9 − 6 =

    69-A 3
    69-B 7
    69-C 14
    69-D 15

70. 4 × 6 =

    70-A 10
    70-B 20
    70-C 24
    70-D 26

STOP!

**IF YOU FINISH THIS PART BEFORE THE TIME IS UP, CHECK OVER
YOUR WORK ON THIS PART ONLY. DO NOT GO ON UNTIL YOU ARE
TOLD TO DO SO.**

PART 3

ATTENTION TO DETAIL

TIME: 5 Minutes

This is a test of your ability to find an important detail. For each problem in the test, there are five possible answers. There is only one correct answer for each problem. Look at each problem carefully, and decide which one of the five answers is correct.

Now look at Sample Problem S1

O O C O C O O O O C O O O O O O O O C O O O O C O C C O O O C O O O O O O O O O
O O O O O C O O O O O O C O O O C O O C O O C O O C O O O O O O O O C O O O O O O O O O

There are two lines of O's with some C's mixed in. You are to count the total number of C's in both lines of the problem. There are 14 C's in both lines of Sample Problem S1, so 14 is the correct answer. After the number S1, below, are five numbers: 11, 12, 13, 14, and 15. The space under the number 14 is blackened out to show that 14 is the correct answer.

S1   11   12   13   14   15
       O   O   O   ●   O

Now look at Sample Problem S2.

O C O O O O O C O O O O C O O O O O O O C O O O O O C O O O O O O O O O O C O O O
O O O O O O O O C O C O O C O O O O O O O O O O O O C O C O O O C O O O O C O O O O O

Count the number of C's in both lines of the problem. You may find 11, 12, 13, 14, or 15 C's. Do this now.

There are 12 C's, so 12 is the correct answer.

This is a speed test, so work as fast as you can without making mistakes.

71. O O O O O O O C O O O C O O O O O O O C O O O O C O O O O O O O O C O O
O O O O O C O O O C O O O O O C O O O O O O C O O O C O O C O O C O O O O C O

72. O C O O O O C O O O O O C O O O C O O O O O C O C O O O C O O O O O O O C O O O O
O O O O O C O C O O O O O O O O C O O O O O O C O O O O O O O O O O O O O O O O

73. O O O O O O O C O C O O C O O O O O O O O O O O O O O O C O O O C O O O O C O O O O
O O C O O O O O O C O O O C O O O O O O C O O O C O O O C O O O O O O O C O O O O

74. O O O O O O O C O C O O O O C O O O O O O O O O O O O O O O C O O O O O O O O O O O
O O O O O O C O O C O O C O O O O O O C O O O O C O O O O O O O O C O O O O C O O C O

75. C O O O O O O O O O C O O O O O O O O O O O O O O C O O O C O O O O O C O O O O O O O
O C O O O O O O C O C O O O O O O O O O O C O O O O O O C O O O O O O C O O O O C O O

76. O O C O O O O O C O O C O O O O O O O O O O C O O O O O C O O O O C O O O O O O O O O
C O O O O O O O C O O O C O O O O O C O O O C O O O O O O O O O O O C O O O O O O O

77. O O O O C O O C O O C O O O O O O O O O O O O O O O O O O C O O C O O C O C O O O O
O C O O O C O O O O O O C O C O O O O O C O O O O O O O O O C C O O O O O O C O O O O

78. C O O C O O O O O C O O O O C O O O O O O C O C O O O O O O O C O O O O O O O O C O O
O O O C C O O C O O O O O O O O O O O O O O O O O O O O O O C O O O O O C O O O O O O O

79. O C O O O O O C O O O O O O O C C O O O O O O O O C O O O O O O O O C O O O C O O O O O
O O O O O O O O C O O O O O C O O C O O O O O O O O C O O O O O O O O O O O O O O

80. O O C C C O O O O O C O O C O O O O O O O O O C O O O C O O O O O C O C O O O O O O
C O O O O C O O O O O O O O O C O O O C O O O O O O O O O O O O O C O O O O O O O O

81. C O O C O O O C O O O O O O O O O C O O O O O O O O O C O O C O O C O O O O O C O O
O O C O O O C O O O O O O O O O O O O O O C O O C C C O O O C O C O O O O O O O

82. O O O O C O O O C O C O O O O C O O C O O O O O C O O O O O O O O C O O O O C O O O C O O
O O O O C O O O C O O C O O O O O O O O O O C O O C O C O O O O O O O C C O O O O O

83. O C O O O O O O O C O O O O C O O O O O O O O C O O O C O O O O O O O O O O O
O O C O O O O O O O C O C C O O O O O O O O C O O O C O O O O C O O O O C O O O C O O

84. C O C O O C O O O O O O O C O O C O O O O O O O O O O C O O O O C O O O O O C O O O
C O O O O O O O C O O C O O O O O O O O O C O O O C O O O O O C O O O O O C O O

85. O O C O O O O C O O O O O O O C O O O O O C O O C O O O O O O O O C O O C O O O C O O
O O O C O O C O O O O O O O O O O O C O O O C O C O O O O O O O O O O O O O C O O O O

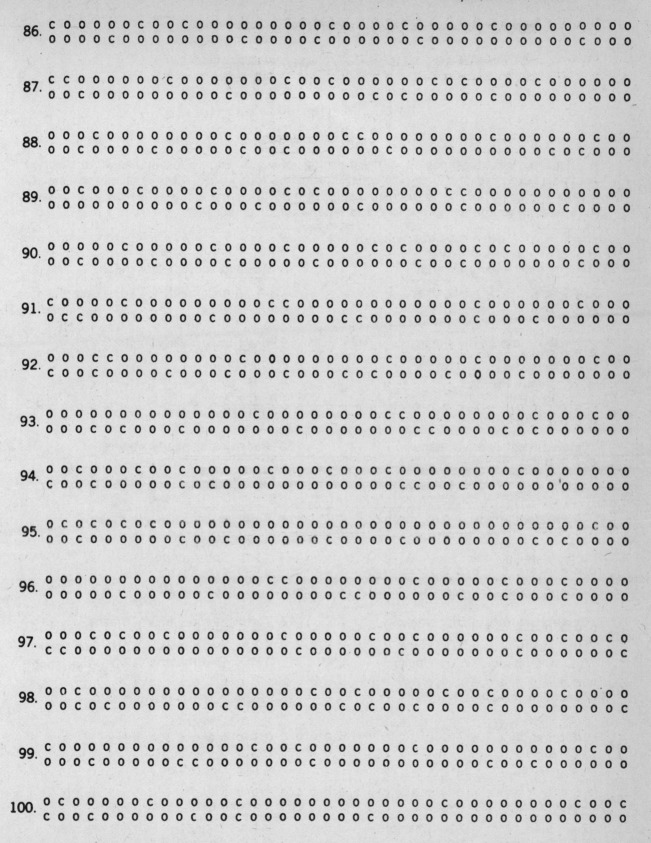

PART 4

WORD KNOWLEDGE

TIME: 10 Minutes. 30 Questions.

This test has questions about the meanings of words. Each question has an underlined boldface word. You are to decide which one of the four words in the choices most nearly means the same as the underlined boldface word, then mark the space on your answer form which has the same number and letter as your choice.

1. **Inform** most nearly means

    1-A Ask. 1-B Heed.
    1-C Tell. 1-D Ignore.

2. **Crimson** most nearly means

    2-A Crisp.
    2-B Neatly Pressed.
    2-C Reddish.
    2-D Colorful.

3. **Caution** most nearly means

    3-A Signals. 3-B Care.
    3-C Traffic. 3-D Haste.

4. **Intermittently** most nearly means

    4-A Constantly.
    4-B Annually.
    4-C Using intermediaries (to stay).
    4-D At irregular intervals.

5. **Occurrence** most nearly means

    5-A Event. 5-B Place.
    5-C Occupation. 5-D Opinion.

6. **Deception** most nearly means

    6-A Secrets.
    6-B Fraud.
    6-C Mistrust.
    6-D Hatred.

7. **Cease** most nearly means

    7-A Start. 7-B Change.
    7-C Continue. 7-D Stop.

8. **Acclaim** most nearly means

    8-A Amazement. 8-B Laughter.
    8-C Booing. 8-D Applause.

9. **Erect** most nearly means

    9-A Paint.
    9-B Design.
    9-C Destroy.
    9-D Construct.

10. **Relish** most nearly means

    10-A Care. 10-B Speed.
    10-C Amusement. 10-D Enjoy.

11. **Sufficient** most nearly means

    11-A Durable.
    11-B Substitution.
    11-C Expendable.
    11-D Appropriate.

12. **Fortnight** most nearly means

    12-A Two weeks. 12-B One week.
    12-C Two months. 12-D One month.

13. **Blemish** most nearly means

    13-A Defect
    13-B Mixture.
    13-C Accusation.
    13-D Decoration.

14. **Impose** most nearly means

    14-A Disguise. 14-B Escape.
    14-C Require. 14-D Purchase.

15. **Jeer** most nearly means

  15-A Peek.
  15-B Scoff.
  15-C Turn.
  15-D Judge.

16. **Alias** most nearly means

  16-A Enemy.
  16-B Sidekick.
  16-C Hero.
  16-D Other name.

17. **Impair** most nearly means.

  17-A Direct.
  17-B Improve.
  17-C Weaken.
  17-D Stimulate.

18. **Itinerant** most nearly means.

  18-A Traveling.
  18-B Shrewd.
  18-C Insurance.
  18-D Aggressive.

19. **Abandon** most nearly means.

  19-A Relinguish.
  19-B Encompass.
  19-C Infiltrate.
  19-D Quarantine.

20. **Resolve** most nearly means.

  20-A End.
  20-B Understand.
  20-C Recall.
  20-D Forget.

21. **Ample** means

  21-A Plentiful.
  21-B Enthusiastic.
  21-C Well shaped.
  21-D Fat.

22. **Stench** most nearly means.

  22-A Puddle of slimy water.
  22-B Pile of debris.
  22-C Foul odor.
  22-D Dead animal.

23. **Sullen** most nearly means.

  23-A Grayish yellow.
  23-B Soaking wet.
  23-C Very dirty.
  23-D Angrily silent.

24. **Rudiments** most nearly means.

  24-A Basic methods and procedures.
  24-B Politics.
  24-C Promotion opportunities.
  24-D Minute details.

25. **Clash** most nearly means:

  25-A Applaud.
  25-B Fasten.
  25-C Conflict.
  25-D Punish.

26. **Camaraderie** most nearly means.

  26-A Interest in photography.
  26-B Close friendship.
  26-C Petty jealousies.
  26-D Arts and crafts projects.

27. **Superficial** most nearly means.

  27-A Excellent.
  27-B Official.
  27-C Profound.
  27-D Cursory.

28. **Tapestry** most nearly means.

  28-A Fabric of woven designs.
  28-B Tent
  28-C Piece of elaborate jewelry.
  28-D Exquisite painting.

29. **Terse** most nearly means.

  29-A Pointed.
  29-B Trivial.
  29-C Oral.
  29-D Lengthy.

30. **Concoction** most nearly means.

  30-A Combination of ingredients.
  30-B Appetizer.
  30-C Drink made of wine and spices.
  30-D Relish tray.

PART 5

ARITHMETIC REASONING

TIME: 20 Minutes. 20 Questions.

This test has questions about arithmetic. Each question is followed by four possible answers. Decide which answer is correct, then blacken the space on your answer form which has the same number and letter as your choice. Use your scratch paper for any figuring you wish to do.

Your score on this test will be based on the number of questions you answer correctly. You should try to answer every question. Do not spend too much time on any one question.

31. A fruit picker gets $2.00 an hour plus 48¢ for every bushel over 40 that he picks in a day. If he works 8 hours and picks 50 bushels, how much will he get?

31-A $16.00
31-B $19.84
31-C $20.80
31-D $24.00

32. How many 36 passenger buses will it take to carry 144 people?

32-A 4
32-B 3
32-C 5
32-D 6

33. A gallon contains 4 quarts. A cartoning machine can fill 120 one-quart cartons a minute. How long will it take to put 600 gallons of orange juice into cartons?

33-A 1 minute and 15 seconds
33-B 5 minutes
33-C 10 minutes
33-D 20 minutes

34. A man who runs a filling station greased 168 cars in 28 days. What was his daily average of cars greased?

34-A 5
34-B 6
34-C 7
34-D 8

35. What is the fifth term in the series: 4½; 8¾; 13; 17¼; _____?

35-A 20¾
35-B 21
35-C 21½
35-D 21¾

36. Three girls assemble 360 switches per hour, but 5% of the switches are defective. How many good (nondefective) switches will these 3 girls assemble in an 8-hour shift?

36-A 2736
36-B 2880
36-C 2944
36-D 3000

37. The butcher made 22½ pounds of beef into hamburger and wrapped it in 1¼-pound packages. How many packages did he make?

37-A 15
37-B 16
37-C 17
37-D 18

38. A car-renting agency charges a fixed rate of $8 per day plus 8 cents per mile. If a family paid the agency $260 for the use of a car on a 2,450-mile trip, how many days was the car used?

38-A 8 days
38-B 24½ days
38-C 26 days
38-D 32 days

39. It cost a boy $13.50 to take a girl out for the evening. Sixty per cent of this was for theater tickets. What was the cost for each ticket?

   39-A $3.95
   39-B $4.05
   39-C $5.40
   39-D $8.10

40. Soap, ordinarily priced at 2 bars for $0.66, may be purchased in lots of one dozen for $3.48. What is the saving per bar when it is purchased in this way?

   40-A 4 cents
   40-B 8 cents
   40-C 16 cents
   40-D 19 cents

41. Twenty men contribute $25 each for a Christmas party. Forty percent of the money is spent for food and drinks. How much is left for other expenses?

   41-A $125
   41-B $200
   41-C $300
   41-D $375

42. A pole 24 feet high has a shadow 8 feet long. A nearby pole is 72 feet high. How long is its shadow?

   42-A 16 feet
   42-B 24 feet
   42-C 32 feet
   42-D 56 feet

43. The price of a $250 item after successive discounts of 20% and 30% is

   43-A $125
   43-B $130
   43-C $140
   43-D $180

44. If the following series will continue in the same pattern, what is the next number in the series 1, 10, 7, 16, _____?

   44-A 10
   44-B 13
   44-C 14
   44-D 25

45. A home has a tax rate of 2%. If the tax is $550.00, what is the assessed value of the home?

   45-A $1,100.00
   45-B $2,750.00
   45-C $11,000.00
   45-D $27,500.00

46. The parcel post rate in the local zone is 18 cents for the first pound and 1½ cents for each additional pound. How many pounds can be sent in the local zone for $1.50?

   46-A 88
   46-B 89
   46-C 100
   46-D 225

47. The minute hand fell off a watch but the watch continued to work accurately. What time was it when the hour hand was at the 17-minute mark?

   47-A 3:02
   47-B 3:17
   47-C 3:24
   47-D 4:17

48. A dressmaker has 3,375 yards of material on hand. If the average dress takes 3⅜ yards of material, how many dresses can he make?

   48-A 844
   48-B 1000
   48-C 1125
   48-D 1250

49. It cost $0.50 per square yard to waterproof canvas. What will it cost to waterproof a canvas truck cover that is 15' x 24'?

   49-A $6.67
   49-B $18.00
   49-C $20.00
   49-D $180.00

50. Mary put in a total of 16½ hours baby-sitting during 5 days of the past week. What was her average work day?

   50-A 3 hours
   50-B 3 hours, 15 minutes
   50-C 3 hours, 18 minutes
   50-D 3 hours, 25 minutes

PART 6

SPACE PERCEPTION

TIME: 12 Minutes. 20 Questions.

This test has questions about folding cardboard patterns into boxes. The first row of pictures below shows what this means. The dotted lines show where folds are to be made. The last picture shows the box that has been made by folding.

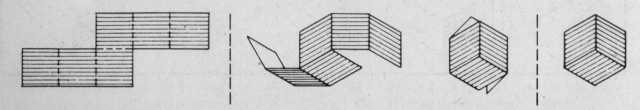

In the test, the first picture in each row shows a cardboard pattern that is to be folded. There are also four boxes in each row, labeled A, B, C, D. Your job is to find which box could be made by folding the pattern.

Look at the sample question. Which box could this pattern make?

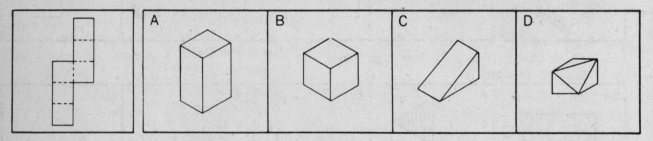

The B answer is correct.

Here is another type of question. Which of the four patterns would result when the box is unfolded?

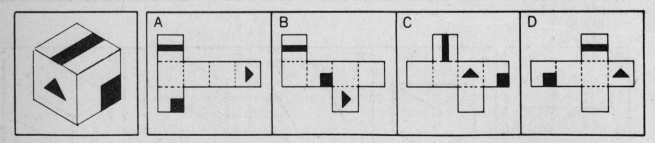

The D answer is correct.

Your score on this test will be based on the number of questions you answer correctly. You should try to answer every question. Do not spend too much time on any one question.

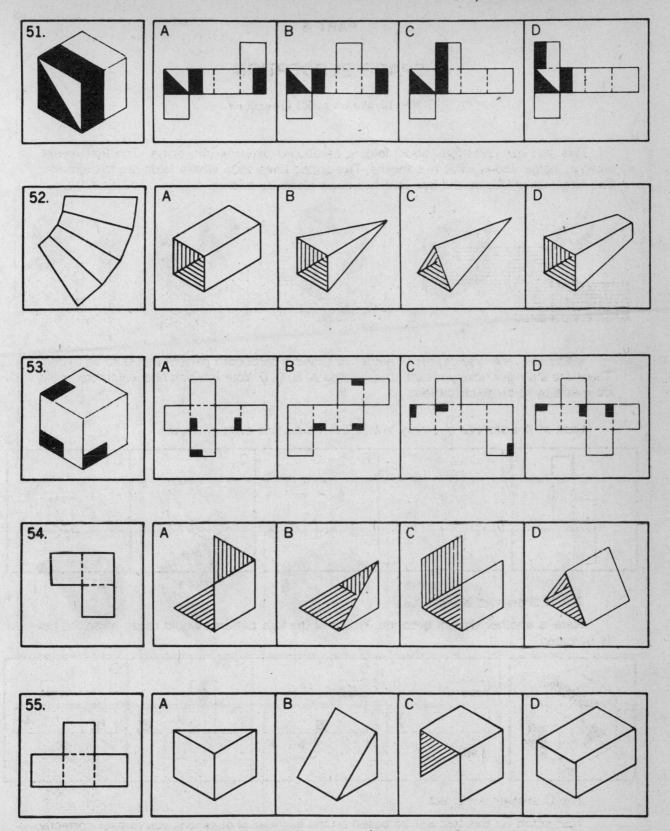

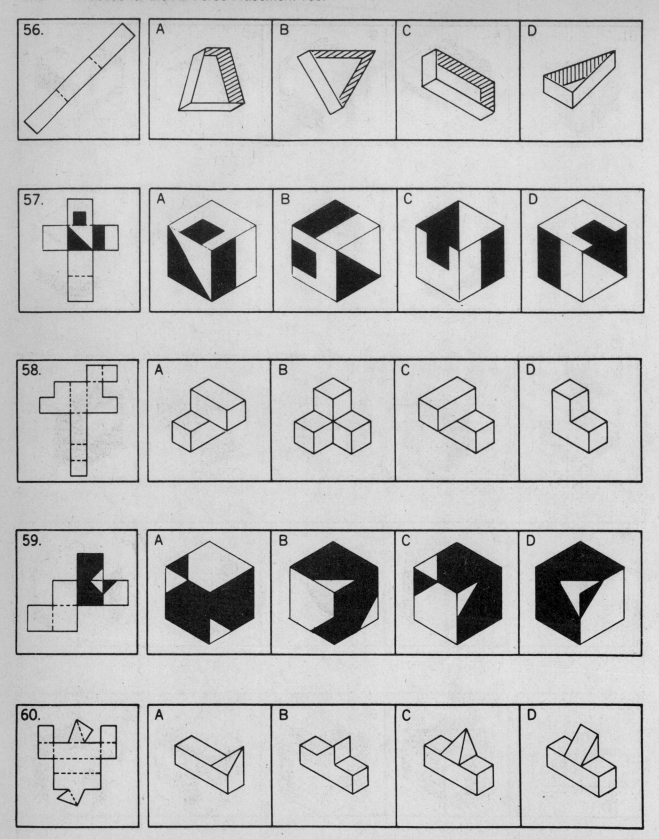

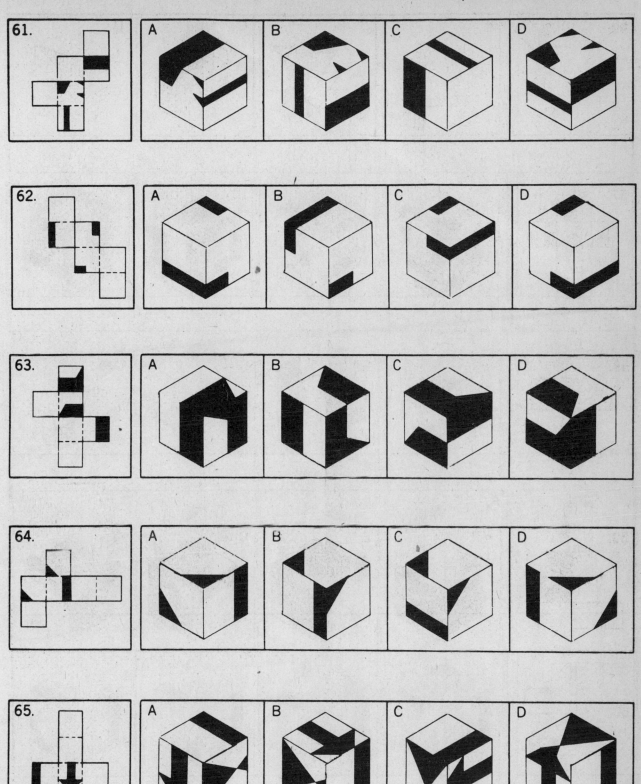

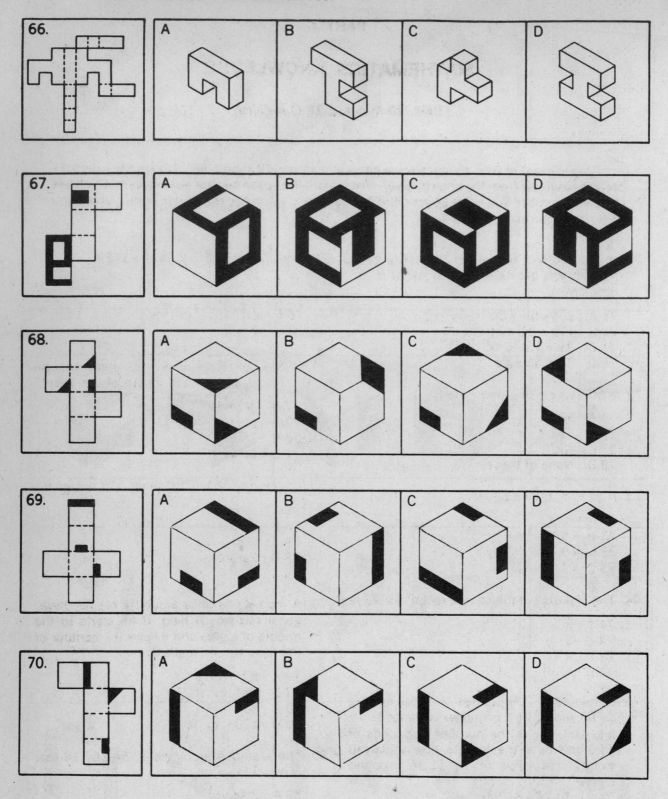

PART 7

MATHEMATICS KNOWLEDGE

TIME: 20 Minutes. 20 Questions.

This is a test of your ability to solve general mathematical problems. You are to select the correct response from the choices given. Then mark the space on your answer form which has the same number and letter as your choice. Use the scratch paper that has been given to you to do any figuring that you wish.

71. If you subtract $6a - 4b + 3c$ from a polynomial, you get $4a + 9b - 5c$. What is the polynomial?

   71-A $10a - 5b + 2c$
   71-B $10a + 5b - 2c$
   71-C $2a + 13b - 8c$
   71-D $2a + 5b + 8c$

72. If 50% of $x = 66$, then $x =$

   72-A   33
   72-B   99
   72-C   122
   72-D   None of these

73. If $3x = -5$, then x equals

   73-A $3/5$
   73-B $-5/3$
   73-C $-3/5$
   73-D -2

74. The first digit of the square root of 59043 is

   74-A   2
   74-B   3
   74-C   4
   74-D   5

75. A mixture of 200 pounds of coffee costing $1.06 and $1.26 a pound was sold for $1.15 a pound. If x is the number of pounds of $1.06 coffee in the mixture, how would you express the value of the $1.26 a pound coffee?

   75-A $\$1.26 - \$1.06x$
   75-B $\$1.26(200 - x)$
   75-C $\$1.15(200) - \$1.26x/\$1.06x$
   75-D $\$1.15(\$1.06x \cdot 200)$

76. The value of $27/8 \times 24/9 \div 3/2 =$

   76-A   6
   76-B $7\ 2/9$
   76-C $8\ 1/4$
   76-D $9\ 5/8$

77. If the perimeter of an equilateral triangle is $6n-12$, what is the length of the base?

   77-A $3(2n-4)$
   77-B $2(3n-6)$
   77-C $3n-6$
   77-D $2n-4$

78. Which one of the following is a polygon?

   78-A   Circle
   78-B   Ellipse
   78-C   Star
   78-D   Parabola

79. A man walks once around a regular hexagonal (six-sided) field. If he starts in the middle of a side and follows the contour of the field, he will make 6

   79-A $30°$ turns
   79-B $45°$ turns
   79-C $60°$ turns
   79-D $120°$ turns

80. The area of a rectangle 12 feet by 18 feet is equal to

   80-A   8 sq yds
   80-B   24 sq yds
   80-C   36 sq yds
   80-D   72 sq yds

81. Given the formulas d = rt and A = r + d/t, which formula below correctly expresses the value of A without using t?

   81-A   A = dr
   81-B   A = r + 2d/r
   81-C   A = 2r + d
   81-D   A = 2r

82. If a + 6 = 7, then a is equal to

   82-A   0
   82-B   1
   82-C   −1
   82-D   7/6

83. The distance in miles around a circular course with a radius of 35 miles is (use Pi = 22/7)

   83-A   156
   83-B   220
   83-C   440
   83-D   880

84. The expression "3 factorial" equals

   84-A   1/9
   84-B   1/6
   84-C   6
   84-D   9

85. If you multiply x + 3 by 2x + 5, how many x's will there be in the product?

   85-A   3
   85-B   6
   85-C   9
   85-D   11

86. Solve for x: $\dfrac{2x}{7} = 2x^2$

   86-A   1/7
   86-B   2/7
   86-C   2
   86-D   7

87. Solve the following equation for C

   $$A^2 = \frac{B^2}{C + D}$$

   87-A $C = \dfrac{B^2 - A^2 D}{A^2 B}$

   87-B $C = \dfrac{A^2 - D}{B^2}$

   87-C $C = \dfrac{A^2 + D}{B^2 - D}$

   87-D $C = \dfrac{B^2 - D}{A^2}$

88. The expression, -1 (3 -2), is equal to

   88-A   −3 + 2
   88-B   −3 − 2
   88-C   3 − 2
   88-D   3 + 2

89. The reciprocal of 5 is

   89-A   1.0
   89-B   0.5
   89-C   0.2
   89-D   0.1

90. What is the area, in square inches, of a circle whose radius measures

   7 inches? (Use $\dfrac{22}{7}$ for Pi)

   90-A   22
   90-B   44
   90-C   154
   90-D   616

STOP!

IF YOU FINISH THIS PART BEFORE THE TIME IS UP, CHECK OVER YOUR WORK ON THIS PART ONLY. DO NOT GO ON UNTIL YOU ARE TOLD TO DO SO.

PART 8

ELECTRONICS INFORMATION

TIME: 15 Minutes. 30 Questions.

This is a test of your knowledge of electrical, radio, and electronics information. You are to select the correct response from the choices given. Then mark the space on your answer form which has the same number and letter as your choice.

91. The most likely cause of a burned-out fuse in the primary circuit of a transformer in a rectifier is

   91-A grounding of the electrostatic shield.
   91-B an open circuit in a bleeder resistor.
   91-C an open circuit in the secondary. winding.
   91-D a short-circuited filter capacitor.

92. The primary coil of a power transformer has 100 turns and the secondary coil has 50 turns. The voltage across the secondary will be

   92-A four times that of the primary.
   92-B twice that of the primary.
   92-C half that of the primary.
   92-D one-fourth that of the primary.

93. The best electrical connection between two wires is obtained when

   93-A the insulations are melted together
   93-B all insultation is removed and the wires bound together with friction tape.
   93-C both are wound on a common binding post.
   93-D they are soldered together.

94. Excessive resistance in the primary circuit will lessen the output of the ignition coil and cause the

   94-A battery to short out and the generator to run down.
   94-B battery to short out and the plugs to wear out prematurely.
   94-C generator to run down and the timing mechanism to slow down.
   94-D engine to perform poorly and hard to start.

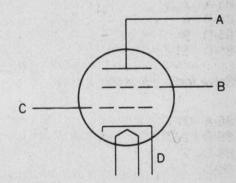

95. In the schematic vacuum tube illustrated, the cathode is element

   95-A A.
   95-B B.
   95-C C.
   95-D D.

96. The main reason for making wire stranded is

  96-A to make it easier to insulate.
  96-B so that the insulation will not come off.
  96-C to decrease its weight.
  96-D to make it more flexible.

97. The oscilloscope image shown above represents

  97-A steady DC.
  97-B resistance in a resistor.
  97-C AC.
  97-D pulsating DC.

98. Voltage drop in a circuit is usually due to

  98-A inductance.
  98-B capacitance.
  98-C resistance.
  98-D conductance.

99. If an increase in grid voltage no longer produces an increase in plate current, the tube has reached its

  99-A inversion point.
  99-B saturation point.
  99-C class C operating point.
  99-D class A operating point.

100. Earphones are generally not used with radio receivers having more than three tubes because

  100-A earphones can handle only alternating current.
  100-B the amplification factor makes them unnecessary.
  100-C only one person may hear them at a time.
  100-D earphones are too delicate for normal use.

101. Of the non-metallic elements listed below, which one is the best conductor of electricity?

  101-A Mica.
  101-B Carbon.
  101-C Formica.
  101-D Hard rubber.

102. If an electric motor designed for use on AC is plugged into a DC source, what will probably happen?

  102-A Excessive heat will be produced.
  102-B It will operate the same as usual.
  102-C It will continue to operate, but will not get so warm.
  102-D It cannot be predicted what will happen.

103. Most electrical problems involving voltage, resistance, and current are solved by applying

  103-A Ohm's Law.
  103-B Watt's Law.
  103-C Coulomb's Law.
  103-D Kirchoff's Voltage and Current Laws.

104. If every time a washing machine is started the circuit breaker must be reset, the **best** solution would be to

  104-A oil the motor in the washer.
  104-B replace the circuit breaker.
  104-C tape the breaker switch closed.
  104-D repair the timing mechanism.

105. In most AC-DC radio circuits when one tube filament burns out, it will

  105-A cause the others to burn out
  105-B open the circuit and keep the others from operating.
  105-C cause the remaining ones to operate at higher current ratings.
  105-D cause the line voltage to drop.

106. The most stable type of radio oscillating circuit is the

  106-A electron-coupled.
  106-B crystal.
  106-C heterodyne.
  106-D colpitts.

107. The ampere is the unit of measurement of

  107-A inductance.
  107-B resistance
  107-C voltage.
  107-D current.

108. Hoping to make his car run faster, a "hot-rodder" decides to try changing the ignition mechanism. He finds all the components in good working order, so he decides to

  108-A use a larger capacitor on the points.
  108-B retard the ignition several degrees.
  108-C put hotter spark plugs in the engine.
  108-D check the ignition timing.

109. A mixer, in radio terminology, would function to

  109-A jumble a carrier wave for security transmissions.
  109-B couple the stages of two succeeding circuits.
  109-C coordinate the triodes in a push-pull power amplifier circuit.
  109-D combine the incoming and local oscillator frequencies.

110. Flux is used in the process of soldering together two conductors in order to

  110-A provide a luster finish.
  110-B prevent oxidation when the connection is heated.
  110-C maintain the temperature of the soldering iron.
  110-D prevent the connection from becoming overheated.

111. Which of the following devices converts heat energy directly into electrical energy?

  111-A A piezoelectric crystal.
  111-B A photoelectric cell.
  111-C A steam driven generator.
  111-D A thermocouple.

112. One use of a coaxial cable is to

  112-A ground a signal.
  112-B pass a signal from the set to the antenna of a mobile unit
  112-C carry the signal from a ballast tube.
  112-D carry grid signals in high altitude areas.

113. Which of the following has the **least** resistance?

  113-A silver.
  113-B aluminum.
  113-C copper.
  113-D iron.

114. A rectifier is used to convert

  114-A alternating current into direct current.
  114-B static current into direct current.
  114-C direct current into alternating current.
  114-D low frequency current into high frequency current.

115. The length of a radio transmitter antenna system is primarily determined by

  115-A transmitter power.
  115-B transmitter frequency.
  115-C oscillator voltage.
  115-D distance from receiving antenna.

116. Which one of the following may best be compared to electrical voltage?

  116-A Tension.
  116-B Resistance.
  116-C Flow.
  116-D Pressure.

117. The extent to which a radio receiver converts the signals received into sounds that are undistorted is called

    117-A fidelity.
    117-B sensitivity.
    117-C selectivity.
    117-D resonance.

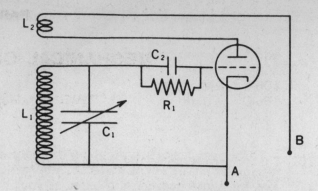

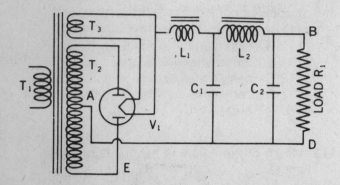

118. The tube in the figure above acts as a

    118-A voltage regulator.
    118-B voltage divider.
    118-C half-wave rectifier.
    118-D full-wave rectifier.

119. The oscillator in the circuit in the figure shown above is known as a

    119-A tuned-grid oscillator.
    119-B tuned-plate oscillator.
    119-C electron-coupled oscillator.
    119-D resistance feedback.

120. The power supply in a vacuum tube equipped auto radio differs from the power supply in an AC home radio in that the former utilizes a

    120-A filter capacitor.
    120-B choke.
    120-C vibrator.
    120-D rectifier tube.

STOP!

IF YOU FINISH THIS PART BEFORE THE TIME IS UP, CHECK OVER YOUR WORK ON THIS PART ONLY. DO NOT GO ON UNTIL YOU ARE TOLD TO DO SO.

PART 9

MECHANICAL COMPREHENSION

TIME: 15 Minutes. 20 Questions.

This test has questions about mechanical and physical principles. Study the pictures and decide which answer is correct. Then mark the space on your separate answer form which has the same number and letter as your choice.

Here is a sample question.

Which bridge is the strongest?

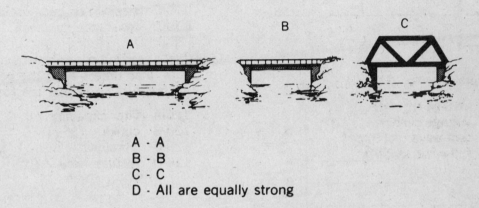

A - A
B - B
C - C
D - All are equally strong

The C answer is correct.

Your score on this test will be based on the number of questions you answer correctly. You should try to answer every question. Do not spend too much time on any one question.

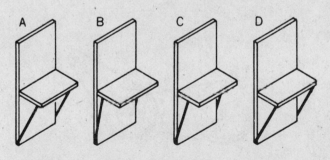

121. Which shelf could support the most weight?

121-A   A.
121-B   B.
121-C   C.
121-D   D.

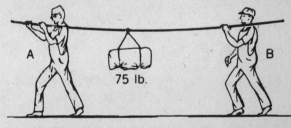

122. The weight is being carried entirely on the shoulders of the two men shown. Which man bears the most weight on his shoulder?

122-A   A.
122-B   B.
122-C   Both men are carrying the same.
122-D   It is impossible to tell.

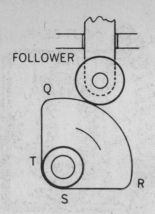

FOLLOWER

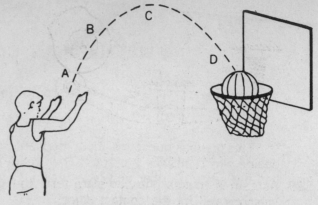

123. The follower is at its highest position between points

123-A   Q and R.
123-B   R and S.
123-C   S and T.
123-D   T and Q.

126. At which point was the basketball moving slowest?

126-A   A.
126-B   B.
126-C   C.
126-D   D.

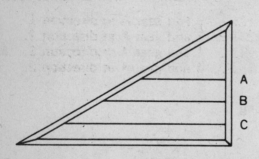

124. All of the wires are of the same substance, the same diameter, and under the same tension. Which will vibrate at the highest frequency?

124-A   A.
124-B   B.
124-C   C.
124-D   They will vibrate at equal frequency

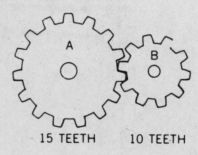

15 TEETH   10 TEETH

127. If gear A makes 14 revolutions, gear B will make

127-A   21.
127-B   17.
127-C   14.
127-D   9.

125. A man in an elevator is carrying a heavy suitcase. The suitcase will feel heaviest to him when the elevator

125-A   has not yet started moving.
125-B   is gaining speed in descent.
125-C   is maintaining a rapid steady speed of descent.
125-D   is gaining speed in ascent.

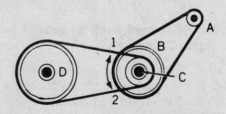

128. If pulley A is the driver and turns in direction 1, which pulley turns fastest?

128-A   A.
128-B   B.
128-C   C.
128-D   D.

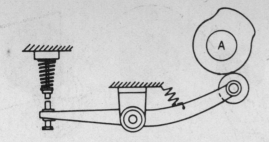

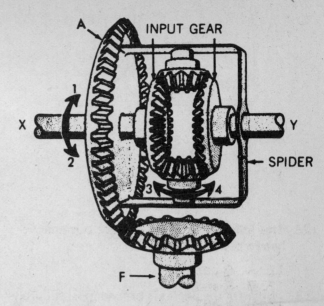

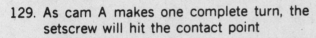

129. As cam A makes one complete turn, the setscrew will hit the contact point

    129-A Once.
    129-B Twice.
    129-C Three times.
    129-D Not at all.

131. If shaft X turns in direction 2 as shaft Y is held fixed, shaft F will turn in direction

    131-A 3 and gear A in direction 1.
    131-B 3 and gear A in direction 2.
    131-C 4 and gear A in direction 1.
    131-D 4 and gear A in direction 2.

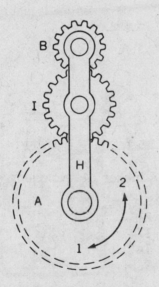

130. If arm H is held fixed as gear B turns in direction 2, gear

    130-A A must turn in direction 1.
    130-B A must turn in direction 2.
    130-C I must turn in direction 2.
    130-D A must be held fixed.

132. A 150-pound man jumps off a 600-pound raft to a point in the water 12 feet away. Theoretically, the raft would move

    132-A 12 feet in the same direction.
    132-B 6 feet in the same direction.
    132-C 3 feet in the opposite direction.
    132-D 1 foot in the opposite direction.

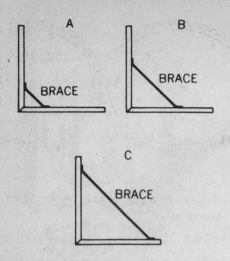

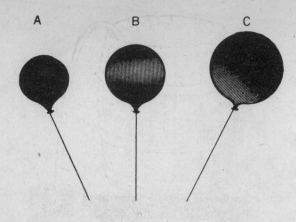

133. Which of the angles is braced most securely?

    133-A A.

    133-B B.

    133-C C.

    133-D All equally braced.

135. The amount of gas in the balloons is equal. The atmospheric pressure outside the balloons is highest on which balloon?

    135-A A.

    135-B B.

    135-C C.

    135-D The pressure is equal on all balloons.

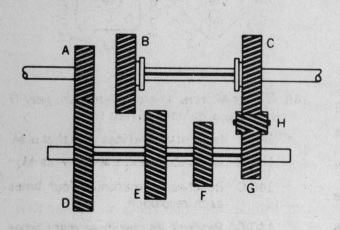

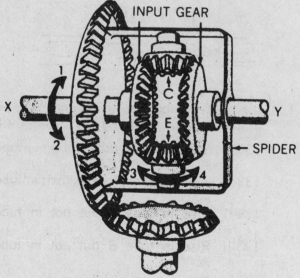

134. Gear B is intended to mesh with

    134-A gear A only.

    134-B gear D only.

    134-C gear E only.

    134-D all of the above gears.

136. If shaft X turns in direction 1 and shaft Y is held fixed, gear C will turn in direction

    136-A 3 and gear E in direction 3.

    136-B 3 and gear E in direction 4.

    136-C 4 and gear E in direction 3.

    136-D 4 and gear E in direction 4.

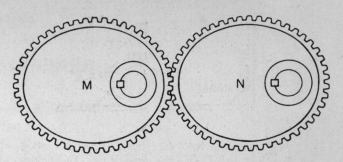

137. Liquid is being transferred from the barrel to the bucket by

137-A Suction in the hose.
137-B Fluid pressure in the hose.
137-C Air pressure on top of the liquid.
137-D Capillary action.

139. If gear N turns at a constant rpm, gear M turns at

139-A The same constant rpm as N.

139-B A faster constant rpm than N.

139-C A slower constant rpm than N.

139-D A variable rpm.

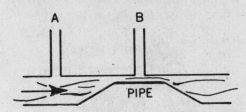

138. If water is pumped rapidly through the pipe in the direction shown by the arrow, it will

138-A Rise higher in tube A than in tube B.
138-B Rise higher in tube B than in tube A.
138-C Rise in tube A but not in tube B.
138-D Rise in tube B but not in tube A.

140. If gear M turns at a constant rpm, gear N turns at a number of rpm that

140-A Is constant and less than that of M.

140-B Is constant and the same as M.

140-C Reaches its maximum four times each revolution.

140-D Reaches its maximum eight times each revolution.

STOP!

IF YOU FINISH THIS PART BEFORE THE TIME IS UP, CHECK OVER YOUR WORK ON THIS PART ONLY. DO NOT GO ON UNTIL YOU ARE TOLD TO DO SO.

PART 10

GENERAL SCIENCE

TIME: 10 Minutes. 20 Questions.

This test has questions about science. Pick the best answer for each question, then blacken the space on your separate answer form which has the same number and letter as your choice.

141. Which of the following operates by suction?

    141-A   A riveting hammer.
    141-B   A balloon.
    141-C   A vacuum cleaner.
    141-D   An electric fan.

142. If a 33 1/3 rpm phonograph record is played at a speed of 45 rpm, it will

    142-A   Sound lower-pitched.
    142-B   Sound higher-pitched.
    142-C   Give no sound.
    142-D   Play louder.

143. The chief nutrient in lean meat is

    143-A   Starch.
    143-B   Protein.
    143-C   Fat.
    143-D   Carbohydrates.

144. Which one of the following metals is a liquid at room temperature?

    144-A   Mercury.
    144-B   Molybdenum.
    144-C   Cobalt.
    144-D   Magnesium.

145. The absence of any gravitational pull on an object is called

    145-A   Weightlessness.
    145-B   Mass.
    145-C   Kinetic energy.
    145-D   Force.

146. "Shooting stars" are

    146-A   Exploding stars.
    146-B   Cosmic rays.
    146-C   Planetoids.
    146-D   Meteors.

147. Two children are seated on a seesaw. The first child, seated 4 feet from the center, weighs 80 pounds. If the second child weighs 40 pounds, how far from the center must he sit to balance the seesaw?

    147-A   1 foot.
    147-B   2 feet.
    147-C   8 feet.
    147-D   16 feet.

148. A test for the presence of oxygen is that it

    148-A   Turns limewater milky.
    148-B   Turns litmus red.
    148-C   Puts out a match.
    148-D   Causes a glowing splinter to burst into flame.

149. An eclipse of the sun throws the shadow of the

    149-A   Earth on the moon.
    149-B   Moon on the earth.
    149-C   Moon on the sun.
    149-D   Earth on the sun.

150. Hearing an echo is most like seeing

    150-A   Around the corner through a periscope.
    150-B   Fine print under strong illumination.
    150-C   Stars at night that are invisible in the daytime.
    150-D   One's image in a mirror.

151. A thermometer which indicates the freezing point of water at zero degrees and the boiling point of water at 100 degrees is called the

    151-A Centigrade thermometer.
    151-B Fahrenheit thermometer.
    151-C Reaumer thermometer.
    151-D Kelvin thermometer.

152. Refraction of light affects the aim one should take when

    152-A Shooting at a fish that has jumped out of the water.
    152-B Spearing a fish in the water from the bank.
    152-C Spearing a fish under water when one is swimming under water.
    152-D Casting a fly on the surface of the water.

153. The primary reason designers seek to lower the center of gravity in automobiles is to

    153-A Reduce wind resistance.
    153-B Provide smoother riding.
    153-C Increase stability.
    153-D Reduce manufacturing costs.

154. Substances which hasten a chemical reaction without themselves undergoing change are called

    154-A Buffers.
    154-B Catalysts.
    154-C Colloids.
    154-D Reducers.

155. The change from ice to water is

    155-A A chemical change.
    155-B An elementary change.
    155-C A physical change.
    155-D A solid-state change.

156. The principle function of an air conditioner, aside from regulating heat, is to regulate the air's

    156-A Speed of motion.
    156-B Moisture content.
    156-C Oxygen content.
    156-D Density.

157. Lack of iodine is often related to which of the following diseases?

    157-A Beriberi.
    157-B Scurvy.
    157-C Rickets.
    157-D Goiter.

158. Why will a given quantity of steam always produce a more severe burn than that produced by the same quantity of boiling water?

    158-A Steam always penetrates the epidermis.
    158-B Steam causes the skin to contract and break.
    158-C Steam always releases more heat per gram than water.
    158-D Steam always covers more area of the skin.

159. A lead sinker weighs 54 grams in air, 23.8 grams in liquid A, and 28.6 grams in liquid B. From this information, what conclusions can be drawn concerning the densities of the two liquids?

    159-A Liquid A has a greater density than liquid B.
    159-B Both liquids are more dense than water.
    159-C Both liquids are less dense than water.
    159-D No conclusions can be drawn concerning the densities of the two liquids.

160. After adding a solute to a liquid, the freezing point of the liquid is

    160-A Lowered.
    160-B The same.
    160-C Raised.
    160-D Inverted.

PART 11

SHOP INFORMATION

TIME: 8 Minutes. 20 Questions.

This test has questions about shop practices and the use of tools. Pick the best answer for each question, then blacken the space on your separate answer form which has the same number and letter as your choice.

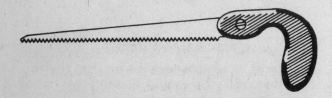

161. The saw shown above is used mainly to cut

161-A across the grain of wood.
161-B along the grain of wood.
161-C plywood.
161-D odd-shaped holes in wood.

162. Concrete is usually made by mixing

162-A only sand and water.
162-B only cement and water.
162-C lye, cement, and water.
162-D rock, sand, cement, and water.

163. The set of a saw is the

163-A angle at which the handle is set.
163-B amount of springiness of the blade.
163-C amount of sharpness of the teeth.
163-D distance the points stick out beyond the sides of the blade.

164. The principal reason for "tempering" or "drawing" steel is to

164-A reduce strength.
164-B reduce hardness.
164-C increase strength.
164-D increase maleability.

165. Sheet metal is dipped in sulphuric acid to

165-A clean it.
165-B soften it.
165-C harden it.
165-D prevent it from rusting.

166. The cut of a file refers to the

166-A shape of its handle.
166-B shape of its edge.
166-C kind of metal it is made of.
166-D kind of teeth it has.

167. In grinding a good point on a twist drill, it is necessary that

167-A the point be extremely sharp.
167-B both cutting edges have the same lip.
167-C a file be used for the entire cutting process.
167-D the final grinding be done by hand.

168. The tool used to locate a point directly below a ceiling hook is a

168-A a plumb bob.
168-B line level.
168-C transit.
168-D drop gauge.

169. The sawing of a piece of wood at a particular angle, for example 45 degrees, is accomplished by using a

169-A jointer.
169-B cant board.
169-C miter box.
169-D binder.

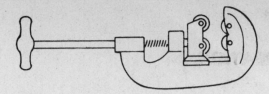

170. The tool above is a

170-A marking gauge.
170-B knurling tool.
170-C thread cutter.
170-D pipe cutter.

171. A high speed grinder operator will check the abrasive wheel before starting the machine because

171-A it must be wetted properly before use.
171-B if cracked or chipped, it could injure someone.
171-C a dry wheel will produce excessive sparks.
171-D previous work may have clogged the wheel.

172. When marking wood, an allowance of 1/16" to 1/8" should be made to allow for

172-A drying of the wood.
172-B absorption of water by wood.
172-C the width of the saw.
172-D knots in the wood.

173. A "pinch bar" is used for

173-A joining.
173-B leveling.
173-C prying.
173-D tightening.

174. The tool shown above is used for

174-A pressure lubricating.
174-B welding steel plate.
174-C drilling small holes in tight places.
174-D holding small parts for heat treating.

175. The primary function of a power driven sabresaw is to

175-A cut angles.
175-B saw heavy wood stock.
175-C cut curves in flat wood.
175-D make perfectly straight cuts.

176. What tool is shown above?

176-A countersink.
176-B keyhole saw.
176-C hole saw.
176-D grinding wheel.

177. The tip of a soldering iron is usually made of

177-A iron
177-B steel
177-C lead
177-D copper

178. Which of the following is used with a miter box?

178-A back saw.
178-B keyhole saw.
178-C coping saw.
178-D compass saw.

179. The length of a six penny nail is about

179-A 1 inch.
179-B 2 inches.
179-C 3 inches.
179-D 4 inches.

180. High oil content or so-called "spar" varnish is used primarily for

180-A Finishing furniture.
180-B Obtaining a high-gloss finish.
180-C Finishing weather exposed surfaces.
180-D Finishing interior trim.

PART 12

AUTOMOTIVE INFORMATION

TIME: 10 Minutes. 20 Questions.

This test has questions about automobiles. Pick the best answer for each question, then blacken the space on your separate answer form which has the same number and letter as your choice.

Here is a sample question.

The most commonly used fuel for running automobile engines is

A - kerosene.
B - benzine.
C - crude oil.
D - gasoline.

Gasoline is the most commonly used fuel, so D is the correct answer.

Your score on this test will be based on the number of questions you answer correctly. You should try to answer every question. Do not spend too much time on any one question.

181. Which of the following devices prevents the generator/alternator from overcharging the battery in an automobile?
    181-A Governor.
    181-B Solenoid switch.
    181-C Current regulator.
    181-D Voltage regulator.

182. A torsion bar might be found in the
    182-A Transmission.
    182-B Distributor.
    182-C Speedometer.
    182-D Suspension.

183. A black gummy deposit in the end of the tail pipe of an automobile indicates that
    183-A The automobile "burns" oil.
    183-B There is probably a leak in the exhaust manifold.
    183-C The timing is late.
    183-D There are leaks in the exhaust valves.

184. What would be the most probable cause if an automobile has a weak spark at the plugs, "turns over" very slowly, and has dim headlights?

    184-A Weak battery.

    184-B Faulty condenser.

    184-C Faulty ignition cable.

    184-D Worn contact breaker points.

185. An automobile engine won't "turn over." If the battery charge is found to be normal, the next test would normally be for

    185-A Defective starter motor.

    185-B Short-circuited switches.

    185-C Faulty battery cable connections.

    185-D Defective generator.

186. The generator or alternator of an automobile engine is usually driven by the

186-A   Camshaft.
186-B   Flywheel.
186-C   Fan belt.
186-D   Cranking motor.

187. What source of trouble can be tested by
removing a spark plug and holding a thumb
over the spark plug hole while the engine
is being cranked?

187-A   Poor ignition.
187-B   Low compression.
187-C   High oil consumption.
187-D   High fuel consumption.

188. If an automobile engine overheats while
the radiator remains cold, the difficulty
probably lies in

188-A   Lack of engine oil.
188-B   Stuck thermostat.
188-C   Improper ignition timing.
188-D   An overloaded engine.

189. It is best for an automobile's gas tank to
be full or nearly full to prevent

189-A   gasoline from vaporizing in the
fuel lines.
189-B   moisture from condensing in the
gas tank.
189-C   drying out of the fuel pump.
189-D   loss of vacuum in the vacuum line.

190. In troubleshooting the rear axle, an automobile is driven on a smooth road at 25
mph, and the accelerator is lightly pressed
and released. If there is a "slapping"
noise, the most probable trouble is

190-A   a worn universal joint.
190-B   an incorrect drive line angle.
190-C   loose accelerator linkage.
190-D   a bent transmission shaft.

191. An automobile handbrake is set tightly and
the engine is idling at 30 mph road speed.
If you shift into high gear, release the
clutch, and the engine continues to run
about the same, what would most likely
need repair?

191-A   clutch.
191-B   throttle.
191-C   high gear.
191-D   carburetor.

192. The pistons of gasoline engines will sometimes increase in size so that they "stick"
in the cylinder. This is often caused by

192-A   low engine operating temperature.
192-B   overheating of the engine.
192-C   worn oil rings.
192-D   worn compression rings.

193. If a 4-speed transmission makes noise when
engaged in low gear, it will likely also make
noise when in

193-A   3rd gear.
193-B   4th gear.
193-C   reverse.
193-D   neutral.

194. The letter "W" in the oil designation SAE
20-W means

194-A   the oil was produced by a refinery
in a western state.
194-B   the oil is adapted for cold weather
starting.
194-C   the oil is water-soluble.
194-D   it is a flushing oil.

195. What will happen if leaded gasoline is used
in a car equipped with a catalytic converter

195-A   intake valves will crack.
195-B   catalytic converter will be damaged.
195-C   engine will overheat.
195-D   engine will begin backfiring.

196. Dual or multiple carburetors are used to obtain

   196-A a richer mixture of air and gasoline.
   196-B a more uniform distribution of fuel charge.
   196-C an overlapping of suction periods on one mixing tube.
   196-D flexibility of firing order.

197. If an automobile air conditioning system fails to cool, the first check to make is for

   197-A leaks in hoses.
   197-B malfunction of the compressor.
   197-C low oil level.
   197-D shortage of refrigerant.

198. If the air cleaner on an automobile engine becomes clogged, the effect on engine performance will be similar to that of a

   198-A partly closed choke valve.
   198-B vapor lock.
   198-C clogged fuel nozzle.
   198-D needle valve stuck in closed position.

199. Which of the following instruments can be used to adjust the air/fuel ratio, valve timing, and check for leaky head gaskets?

   199-A compression tester.
   199-B vacuum gauge.
   199-C timing light.
   199-D dwell meter.

200. In the operation of a gasoline engine, ignition coil failure is most often caused by

   200-A a low battery.
   200-B an overcharged battery.
   200-C burned coil terminal.
   200-D moisture entering coil case.

END OF EXAMINATION!

IF YOU FINISH BEFORE THE TIME IS UP, CHECK OVER YOUR WORK ON THIS PART ONLY. DO NOT GO BACK TO ANY PREVIOUS PART.

CORRECT ANSWERS FOR SPECIMEN ASVAB-5

(Please make every effort to answer the questions on your own before looking at these answers. You'll make faster progress by following this rule.)

PART 1—GENERAL INFORMATION

1.C	5.B	9.C	13.B	17.A
2.D	6.C	10.C	14.C	18.B
3.B	7.D	11.C	15.B	19.D
4.A	8.A	12.D	16.B	20.D

PART 2—NUMERICAL OPERATIONS

21.C	29.C	37.A	45.A	53.B	59.A	65.B
22.A	30.A	38.A	46.D	54.C	60.D	66.B
23.B	31.C	39.B	47.A	55.D	61.C	67.A
24.D	32.C	40.C	48.B	56.A	62.B	68.D
25.D	33.D	41.A	49.D	57.D	63.A	69.A
26.A	34.D	42.D	50.D	58.C	64.D	70.C
27.A	35.B	43.C	51.B			
28.C	36.D	44.B	52.D			

PART 3—ATTENTION TO DETAIL

71.13	76.14	81.15	86.11	91.13	96.12
72.12	77.15	82.15	87.13	92.15	97.15
73.12	78.14	83.13	88.13	93.13	98.15
74.11	79.12	84.15	89.12	94.14	99.11
75.13	80.14	85.14	90.15	95.12	100.11

PART 4—WORD KNOWLEDGE

1.C	6.B	11.D	16.D	21.A	26.B
2.C	7.D	12.A	17.C	22.C	27.D
3.B	8.D	13.A	18.A	23.D	28.A
4.D	9.D	14.C	19.A	24.A	29.A
5.A	10.D	15.B	20.A	25.C	30.A

PART 5—ARITHMETIC REASONING

31.C	35.C	39.B	43.C	47.C
32.A	36.A	40.A	44.B	48.B
33.D	37.D	41.C	45.D	49.C
34.B	38.A	42.B	46.B	50.C

PART 6—SPACE PERCEPTION

51.C	55.C	59.D	63.C	67.D
52.D	56.B	60.C	64.A	68.D
53.A	57.A	61.B	65.D	69.A
54.A	58.D	62.A	66.B	70.C

PART 7—MATHEMATICS KNOWLEDGE

71.B	75.B	79.C	83.B	87.D
72.D	76.A	80.B	84.C	88.A
73.B	77.D	81.D	85.D	89.C
74.A	78.C	82.B	86.A	90.C

PART 8—ELECTRONICS INFORMATION

91.D	96.D	101.B	106.B	111.D	116.D
92.C	97.D	102.A	107.D	112.B	117.A
93.D	98.C	103.A	108.D	113.A	118.D
94.D	99.B	104.B	109.D	114.A	119.A
95.D	100.B	105.B	110.B	115.B	120.C

PART 9—MECHANICAL COMPREHENSION

121.D	125.D	129.A	133.C	137.C
122.A	126.C	130.B	134.C	138.A
123.A	127.A	131.B	135.A	139.A
124.A	128.A	132.C	136.B	140.B

PART 10—GENERAL SCIENCE

141.C	145.A	149.B	153.C	157.D
142.B	146.D	150.D	154.B	158.C
143.B	147.C	151.A	155.C	159.A
144.A	148.D	152.B	156.B	160.A

PART 11—SHOP INFORMATION

161.D	165.A	169.C	173.C	177.D
162.D	166.D	170.D	174.B	178.A
163.D	167.B	171.B	175.C	179.B
164.C	168.A	172.C	176.C	180.C

PART 12—AUTOMOTIVE INFORMATION

181.D	185.C	189.B	193.C	197.D
182.D	186.C	190.A	194.B	198.A
183.A	187.B	191.A	195.B	199.B
184.A	188.B	192.B	196.B	200.D

SCORE SHEET—ASVAB 5

PART	NUMBER CORRECT		NUMBER OF QUESTIONS	
GENERAL INFORMATION	_____	÷ 15 =	_____	× 100 = _____%
NUMERICAL OPERATIONS	_____	÷ 50 =	_____	× 100 = _____%
ATTENTION TO DETAIL	_____	÷ 30 =	_____	× 100 = _____%
WORD KNOWLEDGE	_____	÷ 30 =	_____	× 100 = _____%
ARITHMETIC REASONING	_____	÷ 20 =	_____	× 100 = _____%
SPACE PERCEPTION	_____	÷ 20 =	_____	× 100 = _____%
MATHEMATICS KNOWLEDGE	_____	÷ 20 =	_____	× 100 = _____%
ELECTRONICS INFORMATION	_____	÷ 30 =	_____	× 100 = _____%
MECHANICAL COMPREHENSION	_____	÷ 20 =	_____	× 100 = _____%
GENERAL SCIENCE	_____	÷ 20 =	_____	× 100 = _____%
SHOP INFORMATION	_____	÷ 20 =	_____	× 100 = _____%
AUTOMOTIVE INFORMATION	_____	÷ 20 =	_____	× 100 = _____%
TOTAL	_____	÷ 295 =	_____	× 100 = _____%

COMPARISON CHART

The parts of ASVAB-5 are not in the same order as the parts of the model exams. Skip around to fill in the blanks to compare your scores.

	Exam I	Exam II	Exam III	ASVAB 5
GENERAL SCIENCE	%	%	%	%
ARITHMETIC REASONING	%	%	%	%
WORD KNOWLEDGE	%	%	%	%
PARAGRAPH COMPREHENSION	%	%	%	——
NUMERICAL OPERATIONS	%	%	%	%
CODING SPEED	%	%	%	——
SPACE PERCEPTION	——	——	——	%
AUTO & SHOP INFORMATION	%	%	%	——
SHOP INFORMATION	——	——	——	%
AUTOMOTIVE INFORMATION	——	——	——	%
MATHEMATICS KNOWLEDGE	%	%	%	%
MECHANICAL COMPREHENSION	%	%	%	%
ELECTRONICS INFORMATION	%	%	%	%
GENERAL INFORMATION	——	——	——	%
TOTAL	%	%	%	%